A U.S.–MEXICO–CANADA FREE-TRADE AGREEMENT

Do We Just Say No?

WILLIAM McGAUGHEY, JR.

Thistlerose Publications

MINNEAPOLIS

Copyright © 1992 by William McGaughey, Jr.

All rights reserved including the right of reproduction in whole or in part in any form, except with the prior written consent of the publisher.

International Standard Book Number: 0-9605630-2-4

Library of Congress Catalog Card Number: 91-068572

Printed in the United States of America

Library of Congress Cataloging-in-Publication Data

McGaughey, William

Free-Trade Agreement, a U.S.-Mexico-Canada/ William McGaughey

p.   c.

Includes bibliographical references and index.

ISBN 0-9605630-2-4

1. Free trade—United States. 2. Free trade—Mexico. 3. Free trade—Canada. 4. Nontariff trade barriers. 5. Labor rights. 6. Labor movement. 7. Hours of labor. 8. Totalitarianism.

Thistlerose Publications
1702 Glenwood Ave. N., Suite 11
Minneapolis, MN 55405

CONTENTS

Part One
What is the Issue Here?

Some free-trade promotions   1

Comparisons with the European Economic Union   3

The negotiating agenda   5

Precedent of the U.S.-Canada FTA   8

Two principal types of trade barriers   11

The removal of tariffs   12

Attacking the non-tariff trade barriers: the conservative
    deregulatory agenda   14

Stimulus to trade or locking in access to investment
    opportunities?   18

Export-led development: can this be a "win-win" situation?   26

Sops for labor and environmental groups   31

The doctrine of comparative advantage   36

Historical perspectives on trade and development   41

Part Two
Mexican and Canadian Experiences
with Free Trade

The three North American countries   45

Some elements in Canada's political background   47

Twists and turns in Mexico's economic development   49

Living in the shadow of debt   52

Harbingers of free trade in Mexico   55

Suppression of Mexican labor   56

The Maquiladora program   59

Conditions inside the plants   61

Community squalor and environmental degradation   63

What this bodes for free trade   65

Employment concerns in Canada   67

Economic pressures and threats   72

Some environmental consequences of the U.S.-Canada FTA   75

Talking with our continental neighbors   79

Part Three
Against Business Totalitarianism

Evolution of divided power in western society   83

Rise and fall of political totalitarianism in the Soviet Union 87

How global debt subverted government power   89

Smith, Keynes, and their heirs   92

The nature of business totalitarianism   99

Swing toward a more balanced position   104

The Pope's view of an economically just society   106

Trade unions as an anti-totalitarian force   108

Some functions of government in the approaching age   110

Reduced work time as a way of managing the labor supply   114

The alternative to reduced hours: economic waste   116

A need for political self-reform   120

Part Four
Speculations concerning a Positive Alternative to Free Trade

The battle over "fast track"   123

Alignment of forces since the fast-track vote   125

Alternative agendas   127

The rejectionist alternative   132

Breakdown into regional trading blocs   136

A framework for international cooperation   139

Economic pressures driving the NAFTA   142

The debt-for-nature swap   143

Limiting production capacity by cutting work hours   146

Attitudes in the European Community and Japan   149

Employer-specific tariffs: a brake on exports from
    developing countries   156

The GATT and other structures for international
    cooperation   161

Some precedents in linking labor standards to trade   168

To reaffirm free labor and democracy   175

Concluding Statements

Author's acknowledgments   177

A Declaration   182
Statement of Jim Silver   183
Statement of Hector de la Cueva   186
Statement of Joe Fahey   188
Statement of Raul Escobar   191
Statement of Tom Laney   193
Statement of Susan Spratt   195
 Statement of Jose Quintana   197

Endnotes   199

Index   214

PART ONE

What is the Issue Here?

Some Free-Trade Promotions

A superficial opinion holds that critics of a free-trade agreement with Mexico and Canada, many of them trade unionists, are modern-day "Luddites" who would deny the evident progress being made in integrating world markets. Faced with increasingly fierce trade competition from the European Community and east Asian nations, it seems only natural that the United States would want to join with its two national neighbors to create a North American free-trade zone that would strengthen the competitiveness of producers in this region. "If accomplished," wrote an enthusiastic editorial writer, "the hemispheric powerhouse would include 350 million people and be larger than the European Community."[1] A market of this size might increase production efficiency through economies of scale. It might expose regional producers to world-class competition and, consequently, stimulate better performance. With free trade would come a closer integration of the U.S., Mexican, and Canadian economies. Inevitably, the sense of political and cultural neighborliness among the three nations would be increased. On the other hand, for the U.S. Congress to reject such an agreement would be "to slap our neighbor (Mexico) in the face", another editorialist declared.[2] An assistant secretary in the U.S. Department of Labor went so far as to argue that criticism of the proposed trade agreement with Mexico was "tinged with a degree of racism."[3] To support North American free trade is therefore to support international friendship, its promoters suggest. To reject such ties would be to invite chaos.

"Free trade" has a nice ring to it. If trade is free, we think that forces of the marketplace will work out the best economic arrangement. Unfree or protected trade is like giving a crutch to someone with inadequately exercised legs. We suppose it means letting inefficient producers survive by hiding behind trade barriers. But what if "efficiency" means paying low wages or skimping on environmental protection? The issue then becomes more complicated. With low wages, working people might not be able to afford to buy so many products, and the consumer market would shrink. With environmental degradation, the natural resources to support various forms of life and human activity would become poisoned or destroyed. Upon second glance, then, it would seem that what we call "free trade" does not mean the ability to trade freely but, rather, the ability to trade in the absence of governmental regulation. Whether regulation is good or bad depends upon whether the particular regulations are good or bad. If, for instance, the government restricts importation of certain vegetables that contain toxic chemicals, most persons who buy vegetables at the supermarket might say that this type of regulation was justified. The volume of trade could be just as great in a regulated environment as otherwise.

Mexico's president, Carlos Salinas de Gortari, has framed the issue of free trade in terms of a choice which Americans would have to make between importing Mexican products or Mexican people. Without free trade, he suggested to a group of U.S. newspaper editors, people would be migrating from Mexico to the United States "not by the hundreds or thousands but by the millions."[4] Yet, the topic of Mexican immigration has remained off limits in the trade negotiations. Whether or not Americans are culturally or ethnically prejudiced against Mexicans has nothing to do with the merits of a free-trade agreement between Mexico and the United States. There are opponents as well as supporters in both countries. The personal friendship between the two Secretaries of Commerce, Robert Mosbacher (now President Bush's campaign manager) and Jaime Serra Puche, who shoot quail together, is matched, for instance, by that between two trade-union activists, Tom Laney and Raul Escobar, both opponents of the agreement though friends. Emotional considerations aside, a free-trade agreement between Mexico, Canada, and the United States would involve a commercial union between two First World countries and a Third World country or, in other words, between societies at greatly different levels of economic development. While some see this as an exciting challenge, a report issued by the

U.S. International Trade Commission noted that successful free-trade agreements have tended to be found among countries "at comparable levels of development."[5]

Comparisons with the European Economic Union

Some see the prospective Free-Trade Agreement (FTA) between Mexico, Canada, and the United States as North America's response to the European Economic Union that will be established in 1992. Like the European union, the North American agreement contemplates the complete elimination of tariffs and other trade barriers for products traded internally among the member states. Unlike it, the North American free-trade deal would not involve a common currency or harmonization of tariffs with respect to external trading partners. The European union is, therefore, more than a free-trade agreement; it is a step toward political and social as well as economic integration. The economically stronger nations of Europe have pledged aid and assistance to the weaker nations to bring them up to a common level of development. The European Community nations have adopted a "Social Charter", whose provisions would include such features as the right to adequate wages, the right to job training, and the right to health and safety protection in the work place. A North American FTA, promising none of those things, would likely be patterned instead after the U.S.-Canada agreement of 1988. That agreement has become thoroughly unpopular with the Canadian public for reasons that will soon become clear.

The Canadians, like the Mexicans, place a high value upon preserving their national culture in the face of pressures from the United States. They point out that trade agreements have consequences going beyond "trade", in a narrow sense. Such agreements touch the core of values that make one nation different than another. The European Economic Union has attempted to come to terms with that fact, while the U.S.-Canada and the North American FTA have not. Raymond Hebert, who teaches political science at St. Boniface College in Winnipeg, explains that "Europe is an ideal as well as a set of institutions and policies . . . For the visiting Canadian citi-

zen this kind of idealism is rather breathtaking . . . Indeed, beyond the almost palpable decay of the Canadian dream itself under
the weight of political opportunism, one cannot avoid comparing the
evolution of the European system from a coal and steel community
to a comprehensive political and economic system with common
progressive social values solidly anchored upon the free movement
of goods, services, and people. Canada's free trade association with
the United States pales by comparison, for the simple reason that it
can lead to no further social or political development without endan-
gering the very existence of our country. In addition, many if not
most Canadians cannot share the current dominant American
values, centered upon unfettered individualism and accumulation of
wealth for the few and the lack of concern for the public good among
the many. Our 'trade union' with the American behemoth is thus stillborn as a focus of Canadian political and economic idealism and
creativity."[6]

A principal defect of the North American FTA, in comparison
with the European Economic Union, would be its lack of equality in
the relationship between the prospective trading partners. This inequality takes two forms. First, the peoples of Canada and Mexico believe that their nations would be negotiating the agreement from a
position of weakness vis-a-vis the United States, which has a team of
experienced, hard-nosed trade negotiators and a history of dominat-
ing its two neighbors. Both peoples harbor anti-Yankee sentiments
born of this sense of domination and their opposition to perceived
U.S. values centered in "unfettered individualism" and plutocratic
privilege. Both see the proposed free-trade agreement as furthering
a conservative political agenda and, in fact, allowing U.S. business
firms to take over their industries. They fear for their national identi-
ties, in other words. With respect to the two northern countries, there
is a second type of threat arising from the fact that Mexican workers
earn much lower wages than workers in Canada and the United
States. If an FTA with Mexico accelerates the flight of manufacturing
to that country, U.S. and Canadian factory workers would come into
increasingly direct and brutal price competition with their Mexican
counterparts earning, in many cases, less than $4.00 a day.[7] From
their perspective, this agreement would become a vehicle for more
unemployment, wage concessions, and union busting. Their own

high-priced labor, once considered a sign of social progress, would become a ticket to economic marginality and personal degradation.

While it is true that U.S. and Canadian workers have long faced a threat from production outsourcing, they have not previously had an opportunity to express themselves on this subject. For a long time powerful corporate interests have been allowed to roll over the livelihoods of countless individuals. No particular decision was made to encourage that process; incrementally it just happened. But now a group of 535 human beings, each subject to pressures and appeals from real-life constituents, have an opportunity to decide whether or not to take a further, giant step in the direction of reducing people to expendable factors in the current scheme of international production. That is what makes the Congressional vote on the North American FTA such an historic contest. For once, the human element may be decisive in determining trade policy.

The Negotiating Agenda

We are, of course, at a disadvantage in discussing proposals for a North American FTA while the agreement is still being negotiated. Until the negotiations are concluded, one does not know its final form. One can, however, examine the announced guidelines and other published reports regarding the negotiators' agenda. When Presidents Bush and Salinas announced their intention to pursue an FTA in September 1990, they proposed an agenda for the bilateral talks. As stated in a U.S. International Trade Commission report to Congress in February 1991, this agenda was as follows:

> (1) the full, phased elimination of import tariffs,
> (2) the elimination or fullest possible reduction of nontariff trade barriers such as import quotas, licenses and technical barriers to trade,
> (3) the establishment of clear, binding protection for intellectual property rights,
> (4) fair and expeditious dispute settlement procedures, and
> (5) means to improve the flow of goods, services, and investments between the U.S. and Mexico.[8]

Naturally, each nation has its own public or private agenda in the form of particular concessions which it hopes to extract from the other party during negotiations. An article appearing in *Business Week* on November 12, 1990, summarized what the U.S. and Mexican negotiators wanted to accomplish in the trade talks. The U.S. negotiators wanted "guarantees that Asian and European rivals in textiles, steel, and computers, for example, won't bombard the U.S. market from bases in Mexico. One way to ensure that is to establish tough rules of origin." The U.S. negotiators also insisted that any agreement should provide adequate "legal protection for U.S. patents and technology south of the border." A third negotiating objective was to "wipe out the remaining constitutional restrictions on foreign investment in Mexico." A fourth, and politically the most difficult U.S. objective, was to persuade Mexico "to open up its undercapitalized oil industry to American investment—which is prohibited by the Mexican constitution." This last demand President Salinas publicly opposed. For its part, the Mexican negotiating team wanted the United States "to tear down U.S. quotas on textiles and steel and to open U.S. markets to currently prohibited fruits and vegetables", particularly Mexican avocados which are excluded from the U.S. market because screw worms were found in some products 45 years ago.[9]

When Canada joined the U.S.-Mexico trade negotiations in February 1991, the talks became trilateral. As the negotiations were set to begin in Toronto on June 12, the *Wall Street Journal* disclosed that Canada intended "to press for increased access for Canadian banks to the U.S. and Mexican markets." Canadian banks in the United States were faced with restrictions upon interstate banking, and the Mexican restrictions were tougher still. The Canadians also wanted "improved access to the U.S. government procurement market", including removal of "discriminatory barriers" such as "buy American" restrictions and "various set-aside provisions that favor U.S. interests." The United States, on the other hand, was aiming "to press Canada to abolish allegedly discriminatory laws favoring Canadian 'cultural' industries." As another piece of unfinished business from the 1988 trade agreement, the United States wanted Canada to repeal its "compulsory licensing laws", under which "a generic copy of a patented drug may be imported and sold in Canada after the drug has been on the Canadian market for 10 years." The United States also wanted "to increase to 60% from 50% the North American content requirement for new cars and trucks that are traded duty-free." The Canadian government was expected to oppose that proposal because it would exclude some Canadian-built cars of Japanese make from the U.S. market.[10]

As the trade talks progressed through the session held in Seattle, it became clear that the agreement would not be ready, as originally hoped, by the end of 1991. The new target was to wrap up U.S. Congressional approval of NAFTA before the November 1992 elections. Only in the area of selecting commodities for reciprocal tariff cuts had the trinational negotiators achieved the consensus needed for an agreement. The *Wall Street Journal* reported that there were major unresolved differences in at least four areas. First, the U.S. negotiating team seemed unable to convince the Mexicans and Canadians to adopt tough rules of origin, aimed especially at automobiles. The Mexicans wanted to keep the regional content requirement down to 50% while the United States was pressing for something in the 60% to 70% range. Second, the dispute-resolution procedure was complicated by the fact that the Mexican legal system differed significantly from those in Canada and the United States. Third, the United States wanted to open the Mexican market to increased exports of corn and grain while the Mexicans feared that free trade in this area would wreck their system of small-scale communal farming. Fourth, Mexico was encountering stiff resistance to its demand that the United States reduce barriers to imported textiles and steel. "Powerful Washington lobbies" for those two U.S. industries were holding the line on trade liberalization in their areas.[11]

Corn exports emerged as a principal stumbling block as the trade talks moved into December. U.S. corn growers pressed for more access to the highly protected Mexican market. The Mexican government was meanwhile encouraging the 2.3 million corn growers in that country to diversify into other, more profitable crops. Part of its strategy involved privatizing communal farms. The problem was that any such restructuring of agriculture would bring massive displacement of persons who worked on those farms. "U.S. negotiators," the *Wall Street Journal* observed, "are on the horns of a dilemma. If they force Mexico to open its borders wider to overflowing U.S. corn silos, that could set off a new flood of Mexican farm laborers into the U.S., the very problem that the free-trade pact is meant to help resolve." Federally funded research conducted by Dr. Raul Hinojosa Ojeda of the University of California at Los Angeles and three colleagues estimated that about 850,000 heads of household would leave Mexican farms if corn subsidies fell. More than 600,000 of this group could be expected to head for the United States. Considering that the United States currently absorbs about 100,000 Mexican immigrants each year, the population displacement brought about by the restructuring of a single agricultural sector could, if accomplished in one year, produce a six-fold increase in the number of Mexican immigrants entering the United States. Such reports indicate that, at the least, President Salinas should choose a different selling point in pitching the advantages of free trade to U.S. audiences.[12]

Precedent of the U.S.-Canada FTA

In addition to glimpses of information disclosed in official statements and reports leaked from the secretive talks themselves, we have an idea of what the completed North American FTA might contain from the precedent of the agreement reached four years ago between Canada and the United States. The U.S. Trade Representative, Carla Hills, who is leading the U.S. negotiating team, has said that the prospective trinational agreement would be modeled along the lines of that binational precedent. Of course, the Free-Trade Agreement which the United States negotiated with Canada included numerous detailed provisions covering a variety of industries. Its legal text ran hundreds of pages in length. For an overview of the agreement, we can quote President Ronald Reagan's letter to the Speaker of the House when the U.S.-Canada FTA was presented to the U.S. Congress for approval in July 1988.

President Reagan wrote: "The United States-Canada Free-Trade Agreement is one of the most comprehensive agreements on trade ever negotiated between two nations. It provides for the elimination of all tariffs, reduces many non-tariff barriers, liberalizes investment practices, and covers trade in services. For example, the Agreement:

Significantly liberalizes Canada's foreign investment regime;
Provides secure, nondiscriminatory access to Canadian energy supplies, even in times of shortages;
Establishes the critical principle of national treatment with respect to trade in over 150 services, which will ensure nondis-

criminatory treatment of U.S. services providers under future Canadian laws and regulations;

Removes essentially all existing Canadian discrimination faced by U.S. financial institutions operating in Canada;

Facilitates the temporary entry of U.S. business persons and professionals into Canada;

Freezes coverage of the United States-Canada 'Auto Pact' and limits future Pact-like provisions;

Eliminates Canadian duty remission programs linked to performance requirements;

Removes the current Canadian embargo on imports of used motor vehicles and aircraft;

Expands opportunities to sell U.S. goods to the Canadian Government by extending the coverage of the GATT Government Procurement Code bilaterally to purchases between $25,000 and the Code threshold;

Provides that owners of U.S. television programs should be compensated for the retransmission of their programs in Canada;

Eliminates Canadian export subsidies on agricultural trade to the United States;

Prohibits Canadian Government and public entity sales for export to the United States of agricultural goods at prices below cost;

Generally exempts meat products of one country from the other country's meat import quota laws;

Increases Canadian poultry and egg minimum import quotas;

Sets conditions for the removal of Canadian import licensing of wheat, barley, and oats;

Establishes a forum for discussing the possible harmonization of technical regulations on agricultural trade;

Facilitates the recognition by one party of the other's testing facilities and certification bodies in the area of technical standards; and

Removes barriers to the sale of U.S.-produced wine and distilled spirits in Canada."[13]

To avoid becoming bogged down in details, we can summarize the major provisions of the U.S.-Canada FTA by following a scheme presented in the U.S. Department of Commerce publication, *United States Trade Performance in 1988*. The main areas of provision are as follows:

(1) Tariffs: The "centerpiece" of the 1988 agreement was a provision to eliminate all tariffs on each other country's products within ten years. In 1987, Canadian tariffs on U.S. goods averaged 9.9% while U.S. tariffs on Canadian goods averaged 3.3%. Almost three fourths of U.S. goods entering Canada were duty-free. The U.S.-Canada FTA placed the remaining types of goods on three lists depending on whether duties would be eliminated in 1989, 1993, or 1998. It provided a mechanism for accelerating the timetable of tariff reductions if both sides agreed.

(2) Rules of Origin: While tariffs were eliminated on products originating in Canada and the United States, they were retained for products originating in third countries. The rules of origin established a percentage of Canadian or U.S. content for the products to qualify for duty-free treatment.

(3) Government Procurement: The agreement incorporated the GATT requirement that purchases by specified government agencies valued at more than $171,000 be open to free competition, and lowered the dollar threshold to $25,000 in some cases.

(4) Business Services: The 1988 agreement forbade government to place new restrictions on business services and secured access to the telecommunications network. It applied the principle of "national treatment" — requiring both governments to treat the other nation's service providers the same as their own — to business services. It prohibited regulations that would require the other nation's firms to establish a domestic presence to obtain access to national markets. It required that government regulations be "transparent" to all parties involved.

(5) Investment: The agreement eliminated certain trade-related "performance requirements" which the Canadian regulatory agency, Investment Canada, had imposed on U.S. firms. It narrowed the range of conditions under which Investment Canada could review acquisition of Canadian by U.S. firms. Only acquisitions valued at more than $150 million (1992 Canadian dollars) would be eligible for review. While some exceptions to the rules for investment were allowed, both countries agreed not to add new restrictive regulations.

(6) Border Crossing Procedures: The procedures were simplified for four categories of visitors to Canada: business visitors, traders

and investors, intracompany transferees, and professional service providers.

(7) Energy: The agreement eliminated all remaining tariffs on energy products and forbade introduction of new trade regulations with respect to those products which would put the other party at a disadvantage.

(8) Dispute Settlement: The agreement established a "Canada-United States Trade Commission" to supervise its own implementation and to handle disputes except in the areas of financial services, anti-dumping and countervailing duties. The two nations were to continue to follow their own anti-dumping and countervailing duty laws but establish an independent bilateral panel to assist in the process.[14]

Two Principal Types of Trade Barriers

Any proposal for change has both good or bad features depending upon one's point of view. To assess the prospective North American FTA in those terms, one should identify the broad types of provisions included in the agreement and separately analyze each. One type of provision would be the phased but complete elimination of tariffs. The other major category would be the removal of nontariff trade barriers. Thanks to negotiations concerning the General Agreement on Tariffs and Trade (GATT), average tariff rates in the industrialized world have been dropping steadily since the end of World War II. Japan, with a 2.7% average tariff, has one of the lowest rates. The United States, Sweden, and the European Community nations have tariffs averaging between 3% and 4%. Canada's average tariff runs slightly above 6%. Mexico's is around 10%.[15] Obviously tariff rates are not synonymous with the degree of trade protection; the nontariff trade barriers have become increasingly important. These include quotas, voluntary export restraints, trigger mechanisms, domestic-content requirements, import licenses, official import prices, subsidized exports, and so on. Nontariff trade barriers are also related to the question of unfair trade practices in the form of subsidies, dumping, and so on. They are related to investment regulations, protection of intellectual properties, national energy policy, and other such issues which have become an important part of the free-trade controversy.

The Removal of Tariffs

The most obvious element of free trade would be the complete elimination of tariffs. On July 16, 1991, the U.S. Trade Representative published a notice in the *Federal Register* to the effect that "every article provided for in the Harmonized Tariff Schedule of the United States . . . will be considered for the elimination or reduction of duties . . . provided such articles are of Mexican origin."[16] In general, a tariff is an ad valorem tax imposed upon a foreign product as it enters the country. This tax creates an additional product cost, which is usually passed along to the consumer. The additional cost, imposed on the foreign but not the domestic product, alters the comparative level of prices so that the domestic product becomes more attractive to price-sensitive buyers. All else being equal, then, buyers in a tariff-protected market will tend to buy more of the home-grown product and less of the foreign product. National governments, of course, want to see the domestic producers succeed competitively. They are therefore naturally inclined to impose protective tariffs. Free-trade proponents argue, on the other hand, that tariff protection creates a distortion in the flow of international trade. Tariff-protected industries, chronically sheltered from foreign competition, tend to become inefficient, lazy, and weak. In the larger economic picture, it would be better if some of those weaker, less efficient industries perished, freeing up resources for other purposes. Moreover, unilateral government decisions to raise tariff rates often provoke countermeasures by other governments, which could lead to mutually damaging trade wars and reduce the volume of global trade.

Is it good to eliminate protective tariffs? An advantage would be that the buyer of foreign products will pay a lower price. The price reduction may also, for competitive reasons, be matched by domestic producers. Therefore, consumers as a class stand to benefit from tariff reductions. Another benefit would be that increased competition from foreign producers tends to stimulate better performance among the domestic producers, which, in the long run, improves their competitive posture. Finally, elimination of tariffs simplifies and reduces paperwork, streamlines border-crossing procedures, and generally helps the flow of trade. There are also , however, some disadvantages in eliminating tariffs. First, tariffs are a source of revenue for national governments. As with any tax cut, one should ask whether government can afford the revenue loss. Second, tariffs give governments a powerful yet flexible regulatory tool. Selectively applied to imported products, they can promote certain public-policy objectives. Finally, whatever the theoretical merits of free trade, there is little doubt that, if tariff protection were removed, many domestic businesses facing greater price competition would go out of business. These are not necessarily businesses grown lax with privilege. Their inability to compete may be due less to bad management than to a need to pay their employees higher wages than a foreign producer would or to bear certain state- or federally-mandated costs.

That is especially the case with respect to eliminating tariff barriers between the United States and Mexico. At the U.S. International Trade Commission public hearings in Chicago on April 10, 1991, several U.S. business spokesmen predicted their own inability to survive in a free-trade environment. Harry A. Foster of the Michigan Asparagus Growers testified that, because growing asparagus is a labor-intensive industry, most Michigan growers could not compete against asparagus shipped up from Mexico duty-free. The labor-cost component of asparagus is $.20 of the $.51 price per pound, reflecting the U.S. minimum wage, unemployment insurance, workers compensation, and the need to meet codes for migrant workers' housing. Mexican producers, tapping cheaper labor and less costly regulation, could undercut them substantially on price. William Libman, representing the U.S. broom industry, predicted that if a free-trade agreement were concluded with Mexico, half of the nation's 12,000 jobs in that industry would move south of the border within one year. The 32% ad valorem tax on brooms imported from Mexico provided the margin of price to keep that domestic industry alive. On the other hand, Donald Marquart, a spokesman for the Square D Company, testified that, although a North American FTA would help his particular firm, it would wreak havoc in Mexico. He predicted that "the bottom half of Mexican industry will initially not be able to compete in a world market."[17] A survey taken by a Mexican business group found that "nearly half of Mexican industrialists believe the proposed North American free-trade pact would hurt the country's industrial development," according to the *Wall Street Journal*.[18]

Attacking the Nontariff Trade Barriers: the Conservative Deregulatory Agenda

Nontariff trade barriers would seem, at first glance, to be a lawyerly way of achieving the same protectionist ends as with tariffs. In the context of GATT, they provide a loophole to shelter domestic industries without violating the principle of tariff reduction. Indeed, many nations have used them just that way. However, there is another side to the question of eliminating these barriers. Some nontariff trade barriers, such as numerical quotas or voluntary export restraints, are unmistakably related to the desire to restrict foreign imports. When the French government several years ago required Japanese consumer-electronic products to clear customs through a single port of entry located in central France, that was an obvious trade restriction. Other kinds of restrictions, as they have been construed to be, are not so obviously trade-related. A trade restriction can be anything which, intentionally or unintentionally, serves to impede the flow of international trade or which causes customers to prefer the locally produced to the foreign product. Depending on how broad the legal definitions are, national governments can take each other to court charging that various kinds of domestic laws, regulations, and rulings violate international norms of trade. The U.S.-Canada FTA has brought out some grotesque situations of that sort. The proposal to expand free trade to all North America would produce many more.

What is a nontariff trade barrier? According to draft proposals raised at the "Uruguay Round" of GATT negotiations, such an impediment to international trade might take any of the following forms:

• A draft of the GATT text states that no national government or its subdivision can develop "technical regulations" that create "unnecessary obstacles to international trade." Technical regulations are defined to include "product" and "process" requirements or standards for "all industrial and agricultural products", as well as "packaging and labelling requirements." A nontariff trade barrier therefore might include U.S. or state laws pertaining to waste recycling, pesticide standards, bans on toxic substances, or consumer information in regard to product packaging. For instance, the 1990 Nutrition

Labeling and Education Act, which requires manufacturers to disclose nutritional information on food packages, might come under attack as a trade barrier.[19]

• The agricultural section of the GATT draft states: "Contracting parties shall not introduce or maintain sanitary or phytosanitary measures which result in a higher level of sanitary or phytosanitary than would be achieved by measures based on the relevant international standard, guideline or recommendation, where such exist, without reasonable scientific justification." In other words, the U.S. Government could not set higher standards for food safety than the international norm without presenting adequate scientific justification. What is the international norm? The Codex Alimentarius Commission, located in Rome, has authority over food-safety standards. Its regulations would allow fruits and vegetables to be sold containing, for instance, up to fifty times more DDT than what the U.S. government currently considers safe for human consumption.[20]

• GATT requires that, even where no international norm exists, any signatory nation wishing to enact a new regulation should first notify all other signatory nations and allow sufficient time for comment. All objections received must be taken into account. Failure to follow the proper procedure could invite a legal challenge to the regulation. A further proposal, not yet adopted, would extend this reporting requirement to state and local governments.[21]

• The GATT proposals also require signatory nations, wherever possible, to adopt the same "code of practice" as the others. This means, for instance, that the Administrative Procedure Act, which governs U.S. rule-making and dispute-resolution procedures, might be invalidated and replaced by a GATT code. Considering that the GATT decisions are made in secret, this requirement would remove certain administrative procedures from public scrutiny and turn them over to a supranational bureaucracy.[22]

In effect, the proposed new rules of international trade reflect the conservative agenda of deregulation, which restricts government's ability to make various kinds of rules or legislate in the public interest. Some trade barriers, as they have been construed to be, are not primarily instruments of trade but of social, cultural, or environmental policy. Although one might not imagine that the basic prerogatives of government could come in conflict with trade policy, that assumption does not take into account the ambitious aims of U.S. trade negotiators during the Reagan era. Prodded by business groups, these officials have set about deliberately to create a new world order that would leave business as free as possible to pursue profits throughout the world. The objective was stated by Harry J. Gray, Chairman and CEO of United Technologies, in 1983. He said: "Such barriers as quotas, package and labelling requirements, local-content laws, inspection procedures, and discriminatory government procurement policies all inhibit world trade. We need conditions that are conducive to expanded trade. This means a worldwide business environment that's unfettered by government interference."[23] The ideal of "free enterprise" — business unfettered by government — was thus made the basis of U.S. trade policy. Governments were asked to curb their own regulatory functions so that business could operate more freely on a global scale.

At international trade discussions, the U. S. Government has gained a reputation for being quite hardnosed with respect to social concerns. In 1989, for example, "the United States tabled a proposal to get rid of a (GATT) provision that allows countries to embargo the export of agricultural commodities when people in that country are starving to death," a Canadian attorney reported.[24] Likewise, U.S. diplomats opposed efforts to condemn multinational corporations for socially harmful practices such as Nestle's aggressive marketing of infant formula to mothers in poor nations. When national representatives at the World Health Organization voted 118 to 1 in favor of a code limiting such practices, it was the U.S. Government which cast the lone negative vote.[25] The U.S. free traders have also set a low priority on protecting the natural environment. The U.S.-Canada FTA has pre-empted the constitutionally endowed authority of Canadian provincial governments to make their own rules for developing natural resources. Canada has consented to "work toward equivalence" with the United States in pesticide registration, using a risk-benefit model for making environmental decisions. This decision was widely seen as weakening Canadian pesticide regulation.[26] Stephen Shrybman, counsel for the Canadian Environmental Law Association, has concluded that "the agenda of free trade will undermine any progress in the direction of tougher environmental regulation. And it will undermine the progress we have made in countries that have forged higher standards of environmental protection."[27]

The new approach reverses a long-standing U.S. legal practice by which state or local units of governments can set higher regulatory standards than the federal government. "Critics say the trade negotiations include a conservative plot to undermine health and environmental laws that corporations find burdensome," observed an article in *U.S. News & World Report*. " 'It's a way of achieving in Geneva what they couldn't achieve on Capitol Hill,' says Nancy Watzman of . . . Congress Watch."[28] David Morris, a community-development activist, described the attitude taken by U.S. trade officials toward health and safety standards: "Even if applied equally to domestic and foreign businesses, the Reagan/Bush administration argues, such standards burden commerce by requiring corporations to produce goods to different standards. Corporations are thus forced to produce these goods in shorter production runs, thereby raising prices. When Europe banned the import of beef injected with growth stimulating hormones, Secretary of Agriculture Clayton Yeutter lashed out, even though European producers were held to the same standards. When California enacted strict pesticide standards for food sold in that state, Yeutter again exclaimed, 'How can we get international harmonization when we can't get it here at home,' and accused California of 'going off on a tangent' by writing rules and regulations more stringent than federal standards. The GATT talks are viewed as a way to pre-empt local and state authority in key areas by forcing a uniform, minimum world standard."[29]

The U.S. Government has made legal threats against foreign governments which pursue high social or environmental standards on the grounds that these represent unfair trade practices. For example, U.S. trade negotiators have claimed that Japan's Large Scale Retail Store law, which prevents large department stores from building in neighborhoods adequately served by small retailers, constitutes a trade barrier because U.S. exporters would prefer to sell to a few large retailing firms than to thousands of small ones. The United States has accused Canadian firms of enjoying an unfair trade advantage because Canada's National Health program relieves them of the need to provide health insurance for their employees. Reforestation programs in British Columbia violate trade fairness in the timber industry because they receive government subsidies. Another example of trade "fairness" gone awry, not involving the United States, pertains to a decision handed down last year by the Court of Justice of

the European Community. This court invalidated Denmark's returnable bottle law because importers of beverages would find the reuse
requirements more burdensome than Danish producers would.
"There has to be a balancing of interests between the free movement
of goods and environmental protection, even if in achieving the balance the high standard of protection sought has to be reduced," the
court declared.[30]

Stimulus to Trade or Locking in Access to Investment Opportunities?

Generally, proponents of free trade argue that a bilateral agreement
between the United States and Mexico to eliminate tariffs would
stimulate increased trade between those two countries. That argument would have greater force if tariff rates were high. But the rates
are not high. Thanks to the GATT, the average tariff on manufactured goods has fallen from 40% in 1947 to less than 4% today. The
Salinas government slashed Mexican tariffs on imported goods from
an average of 28.5% in 1985 to 10% in 1991. The United States,
with an average trade-weighted tariff of 3.4%, allows numerous
Mexican goods to enter the country duty-free under the Generalized
System of Preferences.[31] In addition, the Maquiladora program,
which supports industrial development along the US-Mexico border,
brings U.S. raw materials and intermediate products into Mexico
without paying customs duties and imposes them only on the value-
added portion of goods re-entering the United States. Therefore, the
complete elimination of tariffs would have only a modestly stimulating effect on the volume of trade between Mexico and the United
States. The removal of nontariff trade barriers would have a somewhat greater effect. The U.S. International Trade Commission has
admitted: "In all but a few sectors, both countries (the U.S. and Mexico) have relatively low tariff and nontariff barriers to trade with each
other, thus limiting the additional trade liberalization that is
possible."[32]

Trade between Mexico and the United States has already grown
quite rapidly in the absence of a comprehensive trade agreement. It
seems unlikely that removal of the remaining barriers would significantly improve the rate of growth. Total exports to Mexico from

the United States rose from $13.6 billion to $28.4 billion between 1985 and 1990, a 108% increase in five years. Imports from Mexico during that five-year period rose by 58%- from $19.1 billion to $30.2 billion.[33] While pointing out that the United States benefits from increased trade with Mexico, the U.S. International Commission report admitted that "the United States will probably obtain most of these benefits without an FTA."[34] Canada's entrance into the picture would make little difference. Canada is already the United States' largest trading partner. Between 1980 and 1988 (the year when the US-Canada FTA was signed), U.S. exports to Canada rose by 77%, compared with an increase of 36% in U.S. exports to other countries.[35] Therefore, further stimulus to trade between the United States and its two neighbors is unnecessary. Some other explanation for the push for a North American FTA is required .

We can regard the prospective agreement as being, rather than stimulus to further trade, a ratification of events that took place during the 1980s. It is a "locking in" of political gains by business before the tide possibly shifts. During the 1980s, one may recall, conservative governments came to power in all three countries. Ronald Reagan replaced Jimmy Carter as President of the United States. Brian Mulroney replaced Pierre Elliott Trudeau in Canada. Carlos Salinas de Gortari and Miguel de la Madrid replaced Lopez Portillo in Mexico. Economic changes accompanied the changes in political administration, and those in Mexico went farthest. Responding to pressure from foreign banks, the Mexican government launched a vigorous program of privatization and deregulation. Strikes were made illegal. Wages but not prices were controlled. Government spending for social programs plummeted. Workers' real income dropped by 60 percent. Such a program was bound to be unpopular. In the 1988 election, President Salinas won election by a bare 50.1 percent of the vote over the PRD candidate, Cuauhtemoc Cardenas, thanks to computer "malfunctioning" and suspected election fraud.[36] Given a fairly conducted election, it is problematical, then, whether Salinas' political party could hang on to power. The Canadian Prime Minister , too, is in trouble; polls taken in August, 1991, showed Mulroney's approval rating to be about 12 percent.[37] President Bush fares somewhat better in the polls although the recession has done some serious damage.

Nevertheless, these three gentlemen remain heads of state in their respective countries, and, in that capacity, are authorized to enter into trade negotiations with each other. All three are staunch friends of international business and political foes of organized labor. Under the circumstances, then, it makes good strategic sense for them now to negotiate a trade agreement of monumental proportions and embed it in concrete. Such an agreement can be written to reward one's political friends, who, happily, are the same group of friends as those of the other two negotiating parties. (Big business has friends everywhere.) A trinational trade agreement has an advantage over political decisions made at the local or national level in that it cannot so easily be rescinded if someone with a different political philosophy comes to power. A future national leader wishing to be rid of its provisions would find his hands tied. So, in a sense, the agreement becomes stronger than the political process itself. That, then, is the appeal of a U.S.-Mexico-Canada Free-Trade Agreement for business. U.S. business interests want to lock in access to oil and other raw materials in Canada and Mexico, and, in Mexico, to cheap labor. They want to conclude an agreement on favorable terms for themselves—i.e., lacking costly requirements to be socially or environmentally responsible—at an opportune time.

The Action Canada Network, which comprises nearly 40 major Canadian groups, has reported that the United States has two main objectives in its trade talks with Canada and Mexico. The first would be "to secure access to Mexico's petroleum" much as the United States gained access to Canadian petroleum in the 1988 FTA. Ideally, the United States wants U.S. firms to acquire an ownership interest in PEMEX, Mexico's state-owned oil company; but, since that is prohibited by the Mexican Constitution, it is following other avenues of approach. One would be for the U.S. Export-Import Bank to grant PEMEX a $5 billion line of credit with the understanding that it would purchase U.S. equipment and service contracts for exploration and drilling. If these arrangements could be converted from a "pure service" to "risk service" type of contract, then the U.S. firms would effectively "own" part of Mexico's oil business. The U.S. negotiators may also seek to increase U.S. participation in this industry by requesting liberalization of Mexico's government procurement practices. The 1988 agreement with Canada guaranteed continuing U.S. access to Canadian oil and gas. Specifically, articles 902 and 903 of the Agreement prohibited imposing countervailing restrictions on exports or imports of energy products. Canada was forbidden to set minimum energy prices or impose export taxes. Furthermore, article 904 of the Agreement required Canada to continue to supply the United States with petroleum products at a rate of supply not less than that in the preceding three years even if Canada itself has energy shortages. Whatever the means, locking in access to its neighbors' oil has been a prime objective of U.S. trade negotiations.[38]

A second major U.S. objective, according to the ACN report, is "to establish permanent investment and services codes favorable to transnational corporations." Again following the pattern of the 1988 U.S.-Canada agreement, the Bush administration wants "to restrict the ability of sovereign countries to set rules governing foreign investment, culture, patents, services, agriculture and regional development." Repeal of Canada's "compulsory licensing" law for pharmaceuticals would be an example. More broadly, the U.S. negotiators may press Canada to end various "subsidies" left untouched in the 1988 agreement including those pertaining to agricultural marketing boards, public health insurance, government procurement incentives for local businesses, preferential licensing regulations, and regional development grants. The United States wants Mexico to extend "national treatment" to foreign investors, which would mean giving up the right to limit or screen foreign investments, restrict repatriation of profits, specify amounts of domestic content, require transfer of technologies, etc.[39] For their part, the Mexicans and Canadians would gain more secure access to U.S. markets and enjoy the privilege of being a "Major League player" in world trade. Many Canadians, unimpressed with Brian Mulroney's stewardship of their national interests, see the Prime Minister and his associates as being totally dominated by the United States. The cartoon on the next page personalizes that feeling.

The Canadian interest in NAFTA is ambiguous. Business groups have argued that this agreement would give Canada "preferred access to a potentially dynamic Mexican market". The trade talks would also allow Canadian negotiators to open up unresolved issues from the 1988 agreement such as alleged U.S. harassment of Canadian products by use of antidumping remedies. Another, more defensive reason for Canada to participate in a trinational trade agreement would be to avoid allowing the United States to become the center of North American trade. Keith Martin of the Canadian Chamber of

Figure 1.1

Source: Pro-Canada Dossier

Commerce explained that the NAFTA "permits the creation of a continental trade zone as opposed to the creation of two overlapping zones, one between Canada and the United States and one between Mexico and the United States. The latter arrangement would create a hub and spoke system which would give the U.S. an advantage over Canada and Mexico as a destination for investment."[40] Canadian opponents of NAFTA have stressed the conservative deregulatory agenda emanating from the United States. Laurell Ritchie of Common Frontiers argued that the issue of free trade was nothing less than "the future of democracy in this world." In the face of well-organized efforts from the international business community, even governments would become unable to set policies helping their own people. Some of the smaller Canadian firms which supported the 1988 FTA with the United States "have since that time said something quite different. They have said that if they knew then what they know now they would have taken a very different position," she revealed. Free trade, Ritchie said, was "an economic constitution for a new globalism . . . the ultimate form of deregulation," which would cause problems for companies "not at the empire's center."[41]

Calman Cohen, a spokesman for the U.S.-based Emergency Committee for American Trade (ECAN), seemed to acknowledge the validity of the imperial model of trade relations when he assured U.S. audiences that rationalization of production facilities following adoption of NAFTA might work to their national advantage. "U.S. industry," he said, "is a low-cost producer in many sectors. It would more easily be able to supply the Mexican market from its expansive U.S. facilities—in some cases, facilities with unused capacity—were it not for trade barriers maintained by the government of Mexico. Indeed, U.S. firms frequently have set up manufacturing facilities in Mexico to leap over Mexico's barriers . . . What I'm suggesting, then, is that a free-trade agreement will encourage U.S. firms manufacturing in both Mexico and the United States to find ways to rationalize their production and become more, not less, competitive. It will not lead to the wholesale shift to Mexico of U.S. industry."[42] Rationalization or streamlining of production indeed leads to greater efficiency, but at the cost of jobs. In some cases, employees of firms operating "at the empire's center" will benefit from the consolidation because those firms are already set up for large-scale production. In other cases, though, the firms will decide to move out of the high-wage center and into peripheral areas offering cost advantages with respect to labor, taxes, and natural resources. Such areas often have a greater potential for economic growth. Their communities are also more willing to accommodate the demands of business, being "hungrier", so to speak.

The Mexican President, Salinas, wants NAFTA for a different set of reasons. His economic program is driven by financial pressures arising from Mexico's foreign debt. The need to service this debt requires generating large surpluses of hard currency. Since Mexico's domestic economy will be unable to grow rapidly enough, Salinas has decided to accelerate the process by seeking loans and investment from outside the country. While much of this investment money has come from repatriation of funds deposited abroad by wealthy Mexicans, much more is needed from foreign business groups. The problem was that investment opportunities were also opening up in eastern Europe, so Salinas had to move fast. As *Business Week* tells the story, the Mexican President courted foreign investors by placing "dozens of state-owned behemoths, including Telefonos de Mexico, on the block. In 1989, he liberalized foreign investment rules and renegotiated Mexico's $100 billion debt without a hitch. Still, no avalanche of investment poured in. To his dismay, Salinas found his sprint was still too slow for the fast-moving events in Europe after the Berlin Wall fell. Only after a whirlwind tour of Europe's capitals early this year did Salinas see how fast he would have to run, say insiders. If Mexico was to compete for the ever-scarcer aid and investment now drawn to Eastern Europe, Salinas would have to go all the way. Shortly after his return, he dropped two bombshells. He would privatize commercial banks. Then, he announced, long-isolated Mexico would say yes to free trade."[43]

Business investors would be attracted to Mexico for two reasons. Some would be attracted by the once-in-a-lifetime opportunity to buy valuable state-owned enterprises such as the telephone company and airlines at reasonable prices, although the juiciest plum, PEMEX, remains, for now, off limits. Second, foreign investors would be attracted to Mexico in order to produce for the neighboring U.S. market. Normally, investors plan to make money by selling in the national market where the investment is made. In Mexico's case, however, most of its people are so poor that only a small part of the Mexican population would be able to afford the products of foreign companies. Its Gross Domestic Product is only 3.6% as large as that of the United States. By far the greater opportunity for foreign investors would be to produce goods in Mexico, taking advantage of the low labor rates, and then ship them to the United States for sale. Such producers, of course, would want assurances that the United States would always agree to take the production. A comprehensive FTA between the United States and Mexico would certainly do that.

Still, foreign producers already ship a large volume of products from Mexico to the United States paying little or no duty. What additional benefit would a free-trade agreement provide for these firms? Investors, having to commit large sums of money for long periods to build production facilities, want to make sure that their investments are "safe" and free of unusual government restrictions. Since Mexico has a history of restricting capital mobility and even of nationalizing foreign properties, U.S. and other foreign investors needed further assurances that their investments would be secure. The U.S. International Trade Commission report to Congress disclosed that U.S. negotiators will likely press Mexico to repeal its 1973 "Law to Promote Mexican Investment and Regulate Foreign Investment." Even though its provisions were liberalized in 1989, U.S. and other foreign investors felt that the Mexican law unduly curtailed their business prerogatives and made investment in that country less attractive. The USITC report noted in that regard: "Many analysts . . . believe that by codifying liberal trade and investment policies in an international agreement, heretofore adopted only as a matter of national policy, a United States-Mexico FTA would increase the confidence of investors in Mexico's continued economic growth and its resolve to maintain conditions favorable to the profitable operations of businesses. Investors . . . might also believe that an FTA with the United States would ensure Mexico's continued access to the U.S. market."[44]

Investment opportunities lie behind business support for NAFTA as much as opportunities for expanding trade. It is, however, trade-oriented investment that drives the rush to agreement — investment in Mexico and trade directed at markets in Canada and the United States. The idea of permanency or, on its flip side, being impervious to democratic decision-making processes is a critical factor by all accounts. Calman Cohen, for instance, has argued: "Mexico has a government committed to transforming the country into a modern industrial state by unleashing the forces of economic competition . . . It is only prudent to recognize, however, that the changes in Mexico are fully reversible if they fail to receive the support of Mexico's wealthier continental neighbors . . . By working with Mexico to institutionalize them in a regional free-trade agreement, the United States and Canada can help to ensure that they will survive the Salinas presidency."[45] Kay R. Whitmore, chairman of Eastman Kodak, echoed that sentiment when he wrote that the free-trade agreement would "lock in the opening of Mexico's economy so that it can't return to its protectionist ways."[46] A group of U.S. business representatives polled by the U.S. International Trade Commission reported that they favored a FTA with Mexico in part because it offered "some assurance that the executive regulations were permanent, and could not simply be easily changed by the next Mexican administration."[47]

These, then, are two key elements of the agreement: foreign-investor confidence in the permanence of Mexico's investment policies and Mexican producers' continued access to U.S. and Canadian markets. A North American FTA would set those two conditions in concrete. While some business spokesmen have stressed the increased opportunities for exporting goods and services to Mexico and have cited statistics of actual export gains achieved during the last few years, the fact is that the current "boom" in the Mexican economy is largely an expansion based on loan and investment funds rather than on earnings from current production activity. The World Bank is the single largest financial contributor to this boom. The prospective FTA with the United States and Canada is itself Mexico's most persuasive investment incentive.[48] Sylvia Ostry, a former Canadian trade official, told a group of business economists meeting in Washington, D.C., that, from the Mexican perspective, "a North American free trade agreement would enhance export-led growth by 'improving access to the U.S. market and encouraging a return of flight capital as well as new investment.' "[49]

Export-Led Development: Can This be a "Win-Win" Situation?

The expectation that returning Mexican or foreign investors in Mexico will benefit from substantial growth of exports to Canada and the United States in the future is primarily what drives the North American FTA. While no one can quarrel with the need to encourage return of Mexico's considerable "flight capital", the other half of the equation is disturbing from a U.S. perspective. This export-led model of economic growth is a neo-mercantilist trade scheme which can be tolerated, perhaps, in small business enclaves such as Singapore or Hong Kong, but not in a nation as large and populous as Mexico. Such a model is economically unstable because it uncouples production and consumption. A situation is created where production takes place in one country but the primary consumer market is located in another. Healthy consumer markets depend on maintaining large and stable incomes. Such incomes generally depend on producing useful goods and services. The U.S. market was built up by following Henry Ford's philosophy of recycling wealth back to the people who produced it. "The people who consume the bulk of goods are the (same) people who make them," he said.[50] When business instead produces in Mexico to exploit the cheap labor and then sells in the United States, it is depleting one market without creating another. As the U.S. market shrinks with the loss of high-paying factory jobs, it bestows a temporary benefit on persons in the managerial and professional class who enjoy continuing access to income and reap the advantage of low consumer prices. This is a case of short-sighted capitalism cutting its host community's, and ultimately its own, throat.

A possible way out of this situation is to accept the view that Mexico and the United States can have balanced trade relations in the form of exchanging consumer goods for rents on intellectual properties. We will sell the Mexicans Hollywood movies, pharmaceuticals, cartoon-charactered tee shirts, and computer software, while they sell us electronic equipment and cars. Believing that much of our nation's "comparative advantage" lies in intellectual properties, U.S. trade negotiators have moved aggressively to tighten protection in this area. Although the U.S.-Canada FTA does not specifically provide for cultural products, there is a provision in the agreement which gives the United States the right to impose financial penalties if U.S. firms lose money because of government efforts to protect Canadian culture. In contrast, protection of U.S. intellectual properties will certainly be a major concern in the trade talks with Mexico. As a preliminary step to its bid for an FTA with the United States, the Salinas government in January 1990 committed itself to revising certain Mexican statutes which had allowed quick transfer of commercially valuable expressions or knowledge into the public domain. The Mexican proposals, not yet fully implemented, include lengthening the term of patent and trademark protection, Mexico's participating in certain international conventions, repealing a legal provision that gives the right to use licensed technology after the licensing agreement has expired, and agreeing to "grantbacks" to the licenser of subsequent technological improvements.[51]

The idea that rents from intellectual properties can cover the cost of goods received in trade from Mexico is a dubious scheme based, perhaps, upon our national conceit of superior intelligence. It may also account for part of the support which the free-trade proposal has received from U.S. academics. Evidently some educators see an ex-

panded market for their type of service with free trade. Yet these people are deceiving themselves if they think that the Mexicans will be
content to take the back-breaking production jobs while Americans
perform the functions requiring creative intelligence. Mexicans are
not unintelligent people; they are, in fact, graduating more engineers
per capita than we in the United States. Moreover, several large U.S.
corporations have begun endowing Mexican educational programs
in an effort to exploit Mexico's scientific and technological potential.[52] Such developments point up the fact that, contrary to some
loudly trumpeted claims, free trade is not a "win-win situation." It
is instead, most definitely, a win-lose situation. The losers will be
U.S. and Canadian blue-collar workers whose jobs move south of the
border. The winners will be the better educated workers with access
to public and corporate wealth. Moralistically, they can point to the
displaced factory workers and say these people need to be
"retrained". Another group of would-be winners is the horde of U.S.
attorneys set to invade Mexico and do deals. Predictably, the Mexican attorneys are preparing for them less than a warm welcome.
They are instead urging Mexico's negotiating team to exclude legal
services from NAFTA, arguing that "existing judicial systems . . .
are part of the culture and identity of each nation."[53]

Still another win-lose situation pertains to the geographic identity
of communities standing to benefit or suffer under a trade agreement.
An article in *Business Week* reported that "San Diego is abuzz with
financiers spinning deals in Mexico and is landing many white-collar
jobs that the rest of the country is losing. Texans in San Antonio, El
Paso, Houston, and Dallas are bracing for a bonanza from free trade,
not only in white-collar jobs but from relocated parts suppliers."[54]
Senator Lloyd Bentsen of Texas, a strong backer of the FTA with
Mexico, claimed in an article written for the *Dallas Morning News*
that 30% to 40% of jobs created by increased U.S. exports to Mexico
will "go to Texans" and therefore "greater trade with Mexico is one
of the essential building blocks we need to rebuild the Texas economy."[55] With fellow Texans George Bush, James Baker, Robert
Mosbacher, and others occupying key positions in the Executive
Branch of the federal government, Senator Bentsen has powerful support in promoting this parochial interest at the expense of workers
and taxpayers, for instance, in the industrial midwest.

The big winners, though, will be the multinational corporations in their perennial struggle to evade taxes and government regulation. Business operating on an international scale easily outflanks government. A multinational corporation can play one government off against another to its own advantage. Within the United States, we are used to seeing large companies play local or state governments off against each other as they decide where to locate new facilities. The community that offers more tax concessions, fewer regulations, and perhaps some help with financing usually lands the facility. Business locates in communities offering a favorable business climate, which means having low taxes and poor public services, a lack of unions, environmental permissiveness, and so on. The same situation arises on a larger scale as businesses consider whether to leave the United States for sunny Mexico, which President Salinas has turned into a business paradise. No longer need U.S. corporations feel constrained by federal legislation; now even national regulations can be escaped. The only possible hitch is that, having left the United States to produce goods elsewhere, business needs assurance that those goods will be let back into the country where its markets lie. A Free-Trade Agreement gives that assurance. Business is home free.

Some have suggested that an FTA with Mexico is necessary to our national economic welfare even if many or most U.S. production workers lose their jobs. That is because access to cheap Mexican labor is deemed essential to the ability of U.S. firms to compete against Asian or European rivals. Outsourced production would be good for the U.S. or Canadian economies, because the cost savings might allow North American producers to compete with them effectively on price. Therefore, many other, mostly white-collar, jobs could be saved. Furthermore, the Mexican producers would tend to use more U.S.- or Canadian-made parts and supplies, capital equipment, and raw materials than if the finished product came from overseas. There is a possibility, though, that Japanese or other non-North American firms might establish production facilities in Mexico to take advantage of its cheap labor while gaining duty-free access to U.S. and Canadian markets. To guard against that threat, the Bush administration has proposed to write strict local-origin rules into the FTA, requiring that at least 50%, and preferably 60% or 70%, of the manufacturing content be of North American origin for the product to qualify for duty-free treatment. Evidently the word has not yet reached President Salinas. Louis Uchitelle reported in the *New York*

Times on May 21, 1991: "In a recent speech, Carlos Salinas de Gortari, Mexico's President, appealed to Asians to build high-technology
factories in Mexico, arguing that his country was becoming a platform for penetrating the United States market. He did not dwell on
local-origin rules."[56]

Apparently, President Salinas' words were no gaffe but a true indication of policy. Gearing up for approval of NAFTA, Mexican
producers including foreign multinationals have set their eye upon
greatly increased sales in Canada and the United States. The *New
York Times* reported: "Multinational companies with lines in Mexico are expanding their domestic sales focus to include exports to the
rest of North America and other global markets, said the Mexican
Investment Board . . . Two-thirds of those surveyed, and almost
all the Japanese concerns that responded, are expanding their Mexican lines by adding capacity, building plants, entering joint ventures
or acquiring local companies. Nearly all the respondents are profitable in Mexico . . . The prospect of a free trade accord among the
U.S., Canada and Mexico underpinned the companies' confidence in
expanding to serve international markets."[57] In contrast, General
Motors announced in December 1991 that it would close 21 North
American plants and lay off 74,000 workers, including white-collar
employees, to deal with the problem of production overcapacity in
the automobile industry. Speculation was that these cut-backs would
affect operations only in Canada and the United States, while GM's
Mexican facilities would be spared. "The uncertainty (of which facilities would be closed) is touching off an economic free-for-all pitting
worker against worker, community against community, and the
U.S. against Canada," the *Wall Street Journal* disclosed.[58]

A misconception about the prospective North American FTA is
that the negotiations will be conducted between nations. Presumably, the U.S. negotiators will be representing the interests of our national community, as the Mexicans and Canadians will be representing the interests of theirs. In reality, international trade takes place
increasingly, not between nations, but among or within nationless
corporate entities. For example, the Ford Motor Company, headquartered in the United States, is one of the largest "Mexican" exporters of products to the United States. In fact, the three largest private firms exporting products from Mexico are General Motors,
Ford, and Chrysler, with IBM and Kimberly-Clark not far behind.[59]

In the new world of global business, corporations position themselves to best advantage regardless of historic ties to workers, investments, or national communities. "All such allegiances are viewed as
expendable under the new rules. You cannot be emotionally bound
to any particular asset," declared Martin S. Davis of Gulf & Western
Industries.[60] While governments have closer ties to the community,
politicians tend to be bound to their dominant constituencies. For
that reason, we may be sure that a "winner" under any negotiated
FTA between the United States, Canada, and Mexico will be the
international-business groups which support the Bush, Mulroney,
and Salinas governments. The ideology of the free-enterprise system
and of limited government control will become the blueprint for "reform" of their respective national economies to make them acceptable to the other two negotiating parties.

Sops for Labor and Environmental Groups

Trade has long been considered to be an area of interest mainly for
business. The Advisory Committee on Trade Policy and Negotiations, created to give groups outside the government input into trade
negotiations, contains 44 members, of which two are labor unions
and the rest large corporations.[61] Yet, international trade policy has
become a means of circumventing public discussion of issues that
concern other groups as well. The public outpouring of opposition
to extending presidential "fast-track" authority in May 1991 involved interest groups ranging from environmentalists to child-labor
opponents to consumer advocates. To be sure, following this ground
swell of opposition, President Bush made certain promises to environmental, labor, and other groups, pledging to heed their concerns. As reported in the *New York Times*, the President promised
"to work with Congress to fashion an 'adequately funded' program
of assistance for workers dislocated as a result of increased foreign
competition; to exclude changes in immigration policy from the trade
pact; to prevent Mexican products that do not meet United States
health or safety standards from entering this country; (and) to put in
place an integrated environmental plan for the border between the
United States and Mexico and appoint representatives of environmental organizations to official trade advisory bodies."[62] President

Bush also pledged to support special trade restrictions to benefit the fruit-and-vegetable, peanut, and pork industries.[63]

Organized labor is to be placated by promises to fund adjustment-assistance programs for workers who lose their jobs because of trade liberalization. While the AFL-CIO supports this type of approach, its spokesmen point out the inadequacy of such programs in the past. The Trade Expansion Act of 1962 provided compensation and adjustment services to workers whose layoffs could be traced to tariff reductions. With the recession of 1981–82, however, came a sharp increase in Trade Adjustment Assistance (TAA) expenditures and mounting criticism that the program was too costly. Reagan budget-cutters slashed its expenditures drastically and tried to kill the program. Although that attempt failed, Figure 1.2 shows that there has been a sharp decline in the number of workers applying for TAA, and an even sharper drop in the number of workers certified and receiving

Figure 1.2

Trade Adjustment Assistance

Participation in 1986–90, compared with 1976–80

	1976–1980 (annual average)		1986–1990 (annual average)	
	number	percentage of applicants	number	percentage of applicants
workers applying	393,000	100%	162,000	100%
workers certified	252,000	64%	73,000	45%
workers receiving benefits	199,000	51%	37,000	23%
trade deficit	$21 billion		$124 billion	

Source: "Trade Adjustment Assistance: Time for Action, Not False Promises", AFL–CIO Reviews the Issues, Report No. 53, Sept. 1991.

benefits under this program. It has substantially been replaced by the Economic Dislocation and Worker Adjustment Act (EDWAA), whose modest level of funding limits the program to such activities as teaching displaced workers how to write resumes. One participant has described this as "little more than . . . an orderly process by which a worker accustomed to earning $14 or $15 an hour can find jobs where they can make $7 or $8." Unlike the previous program, EDWAA provides virtually no income support or medical coverage for displaced workers while they receive job training and referral services. EDWAA reaches fewer than 300,000 workers each year although nearly two million workers annually are displaced. Yet, the Bush administration apparently is offering this type of assistance to U.S. workers who might be "rationalized" with free trade.[64]

A more serious objection to this approach is that it neglects the fundamental goal of providing more jobs. There is no assurance that the retrained workers can reasonably expect to find jobs or that their post-training incomes will nearly match what has been lost. There is no guarantee that in a future budget crunch this type of program will not become an easy casualty as trade-adjustment programs in the past have been. To retrain displaced workers for nonexistent or low-paying and marginally useful jobs is certainly not a new initiative. This has been the dominant strategy to handle U.S. employment problems for almost thirty years. Yet, it is one whose benefits seem to have reached sharply diminishing returns:

• At the U.S. International Trade Commission hearings in Chicago, a Bloomington, Ill. alderman told of a federally funded job-training program which had managed to place two of its twelve graduates in jobs.[65]

• When Green Giant closed down most of its Watsonville, California, operation several years ago, the president of its corporate parent promised to help retrain the displaced employees through the Job Training Partnership Act (JTPA). He set a goal of placing at least 80% of the retrained employees in jobs paying at least $8.00 an hour. As of November 1991, 256 people had enrolled in the JTPA program. Of this group, 166 persons were still being trained, 57 had dropped out of the program and were employed in mostly minimum-wage jobs, while only 33 had graduated and found positions comparable to what they had lost.[66]

- A study conducted by researchers at the University of Tennessee concluded that federally funded job-training programs were of no help to a group of female workers who became unemployed when Levi Strauss closed a manufacturing plant in Blount County, Tenn., in 1988. Those who received training under the JTPA were found to be no better off 20 months later than those who had not received such training.[67]

The environmental problems relating to U.S. trade with Mexico have attracted more public attention. Much of this concern centers on business activities in the "maquiladora" free-trade enclaves located along the U.S.-Mexico border. Unregulated industrial development in this area has created what an American Medical Association report calls "a virtual cesspool and breeding ground for infectious diseases." The report refers to "uncontrolled air and water pollution (that) is rapidly deteriorating and seriously affecting the health and future economic viability on both sides of the border."[68] Although the Mexican government adopted a comprehensive environmental law in 1988 to deal with such problems, the program is in its infancy. The Bush administration itself admits that "Mexico has lacked the resources to fully enforce its regulations."[69] In that context, agreements between the United States and Mexico to clean up the environment will be ineffective, whether or not incorporated in a North American FTA. But, in fact, the trade negotiators have no intention of dealing with environmental issues. "We're negotiating a trade agreement," Carla Hills explained.[70] As for the parallel discussions between Mexico and the United States to address industrial pollution in the maquiladoras, Public Citizen has characterized the Environmental Protection Agency's proposal as being "not a commitment to clean up the Mexican border and a program to promote environmentally sound development, but merely a plan to make plans." The national chairman of Sierra Club, Michael McCloskey, has called the plan "pathetically weak."[71]

International trade agreements directly impinge upon the ability of environmental groups to take effective action since environmental problems often extend beyond national borders. For example, a proposal at GATT that would prevent countries from restricting exports of their own natural resources would invalidate the Forest Resources Conservation and Shortage Relief Act of 1990, which prohibits export of unprocessed timber from certain public lands. The Pack-wood-Magnuson Amendment to the Fisherman's Protection Act, authorizing restrictions upon foreign fishing in waters subject to the exclusive authority of the U.S. Government, would also be in jeopardy, as would certain measures to protect whales.[72] One of the most visible environmental irritants in U.S.-Mexico trade relations was Mexico's challenge to a U.S. law protecting dolphins from indiscriminate methods of tuna fishing. The Marine Mammal Protection Act bans the sale of tuna caught in huge nets that also ensnare dolphins. It requires "dolphin safe" labels to be displayed on cans of tuna. Because Mexico's tuna fishermen commonly use the prohibited fishing techniques, the Mexican government brought suit against the United States before a GATT dispute-resolution tribunal charging that the U.S. law banning Mexican tuna imports was illegal under GATT rules. The tribunal ruled in Mexico's favor on August 16, 1991. This ruling was a particular embarrassment to the Bush administration, which had pledged in May that no U.S. environmental standard would be weakened as a result of the Mexican trade pact.[73]

Several major environmental groups in the United States have demanded that the U.S. Government prepare an environmental impact statement pertaining both to the Uruguay Round of the GATT negotiations and to NAFTA. Such an assessment of environmental impact is required by the National Environmental Policy Act (NEPA) as well as regulations issued by the President's Council on Environmental Quality. The Bush administration presented a plan in July for a limited review of environmental issues which did not comply with the NEPA requirements. On August 1, 1991, Public Citizen, the Sierra Club, and Friends of the Earth filed suit in a federal district court to force the Office of the U.S. Trade Representative to prepare environmental impact statements covering both trade agreements.[74] In a position paper issued on August 1, Public Citizen charged that the Trade Representative's environmental review "avoids public input as to the agreement's scope, does not consider differing environmental impact of alternatives to NAFTA, does not consider mitigation of possible effects, and is planned to be completed before the U.S. has a complete proposal to analyze. Specifically, the USTR plan fails to give consideration to impacts that might result from increases in logging, mining and other extractive industries under NAFTA; it does not analyze the existing free trade agreement with Canada; it

does not examine the relationship between NAFTA and the environmental protection capabilities of the three countries; nor does it offer
predictions on how NAFTA will affect intensity and geographical
distribution of development in all three countries. By these and other
signs, it has become apparent that USTR is unwilling to fairly examine the environmental impact of the trade agreements that it has
responsibility to negotiate."[75]

The Doctrine of Comparative Advantage

Even if compelling arguments can be presented against free trade,
supporters have an argumentative "ace" obtained from their friends
in academia which is called the "theory of comparative advantage."
Paul Samuelson, the Nobel-prizewinning economics textbook author, has written that "the theory of comparative advantage is a
closely reasoned doctrine which, when properly stated, is unassail-
able. With it we can identify gross fallacies in the political propagan-
da for protective tariffs aimed at limiting imports."[76] The doctrine of
comparative advantage, which British economist David Ricardo first
proposed in 1817, maintains that it is in every nation's interest to participate in a world economy, to accept international specialization of
production, and to trade freely for products, rather than attempt to
produce everything itself. The nation which is best suited to produce
a certain product because of natural or other advantages should
specialize in producing that product and export the surplus. In return, it should import from other nations other kinds of products
which they were better able to produce. This argument remains valid
even if a nation can produce all or most goods more efficiently than
other nations; it should still specialize in its strongest products and
obtain the others in trade.

Almost with zeal, some free-trade advocates have espoused the
related doctrine of the "creative destruction" of certain industries as
worldwide capitalism redistributes production according to supposed new schemes of comparative advantage. If, for instance,
foreign-produced steel becomes more economical than steel
produced in the United States, then, they contend, the U.S. Government should not attempt to prop up the domestic steel industry arti-
ficially by subsidies and import protection but accept the fact that
steel in this country is a dying industry. Government should instead

devote resources to promoting industries of the future. A decade ago, an ideological faction in Congress favoring selective assistance to firms in the "high tech" field was known as the "Atari Democrats", until the real-life producer of Atari games announced in early 1983 that it was laying off 1,700 employees in California and relocating production to Hong Kong and Taiwan.[77] Still, many policymakers of this persuasion have continued to watch serenely as foreign producers made significant inroads into the U.S. market for products such as steel, clothing, and automobiles. In the back of their mind, they have imagined that U.S. industry would survive the shakedown in international markets, as it always has, by mastering new technologies. And more education would be the key!

Fundamentally, the theory of comparative advantage is a doctrine better suited to a world economy based on mining and agriculture, where regional production advantages or disadvantages exist, than to one based on manufacturing, services, and finance. An advantage in manufacturing is conferred by such factors as capital investment, technological know-how, skilled labor, low-cost labor, and environmental permissiveness. Some of these elements are easily transferred in a global economy, while others—low-cost labor and environmental permissiveness—are socially undesirable. The political or legal climate also plays a part in trade competitiveness. The new situation in world trade is illustrated by a luncheon conversation between a Canadian proponent of free trade and an American opponent. In the course of the conversation, the Canadian complained that U.S. attorneys customarily restricted trade by filing harassing lawsuits against Canadian products. "Yes", the American facetiously replied, "we have a comparative advantage in harassing attorneys."[78]

Proponents of free trade envision that the United States can exploit a comparative advantage in intellectual properties, services, and agriculture. Unfortunately, Japan and the European Community nations are fiercely protectionist with respect to agriculture; the GATT talks broke down in December 1990 over the issue of European agricultural subsidies and, a year later, were still at an impasse. Intellectual properties, such as patents and copyrighted films or tapes, are easily pirated. Dataquest, a market-research company, reports that it takes Asian imitators about three weeks, from the time when a new product is introduced in the United States, to copy the product, manufacture it, and ship a specimen back to the United

States from Asia.[79] Some of the services which U.S. professionals have developed to a high degree of sophistication — legal expertise, financial wizardry — the other nations may not want. Therefore, if we concede the bulk of our manufacturing industries to foreign producers while meanwhile switching from a net-creditor to net-debtor position in asset holdings, the United States may have little left to offer its trading partners. The time has passed when we as a nation could contemplate living off our foreign investments.

In reality, the world economy has become rather homogenized from a manufacturing-production standpoint. We do not have separate nations trading for products which they are uniquely able to provide, but, instead, multinational corporations establishing a presence simultaneously in several different nations and trading among themselves. The corporations can or do produce the same kinds of products in each country. Peter F. Drucker, noted U.S. business theorist, has observed that, while "international trade" has recently been declining, "international investment" is booming. More than one-third of all trade across national borders is intra-company trade. About one-fifth of the capital of U.S. manufacturing firms is invested in facilities outside the United States. Japanese firms are starting to follow suit. The reason that large corporations invest so heavily in foreign facilities is that they need to establish dominance in the world market to survive in their own national market. These corporations want a "feel" for the national markets in which they will be selling. They also want to take full advantage of changing conditions in the global economy which may favor production in one or another nation at various times.[80]

Wage differentials for blue-collar workers have long been an element in corporate-investment decisions, but, with the labor-cost content in many products down to 15% or less, Drucker claims that a nation's low wages will cease to be the drawing card for manufacturers that they have been. Instead, the parochial tax and regulatory climates and the vagaries of the world financial market will determine where to build plants. In the 1980s, the fluctuating currency-exchange rates became a major element in world trade. Corporations whose operations were concentrated in a single nation took a financial beating when their nation's currency rose sharply (as the U.S. dollar did in the middle of this decade), while corporations with foreign subsidiaries were able to weather such changes by shifting funds back to the mother country. Thus, a worldwide presence became a means of currency hedge. Contrary to classical economic theory, currency-exchange rates can be affected by the demand for short-term investments in a country as well as by its merchandise balance of trade. "Increasingly," Drucker wrote, "world investment rather than world trade will be driving the international economy. Exchange rates, taxes and legal rules will become more important than wage rates and tariffs."[81]

Because many of these factors will be short-lived, corporations, to cut costs to the minimum and reap maximum profits, must be prepared to jump across national boundaries at a moment's notice. Peter Drucker has sketched the ideal corporate structure for this environment. "With currency fluctuations a part of economic reality, business will have to consider them as just another cost," he told readers of the *Wall Street Journal*. "Specifically this means that businesses, and especially businesses integrated with and exposed to the world economy, will have to learn to manage themselves as composed of two quite dissimilar parts: a 'core business' permanently domiciled in one country or in a few countries, and a 'peripheral business' capable of being moved, and moved fast, according to differentials in major costs—labor, capital, and exchange rates. A business producing highly engineered products might use its plants in its home country to produce those parts that the quality, performance and integrity of its products demand—say 45% or 50% of the value of the finished product . . . The remaining 50% to 55% of its production would be peripheral and quite mobile, to be placed on short-term contracts wherever the costs are lowest, whether in developed countries with favorable exchange rates or in Third World countries with favorable labor rates."[82]

If comparative advantage continues to exist in the world economy, it may be found more in the relationship between governments and business than in innate characteristics of national producers. Taxes, legal rules, and even currency values are products of governmental policy. The enforcement of environmental standards is a product of governmental policy. Government also favors or opposes the right of workers to form democratic unions. Since these all relate directly to product cost, business will be looking for an "advantage" in governmental attitudes that will minimize the damage. A "favorable" business climate will be one in which government accommodates the financial interests of business even when those interests conflict with human or environmental needs. What, then, is comparative advantage if all it means is that private business can act at the expense of the rest of society? We have reached the end of the line in classical economic thinking. Free trade was supposed to be a winning proposition for all parties concerned; it has instead turned into a clash between opposing economic and political philosophies, pitting business profits and managerial prerogatives against popular living standards, democracy, and environmental protection. The imperative of free trade, supposedly grounded in hard economic facts, is certainly undermined if the advantage of one nation's products over another's lies in the willingness of its government to put business interests ahead of its other responsibilities to the community.

Some argue that free trade brings increased efficiency through global specialization and that producers must play this game to remain competitive with respect to costs. "In order to survive," said George Ball, an Under Secretary of State in the Kennedy Administration, "man must use the world's resources in the most efficient manner. This can be achieved only when all the factors necessary for the production and use of goods — capital, labor, raw materials, plant facilities, and distribution — are freely mobilized and deployed according to the (globally) most efficient patterns."[83] Such an argument ignores the cost of transporting goods over long distances and the response time in filling customer orders. Peter Drucker cites "a well-tested rule (which) says offshore production must be at least 5%, and probably 7½%, cheaper than production nearby to compensate for the considerable cost of distance."[84] Perry D. Quick of Quick, Finan & Associates has challenged Drucker's estimate of costs. "In a recent study for the National Tooling and Machining Association," he wrote, "we found that the total cost of sourcing a product or service abroad was as much as 30% to 35% higher than a foreign company's originally quoted price. The hidden costs of foreign sourcing include freight, packaging, insurance, customs duties and communications costs, as well as others that are harder to quantify — such as the costs of larger inventories, additional internal rework, lost time for delayed deliveries, exchange-rate risks and the costs of additional features required to bring foreign products in line with U.S. standards."[85]

Historical Perspectives on Trade and Development

Some make the argument that, historically, free trade has been the only real basis of economic growth, while protectionism is at best a short-term fix. A consultant to the Hudson Institute, B. Bruce-Briggs, offered this perspective: "No country has adopted free trade because of the plausible arguments of economic science; rather, free trade became policy when nations found it in their economic interests. The Dutch upheld free trade when they had comparative advantage in the carrying trade of Europe. The English fought them with their mercantilist system. After the Dutch were crushed, the English invented the Industrial Revolution, a wonderful advantage, and Adam Smith easily convinced them of the benefits of free trade. Alas, competitors developed their industrial potential within systems that looked much like discredited mercantilism, and England abandoned free trade. One of those competitors—Germany—went through the same stages rather later; another—Japan—is just now switching from a protectionist to a free-trade position. The U.S. has followed much the same pattern . . . The young republic needed open markets for its agricultural goods and its farmers wanted cheap manufactures from Europe, so the policy was free trade. As factories appeared, other interests came to the fore. The emigre German economist-entrepreneur Friedrich List argued for 'infant industries' protection, and found an eager audience. This was the golden age of American capitalism—an era of breakneck economic growth."[86]

Historically, U.S. manufacturing industries were allowed to develop in an environment of tariff protection combined with generous government subsidies for internal infrastructure. In colonial times, American traders had owned one of the world's largest fleets of sailing vessels. The first U.S. Secretary of Treasury, Alexander Hamilton, produced a report recommending that the federal government instead encourage the growth of domestic industries by imposing tariffs on imported goods—a direct threat to those economic sectors dependent on foreign trade. What "creative destruction" Hamilton began his political rival, Thomas Jefferson, finished through the trade embargo of 1807. Jefferson's embargo virtually ruined the U.S.

shipping industry. As that industry was centered in Massachusetts, Jefferson's policies led to a bitter regional dispute between New England and the rest of the country. A threat was made to secede from the union at the Hartford Convention in 1814–15. A tariff bill passed in 1832 aroused similar opposition in the South. The South Carolina legislature declared the federal tariffs to be "null and void", precipitating a constitutional crisis which President Andrew Jackson was able to resolve.

Bernard Lewis, professor emeritus of history at Princeton, has drawn a useful parallel between the decline of commerce and industry in the Ottoman empire during the 18th century and the situation in the United States at the present time. The Ottoman Turks did not lose out to economic competition from the west due to protectionist policies or a lack of free-market institutions but because "(a) rise of mercantilism in the producer-oriented West helped European trading companies, and the states that protected and encouraged them, to achieve a level of commercial organization and a concentration of economic energies unknown and unparalleled in the East . . . Western merchants, later manufacturers, and eventually governments, were able to establish an almost total control of Middle Eastern markets." The Turks then were in a situation analogous to that of today's "consumer-oriented societies of Western Europe and even more, North America, where manufacturers and merchants are faltering or failing in the struggle in the open market against the new mercantilism of competitors (in Asia) who have found new ways of mobilizing and deploying the economic power of their societies."[87] Indeed, noted an article in *U.S. News & World Report*, "Japanese economists are (now) arguing that Japan is a better model for developing nations than America's excessive reliance on market mechanisms, liberalization and deregulation. In fact, Japan is now openly pressing the World Bank to alter its U.S.-inspired development strategy, arguing that the organization should encourage nations to target certain industries and shelter them from foreign competition until they can stand on their own."[88]

According to Peter Drucker, the classic development pattern in the 19th century was for the less developed nations to ship food and raw materials to the advanced industrialized nations in exchange for finished products. Another pattern, pursued by Japan and the four Asian "tigers"—South Korea, Taiwan, Hong Kong, and Singapore—after World War II, was to convert unskilled labor into a low-paid though highly productive work force through training, and thus compete with the industrially more advanced countries on the basis of labor costs. Their specialty was to manufacture products for the export market. The maquiladora program is an attempt to apply this developmental pattern to Mexico. Unfortunately, Drucker noted, few nations today import significant amounts of food, and the raw-material content of most manufactured products has dropped dramatically. The appeal of low wages for skilled and unskilled labor has also diminished as the labor-cost content of products has dropped. Therefore, neither of these two traditional routes to economic development is available to the currently underdeveloped nations. Drucker foresaw that "the Third World may . . . have to find new development strategies based probably on the domestic market . . . Northern Italy and India, rather than Japan, may become tomorrow's development models."[89] In other words, a free-trade policy aimed at increased global specialization to exploit cheap labor may no longer help those poorer nations so much.

It should be mentioned, finally, that a principal architect of the post-war trading order, John Maynard Keynes, had a change of thinking as he approached old age. "I sympathize with those who would maximize economic entanglement among nations," he said. "Ideas, knowledge, science, hospitality, travel—these are the things which should by their nature be international. But let goods be home-spun whenever it is reasonably and conveniently possible and, above all, let finance be primarily national."[90] The debate concerning free trade is certainly not new. What is new is the prospect of economic integration between a developing nation such as Mexico and developed nations such as Canada and the United States. The next part of this book will provide background information on social and economic conditions in our two neighboring North American countries as they relate to trade agreements.

PART TWO

Mexican and Canadian Experiences with Free Trade

The Three North American Countries

Although Canada and Mexico border upon the United States, many Americans are less aware of events occurring in those countries than in more distant places such as the Middle East. The Canadians and Mexicans, on the other hand, are well aware of their common neighbor. That anomaly may, perhaps, be explained by the fact that the United States has tended to dominate the other two North American countries and take them for granted. The U.S. population is roughly three times the population of Mexico. Mexico's population is three times Canada's. Both Canada and Mexico were invaded by U.S. troops in the 19th century. In the 20th century, they have been penetrated by U.S. economic, political, and cultural influences. A remnant of British colonial rule, Canada has a relatively small and static population residing in a large, well-irrigated territory that extends northward beyond the Arctic Circle. Mexico, with its Spanish colonial heritage, has a large and fast-growing population in a relatively small, semi-tropical, and mostly arid territory. Yet the two countries both border upon the United States, and that gives them something in common. The U.S. economy is ten times the size of Canada's, and more than twenty times the size of the Mexican economy. Canada and the United States are each other's largest trading partners. Mexico is the third largest trading partner for the United States, but the United States is Mexico's largest.

Figure 2.1

Population, Territory, and Gross Domestic Product
In Three North American Countries

	United States	Mexico	Canada
population (est. 1990)	248,709,873	88,335,000	26,620,500
territory (sq. miles)	3,618,770	761,604	3,849,000
G.D.P. (billions $US)	$5,167	$187	$543
population per square mile	68.7	116	6.9
per–capita GDP	$20,775	$2,120	$20,400

Source: U.S. International Trade Commission,
the World Almanac and Book of Facts

Politically, all three countries are independent sovereign states having their own Constitution and a democratic form of government. The U.S. Constitution is two centuries old. The British North American Act of 1867 served as Canada's Constitution until 1982 when a new one was adopted. The Mexican Constitution was written in 1917 following a revolution that overthrew the dictatorship of Porfirio Diaz. Today, Canada has three major political parties: Liberals, Conservatives, and New Democratic Party (NDP). This last-named party, supported by the unions, controls Ontario's provincial government. In the United States, there are two major parties, Democrats and Republicans. Mexico has been a one-party state since the 1920s, ruled by the Institutional Revolutionary Party (PRI). Several other political parties have been formed to challenge PRI's rule. The most important are a left-of-center party called Party of the

Democratic Revolution (PRD) led by Cuauhtemoc Cardenas and a right-of-center party called National Action Party (PAN).

The political pendulum swung to the left in all three countries during the 1930s. Lazaro Cardenas, father of Cuauhtemoc, was then President of Mexico. He nationalized Mexico's oil industry and reorganized its ruling political party, bringing labor into the fold. Franklin D. Roosevelt's "New Deal" program in the United States helped organized labor while seeking a way out of the depression. Roosevelt's Canadian counterpart was the Liberal prime minister, Mackenzie King, who served from 1935 until 1948. He brought Canada into World War II on Britain's side, and later played an active role in the formation of the United Nations. The three North American countries stood together during World War II and have been political allies in the postwar era. Moderately left-of-center governments were in power much of that time in Canada and Mexico, while the U.S. administrations have tended to be more mixed. Since the mid 1980s, conservatives have governed the three countries. The North American FTA is intended to be a fruit of that political convergence.

Some Elements in Canada's Political Background

Canadian and U.S. history were once part of the same colonial experience, which involved a power struggle between England and France and encroachment upon the red man's territory. In what we call the "French and Indian War", the British wrested control of French possessions in North America, capturing Quebec in 1759 with Wolfe's victory over Montcalm. A decade and a half later, rebellion broke out against British rule in Massachusetts and other colonies to the south. Canada became a haven for Loyalists who supported George III during the American Revolution. The Canadian provinces remained a British possession until they were organized as an independent confederation in the late 1860s. As such, they came in conflict with the United States during the War of 1812. The territorially ambitious Americans invaded lower Canada that year, but were repelled by British forces including a contingent of Indians led by Chief Tecumseh. Otherwise, Canadian history has paralleled that of the United States with respect to territorial explorations, westward migration, and absorption of European immigrants. While lacking the element of the struggle against slavery, it includes conflict between the English- and French-speaking segments of the population, a remnant of Canada's colonial past.

Canada is organized along a geographical line east to west. The Canadian Pacific Railway completed the last section of track between Montreal and the Pacific coast in 1885. The country is rich in agricultural and natural resources. Its major commodities include fish from the maritime provinces, nickel and iron from upper Ontario, hydroelectric power from northern Quebec, wheat from Manitoba and Saskatchewan, oil from Alberta, and timber and fish from British Columbia. Canada also has a strong manufacturing sector, concentrated in Ontario and Quebec, which is well integrated with the U.S. economy. During the 1930s, hard times in the western provinces brought increased militancy among Canadian farmers, who organized cooperatives to market their products and supported radical political programs. The Social Credit movement, based on the ideas of British economist C.H. Douglas, proposed to replace the banking system with a national bookkeeping scheme that would extend unlimited credit to producers of various goods and services. The Social Credit party won a landslide victory in the 1935 Alberta provincial elections, but the Canadian Supreme Court struck down its financial program. The Cooperative Commonwealth Federation, an agrarian socialist organization, won a majority of seats in the Saskatchewan legislature in 1944. In 1961, it merged with the Canadian Labor Congress to form the New Democratic Party.

Canada has been governed by Liberal administrations since the mid 1930s with the exception of the periods between 1957 and 1963 and since 1984, when Conservative prime ministers held office. Tension between the French-speaking population in Quebec and the English-speaking population in the rest of the country has put a strain on national unity. The Canadian and American labor movements have been integrated since the 19th century. The great May Day strikes were a product of their combined organization. In 1985, however, the Canadian auto workers split from the U.S.-based United Automobile Workers, criticizing its willingness to engage in "concession bargaining." Canadian unions have generally been more aggressive than their U.S. counterparts in seeking gains in wages and benefits, improving public pensions, protecting part-time workers, and demanding better occupational health and safety standards. They have also forged a link to a political party. Workers in unions belonging to the Canadian Labour Congress pay a portion of their dues to the NDP. About 30% of both Canadian and U.S. industrial workers belonged to unions in 1965. By 1988, this had climbed to 39% in Canada but dropped to 17% in the United States.[1]

The Canadian government has been both internationally minded and protective of domestic economic, social, and cultural interests. Canada has, for instance, a national health-insurance program and relatively generous benefits for unemployed and injured workers. Like the French government, it has moved to protect its own national culture from U.S. domination. For that reason, the proposal to enter into a Free-Trade Agreement with the United States aroused a firestorm of political opposition in Canada during the late 1980s. A coalition of labor, religious, peace, women's, environmental, and aboriginal groups fought the proposal put forth by Conservative Prime Minister Brian Mulroney, which was generally supported by Canadian business interests. The Conservatives won the 1988 national elections, and the U.S.-Canada Free-Trade Agreement went into effect on January 1 of the following year.

Twists and Turns in Mexico's Economic Development

Mexico's political past has been equally turbulent. During the long dictatorship of Porfirio Diaz, foreign investors, mainly American, owned 77% of Mexican industries and nearly all its mines and oil-production facilities. Four-fifths of all agricultural land was owned by 834 landlords. The Mexican Revolution of 1910, led by Emiliano Zapata and Pancho Villa, returned the communal lands, or ejidos, to the peasants. The new Constitution, written in 1917, prohibited foreign ownership of oil and other mineral resources and protected the rights of industrial workers.[2] Mexico experienced a period of political instability following a Roman Catholic rebellion in the 1920s. A Christian fanatic assassinated President Alvaro Obregon in July 1928. Because the leader of the state-supported trade union, CROM, was implicated in the assassination plot, the government withdrew its support from this organization, and it fell apart. Several new trade-union groups were created. Meanwhile, a split developed within the ruling political party between former President Elias Plutarcho Calles and the newly elected President Lazaro Cardenas. Leaders of several trade unions formed a "Committee of Proletarian Defense" to support Cardenas. After defeating Calles, President Cardenas reorganized the ruling party and merged the unions that had backed him in the struggle to form the Confederation of Mexican Workers (CTM). To keep labor from becoming too powerful, Cardenas created a separate union for farmers and small property owners, and another for public employees. He then merged these different groups into the ruling party.[3]

During World War II, the government-controlled unions in Mexico signed a pact with management groups pledging not to strike. The U.S. Government, needing replacements for Americans who had been drafted into the war, brought thousands of Mexican workers into the United States to perform agricultural labor under the "bracero" program. This program lasted from 1940 to 1965. It exposed Mexicans to the economic advantages of living in the United States, and exposed U.S. employers to the financial rewards of employing cheap Mexican labor. In 1965, the Mexican government established the Mexican Border Industrialization Program to absorb the terminated bracero workers returning to Mexico. Under this arrangement, businesses could build factories in the 12.5-mile-wide strip of land running along the border with the United States, and import capital goods or raw or semi-finished materials for use in these factories duty-free. Furthermore, foreigners were allowed to have majority ownership. In return for these concessions, the Mexican government required that 100% of the goods produced in the border factories be exported back to the United States or sent to another country. The U.S. Government responded to this program by allowing metal and other products manufactured outside the United States to re-enter the country with a tariff levied only on the value-added portion of the product. The export-production factories became known as maquiladoras.[4]

Mexico's program of industrialization originally focused on the domestic market. Major sectors of industry including oil, telephone service, and the airlines were state-owned. Agriculture underwent a transformation from small-scale production on communal lands to specialized farming on larger, privately owned lands. Chemical fertilizers were introduced. Many peasants, forced off the land, went to work in the cities. Aiming at economic self-sufficiency, the Mexican government limited foreign ownership of business and protected domestic businesses with high tariffs. At the same time, though, the Mexican economy underwent what some have called a "silent integration" with the U.S. economy. Many Mexicans crossed over the U.S. border to pursue better employment opportunities. Mexico continued to import large quantities of capital goods from the United States, thus increasing its dependency upon U.S.-made products. Despite restrictions upon foreign ownership of business, Americans in 1970 controlled more than 50% of Mexico's automobile, chemical, mining, rubber, tobacco, computer, and pharmaceutical industries. Nevertheless, the Mexican economy was booming. The pace of industrialization picked up around 1955. Mexico's GNP grew at an average annual rate of 6.5% for the next three decades. Real wages steadily increased. One spoke of a "Mexican miracle".[5]

A worldwide "oil shock" occurred in 1973 as OPEC producers conspired to drive up the price of petroleum. Suddenly, Arab kings, sheiks, and emirs were awash in funds needing to be invested or spent. The U.S. banks with whom large amounts of their money were deposited needed to recycle these "petrodollars" in some profitable way. Loans to Latin American governments were popular with international bankers in the 1970s because their countries had a history of rapid and sustained economic growth and the governments' full taxing authority underlay repayment. Besides, the interest rates, commissions, and fees for such loans were quite high. So in those "go-go" years of international banking, U.S. and other foreign banks pressed additional loans on Mexico. Its long-term debt rose from $5.9 billion in 1970 to $88.7 billion in 1988. The Mexican government used the proceeds from the loans to finance development projects which often involved purchases of capital equipment and skilled labor from the United States. Facing popular unrest, it also spent money on social-service programs.[6] Mexico's business and political elite skimmed off large sums of money, which were often transferred to foreign banks for safekeeping. It is estimated that by 1990 more than $60 billion had fled the country in this manner.[7]

Living in the Shadow of Debt

As Mexico's debt load mounted, so did interest payments to foreign banks. Annual payments on the long-term debt rose from $283 million in 1970 to $7.6 billion in 1988. It became necessary for the Mexican government to borrow short-term funds from the International Monetary Fund and commercial banks to pay the interest. A crisis occurred in 1976, when the government of Lopez Portillo was forced to meet various IMF-imposed conditions for continued borrowing, which included wage controls, devaluation of the peso, and cuts in government spending. After the Portillo government announced that Mexico had larger oil reserves than expected, bank credit again became plentiful. The price of oil rose in the late 1970s, giving Mexican leaders a renewed sense of confidence. They continued to borrow. In 1982, however, oil prices plunged, while interest rates remained at historically high levels. Mexico's total earnings from oil exports barely covered the interest on its external debt. The Portillo government announced that Mexico could not meet its debt obligations. A confidential U.S. State Department memo leaked then to the *New York Times* revealed the Reagan Administration's hopes that "Mexico 'might sell more gas and oil to us at better prices.' Mexico 'with the wind out of its sails' might be more willing to ease restrictions on foreign investment . . . and 'be less adventuresome in its foreign policy'." President Portillo responded to the financial crisis by nationalizing the banks. He also negotiated a humiliating agreement to sell oil to the United States for its strategic petroleum reserve for $4 a barrel less than the world price.[8]

After struggling for another four years, the Mexican government disclosed in June 1986 that it was considering a moratorium on debt payments. Chairman Paul Volcker of the U.S. Federal Reserve Bank flew down to Mexico City to warn his colleagues there against making such a rash move. President Miguel de la Madrid backed off his threat. Instead, he appointed a new Finance Minister, Carlos Salinas de Gortari, who was more sympathetic to U.S. interests. Mexico subsequently loosed its restrictions on foreign investment and joined GATT. Meanwhile, the U.S. Treasury Secretary, James Baker, unveiled a new program to deal with Third World debt, which called for private commercial banks to make new loans to the debtor nations in exchange for accepting "structural adjustment programs" or SAPs. These SAPs gave the banks unprecedented control over the nations' economic policies. Specifically, they encouraged debtor nations to privatize state-owned businesses, devalue currencies, control wages, and liberalize trade. Even this failed to attract new money from the banks, so a subsequent Secretary of the Treasury, Nicholas Brady, came up with another plan which offered minor debt relief in exchange for collateral guaranteeing the remaining loans. The SAPs were continued.[9]

Mexico, at any rate, had turned the corner. There would be no more talk of defaults or debt moratoriums, but only of full-hearted cooperation with the banks. Whatever it took, Mexico would come up with the money to service its foreign debt. Domestic consumption would have to be restrained, and exports pushed. There would have to be a reversal, in other words, of Mexico's previous policy of inward development aiming to improve Mexican living standards. President Miguel de la Madrid and his young protege, Carlos Salinas de Gortari, who succeeded him as President, were architects of the new approach. Their immediate task was to slash government spending and bring inflation under control. In the long range, they hoped to attract enough foreign capital to Mexico that the Mexican economy could grow faster than the debt obligations and living standards eventually would improve. Abandoning the old approach, they pursued instead what a World Bank report in 1985 called "a fast and far-reaching liberalization of the trading regime, aimed at expanding the tradables (export-KM) sector." Average tariff rates on imported goods were reduced from 28.5% to 11% between 1985 and 1988. The reference pricing system, which set minimum prices for imports, was eliminated in 1988. The number of products requiring import licenses declined from 92.2% of the total in 1985 to 23.2% in 1988.[10] An aggressive program of privatization reduced state ownership of business and relaxed restrictions on foreign investment. Between 1982 and 1989, 80% of 773 government-owned enterprises were sold to private investors, mainly foreigners. They included the telephone company, banks, airlines, mines, steel mills, food-packing plants, and roads. The international bankers and business executives loved it.[11]

These moves to open up Mexico to foreign investment and trade were accompanied by a strenuous regimen of domestic belt-

Figure 2.2

Average Wages per Hour
in Mexico

1982	$1.38
1984	$.69
1986	$.58
1988	$.69
1990	$.45
1991	$.51

Source: Daniel LaBotz

tightening. To fight inflation, the government controlled wages and cut public spending while allowing other prices to rise. The "Solidarity Pact" which the government imposed upon workers in December 1987, did finally bring inflation down. Even so, the real wages of Mexican workers declined by more than 60% between 1982 and 1989. The average hourly manufacturing wage declined from a high of $3.81 in 1981 to $1.57 in 1987 in terms of U.S. dollars. In the maquiladoras, manufacturing wages were substantially lower than that—between $.55 and $.60 an hour.[12] Another element of the anti-inflationary policy was to cut government spending for social programs. Real spending for programs in the areas of education and health care dropped by more than 50% between 1982 and 1990 as the need for them increased. Meanwhile, the percentage of public spending allocated to the rural areas, where poverty was worst, declined from 19% to 5%. The system of communal farming broke down due to lack of government credits, and much of the land was rented to private interests. As a result, corn production in Mexico, providing a staple of the Mexican diet, dropped from 14.6 million tons in 1981 to 11.6 million tons in 1987. Mexico had to import 41% of the beans its people consumed. The Salinas government created a new program called PRONASOL to coordinate government efforts to treat cases of extreme poverty. However, its annual budget of 2.8 trillion pesos represented only 0.12% of Mexico's federal budget.[13]

In 1986, as the Mexican government's austerity program went into effect, two front-page articles in the *Wall Street Journal* reported that the budget cuts seemed to be directed in ways that would cause lasting damage to Mexico and its people. One article called this approach "the wrong kind of austerity", adding that "governments have generally been reluctant to handle political hot potatoes . . . (but) instead . . . have cut capital spending for development projects to the bone and trimmed outlays for maintenance as well. The result: Latin America's existing transportation and other facilities are falling apart, and new development projects lie unfinished or unbuilt." For instance, a new highway from Altamira to Tampico, excavated in 1981, had become a bed of wild flowers five years later.[14] The other article told of the intense human suffering that accompanied the cuts in social programs. To "experts working in Latin America," the article said, "the empirical evidence lead to an inescapable conclusion: A whole region is being pushed backward, so that what was once the middle class now plunges toward poverty, and what was once the poorer class now lives hand to mouth." The intense poverty was producing "severe malnutrition" in children. Many died or incurred mental retardation. In contrast, the article also described a meeting between Richard Webb, former president of Peru's central bank, and creditors in New York where "one banker began expounding on his warm feelings for Peru and on the 'human cost' of its predicament. Mr. Webb first thought he was talking about starving Peruvians. Then he realized, to his horror, that the man was referring to the strain on bankers like himself."[15]

Harbingers of Free Trade in Mexico

Mexico has, in a sense, already experienced free trade in its 25-year-old maquiladora program and more recent dealings with international bankers. The maquiladora program, a creature of trade regulations, is seen as a harbinger of events likely to occur under a North American FTA. In advance of the formal agreement, it shows how trade incentives for foreign corporations to build export-oriented production facilities in Mexico will likely affect wages and working conditions, environmental protection, community development, and other aspects of Mexican life. The report which the U.S. International Trade Commission submitted to Congress in February, 1991, noted that "(m)aquilas, which are principally U.S.-owned, have constituted a trade link of steadily growing importance between the United States and Mexico and are widely considered to have established a basis for more intensified economic cooperation anticipated under an FTA." The other type of experience has arisen from the Mexican government's need to squeeze labor and social programs in order to service the nation's large foreign debt. When Mexico and the United States initiated their bilateral trade relationship in November 1987, they signed an accord which, according to the USITC report, "focused on Mexico's need for export earnings to repay its foreign debt and on the creation of a mechanism for trade consultation, dispute resolution, and mutual reduction of trade and investment barriers."[16]

Suppression of Mexican Labor

How might free trade affect the condition of Mexican labor? First, one should realize that Mexico has excellent guarantees of labor protection built into its Constitution. Among workers' rights protected under Article 123 of the Mexican Constitution are the right to form unions and to strike, the right to work an 8-hour day, the right to a minimum wage and overtime pay, and the right to a share of employers' profits. Since the economic turning point of 1985–86, however, the Mexican government has gone along with bankers' demands that workers' pay, unions, and government spending be brought under tight control to produce funds for debt service. From behind the fascade of legal protection for worker rights has emerged the reality of a totalitarian political structure, dominated by the Mexican President, whose labor component has degenerated into a corrupt and servile bureaucracy. Mexico has what is called a "corporative" structure of state. Distantly related to fascism, this political system includes rule by a single party. A strong President controls the government and the party bureaucracy. The government acts in partnership with labor and management to run the various industries. State-affiliated unions, increasingly undemocratic, have thus become an important part of the control apparatus. Instead of representing workers against management, they function more as an instrument of worker suppression and control.[17]

In Mexico, the millions of workers belonging to state-controlled unions are required to belong to PRI, the ruling party, as a condition of employment. They contribute financially to the party through a dues-checkoff system. Following the structure set up by Lazaro

Cardenas in the 1930s, PRI contains a labor section known as the "Congress of Labor". This body consists of several major confederations, of which the Confederation of Mexican Workers (CTM) is the largest and most important. Other organizations in the Congress of Labor include the Regional Confederation of Mexican Workers (CROM), the Revolutionary Confederation of Workers and Peasants (CROC), and the Revolutionary Workers Confederation (COR).[18] The most powerful labor official in Mexico is Fidel Velazquez, general secretary of the CTM, who has been in his present position since 1940. With sunglasses and slicked-back hair, Velazquez has been called "the Al Capone of Mexico's labor relations." A phrase more often used in Mexico is "El Charro", or "The Cowboy". Originally this term referred to Jesus Diaz de Leon, a colorfully dressed union leader who was bought off by the government in the 1948 railroad strike. The "El Charro" type of union leader mixes bureaucratic corruption with violence. In the course of those activities, he serves a useful function for the foreign business managers whom President Salinas has so assiduously courted. Nicholas Scheele, Ford of Mexico's managing director, summed up the situation in these words: "It's very easy to look at this in simplistic terms and say this is wrong. But is there any other country in the world where the working class . . . took a hit in their purchasing power of in excess of 50% over an eight-year period and you didn't have a social revolution?"[19]

Labor naturally became restive under those conditions. After all, Mexican workers have a constitutionally protected right to organize and to strike, which even President Salinas would find hard to deny. The challenge was met with audacity and violence:

• When workers at the Cananea copper mines in northern Mexico decided to strike for better wages in August 1989, the state-owned firm declared bankruptcy. On the same morning, between 3,000 and 5,000 soldiers of the Mexican army seized the mines and turned away miners reporting to work. The government proceeded to terminate all employees, offering minimal severance pay. Only after workers blocked highways and occupied government offices in the town of Cananea was the union able to negotiate a rescission of the bankruptcy decision and restore most workers' jobs.
• The 1990 strike at the Modelo Brewery in Mexico City involved the national union's refusal to let workers elected their own

local leadership, and the government's refusal to recognize their right to strike. CTM's general secretary, Fidel Velazquez, miffed at the removal of a crony, abolished the local union, created a new one, and aggressively recruited replacements for the striking brewery workers. A judge made the union post a bond of one billion pesos to cover possible property damage to the company. Armed riot police and firemen attacked pickets outside the brewery on the morning of March 17, 1990, and hauled the strikers away to a distant place where they were dropped off at the side of the road. In the end, the persistent union saved all but 100 jobs.

- President Salinas himself may have had a grudge against the national head of the Petroleum Workers Union, Joaquin Hernandez Galicia, who had supported Cardenas in the 1988 election. On January 10, 1989, police officers and army units attacked the labor leader's home in Ciudad Madero, using a bazooka to blow off the front door of the house. Hernandez was arrested and charged with murder in the death of one of the attacking officers. Later, rejecting the choice of local union leaders, the government orchestrated the election of a new national union president. This official agreed to significant contract concessions and raised no objection to the government's sale of PEMEX subsidiaries to foreign investors.

- When workers at the Tornel Rubber Company petitioned to change their union affiliation from CTM to CROC, the Federal Board of Conciliation and Arbitration postponed the election date five times in one year. On May 3, 1990, five Tornel workers including the union's principal leader were kidnapped at gunpoint, beaten, and then released. When the certification election was finally held in August 1990, workers arriving at the polls were attacked and beaten by a gang of 200 men wearing CTM tee shirts, accompanied by local police officers and the mayor. CTM won a subsequent election in November because the workers, fearing violence, boycotted it. In the meanwhile, the company fired 650 of 1,200 workers at the plant and replaced them with CTM recruits.[20]

- In 1987, Ford of Mexico laid off all 3,400 workers at its Cuautitlan assembly plant near Mexico City, terminated the labor contract, and then rehired many of the workers at greatly reduced wages. When the workers elected their own negotiating committee, Ford fired its members. Workers staged a work stoppage at the plant in December 1989 to protest a reduction in the amount of the Christmas bonus and to demand that CTM's local representative be replaced. On the morning of January 8, 1990, workers were attacked inside the plant by a group of thugs hired by CTM. Nine workers were injured by gunfire, one fatally. Dozens were beaten with clubs. Enraged workers occupied the Cuautitlan plant for two weeks until the police evicted them. Ford fired 700 of those workers and CTM found replacements. When a rival union, COR, filed a petition of entitlement to the Ford contract at the workers' request, the Federal Board of Conciliation and Arbitration repeatedly failed to act on the petition.[21] A court-ordered election was finally held on June 3, 1991. This election, which CTM narrowly won, was marked by intimidation and fraud. Workers who had voted "wrong" in the election were required to sign a loyalty oath as a condition of continued employment.[22]

One might gain the impression from this that Mexico's union workers are among its least fortunate people. In fact, they are comparatively well off. The unions are a relic of those happier days when Mexican economic policy was directed toward achieving domestic prosperity. With increased debt came a shift in priorities. IMF conditions for extending further credit called for Mexico to devalue the peso and control wage increases so that Mexican goods might become more competitive. Union wages and benefits, reflecting the fruit of labor struggles over the years, represented a type of privilege that had to be cut down to size: hence, the wave of privatizations, wholesale layoffs, and terminations or adjustments of labor contracts.

The Maquiladora Program

An important influence in that direction has been the maquiladora program concentrated along the U.S.-Mexico border. Originally intended to absorb returning bracero workers, this program has grown into a network of plants in which foreign corporations—90% of them U.S.-owned—could produce goods for export in an environment of cheap labor, low duties and taxes, and a lack of regulatory requirements. There has been a virtual explosion in the number of maquilas and of workers employed at such plants. From 3,000 workers employed in 1965, its first year of operation, the number of per-

Figure 2.3

Number of Maquiladora Workers

1965	3,000
1970	30,327
1975	67,214
1980	119,546
1985	211,968
1988	389,245
1990	459,837

Source: Wall Street Journal,
Daniel LaBotz

sons including administrative employees working in maquiladora fa-cilities has increased to 459,837 in 1990. The Mexican Secretary of Commerce has predicted an additional employment gain of 17% in 1991. The number of maquila plants has increased from roughly 300 in 1982 to 1,000 in 1986, to 1,900 in 1991.[23] Many large U.S. corpo-rations participate in this program including General Motors, Ford, Chrysler, Zenith, General Electric. A.C. Nielsen, and Kimberly-Clark. The Mexican border towns and cities in which these plants are located have grown rapidly. The combined populations of Juarez, Mexicali, and Tijuana, for instance, have increased five-fold since 1960.[24]

A common belief is that, when a First World employer opens fac-tories in a developing country, it attracts labor by offering superior wages and benefits. In the case of the maquiladora plants, however, their prevailing wages are generally below the wages paid elsewhere in Mexican industry. Some estimates put the average wage of a un-ionized worker in Mexico's domestic economy at a level three to four times higher than the wages paid in the maquilas.[25] According to the *New York Times*, a typical starting wage for a maquiladora worker is 82,000 pesos, or $27, for a 49-hour workweek, which averages about $.55 an hour. A more experienced worker might earn 140,000 pesos, or $47 a week, and also receive a subsidized lunch.[26] The ma-quilas show a lower rate of unionization than in Mexican industry as a whole. Those in the east, south of the Texas border, tend to be more unionized than ones out west. Some plants are covered by "protection contracts" — so named because they protect employers from organizing attempts by other unions — which set wages and benefits at a level below the requirements of federal labor law. Some workers in the maquila plants are simply unaware of being covered by a union contract. The Federal Board of Conciliation and Arbitration often refuses to register independent or democratic unions, preferring the established, "charro" type.[27]

Conditions Inside the Plants

Working conditions are such that employee turnover at some maquiladora facilities exceeds 180% per year. Conditions may vary, of course. Alan Brown, who toured several plants in Juarez, returned home to Minnesota to report to his local newspaper: "I saw very clean factories, with gleaming cafeterias that provide subsidized, practically free meals to the workers. I saw free in-plant medical services. I saw lifetime labor contracts provided to each employee after a 90-day probationary period . . . Everywhere I saw an enthusiastic and happy work force."[28] Jack Hedrick, a union official from Kansas City, told of having seen female workers in the factories who wore high-heeled shoes and expensive-looking dresses: this was apparently part of the company dress code.[29] While one should not dismiss the possibility of pleasant working conditions inside some plants, other reports tell of production speedups, long and tedious work, poorly ventilated or overheated work areas, and safety hazards. Jorge Carrillo and Alberto Hernandez have described the work at certain maquilas in Ciudad Juarez as being "monotonous and repetitive. A woman worker in the electronics industry, for example, in one day has to solder 2,000 pieces of a size which is hardly visible. The intensity of the work has to be hard and constant in order to achieve the established production goals, which are generally based on the standards of production of the fastest workers." Most employees there work more than the standard nine hours a day, including much overtime and some double shifts.[30]

An article in the *Wall Street Journal* acknowledges the poor working conditions that exist in many maquiladora plants. Quite candidly, it reports: "Maquilas are generally non-union, set production quotas at rates at least 10% above those in similar factories north of the border, and grant little or no extra pay for seniority . . . (S)ome maquilas resemble sweatshops more than factories. They lack ventilation, and workers may pass out from the heat and fumes. Production demands can put them at risk; Edwviges Ramos Hernandez, a teacher in Juarez, worked at one factory where in a year three workers had fingers sliced off. The machines, she says, were set at a maddening pace. In Tijuana, Zenaida Ochoa . . . sews garments for nine hours straight in a tin-roofed enclosure that sizzles in the summer heat. She makes $60 a week, which is higher than most—but a chicken costs a tenth of that. She is plagued by back pain from hunching over her sewing machine all day, and says, 'My eyes burn from staring at the needle.' A fellow worker, she relates, tried to organize a union to get better pay and working conditions—including toilet paper in the restroom—and was fired."[31]

A noticeable feature of employment in maquilas is the prevalence of female workers, said by some plant managers to have "more patience and manual dexterity" than male workers. Today about two thirds of such workers are female—down from 87% in the period between 1974 and 1982.[32] The predominance of women in the maquiladora program has puzzled some who recall that the program was originally created to employ returning bracero veterans, who were mostly male. A possible explanation is that this system continues the tradition begun by export-production factories in the Far East. Those plants typically employed young, unmarried women who were interested in accumulating a dowry and would often quit after a few years.[33] In any event, the situation of employing mostly women and making men economically redundant has caused some problems in Mexico with fatherless families and delinquency, similar to what the welfare system in the United States has often created. Moreover, female employees are reported to be frequent victims of sexual harassment by male supervisors. There are, reportedly, "Friday night rape parties" and weekend outings involving "use of the women workers by the supervisors and managers . . . (which) . . . creates divisions among the women workers themselves, as they determine who went out with whom and who would not."[34] A Canadian postal worker returning from Ciudad Juarez , Deborah Bourque, reported that "(w)omen routinely face dismissal on becoming pregnant. In some factories women are required to show proof to staff doctors that they are menstruating."[35]

Community Squalor and Environmental Degradation

Outside the maquiladora plants, there is abundant evidence that both nature and humanity are suffering . The above-quoted *Wall Street Journal* article described the border region between Mexico and the United States as "a sinkhole of abysmal living conditions and environmental degradation. A huge, continuing migration of people looking for work has simply overwhelmed the already-shaky infrastructure. Shantytowns spring up overnight around border cities where there is little or no living space left; some of the 400,000 maquila workers pay more than a third of their monthly income to share a bed in one room occupied by six others." In Nogales, there were seven people for every available room. Some workers and their families constructed primitive huts of cardboard or cinder blocks. Some slept outdoors, huddling against each other for warmth.[36] The homeless workers scrounged for building and other materials from the refuse of the maquilas. One family kept its water supply in a 55-gallon drum with a brightly colored label warning that its former contents were fluorocarbon solvents whose vapors were fatal if inhaled.[37] The maquiladora communities could not provide public facilities for these people because, paradoxically, they lacked a tax base. When the Mexican government in 1988 proposed to levy a 2% tax on maquiladora wages to pay for infrastructure improvements, factory owners killed the idea. "Several say that they are in Mexico to make profits and that infrastructure is Mexico's problem, not theirs," the *Wall Street Journal* explained. The local government officials were fearful that if they pushed the tax issue, the foreign employers would pack up and leave.[38]

While low labor costs remain the chief incentive, employers are increasingly attracted to the maquiladora communities by the favorable regulatory climate , especially with respect to the environment. Richard Metcalf, a textile union organizer, explained: "The first maquiladoras were almost exclusively devoted to hand assembly operations. But now we're seeing a second wave in which capital investment is being made in machines and technology. It costs money to set them up, but it solves a very expensive waste disposal problem for U.S. companies. Once they are operating, they can simply dump their poison down there."[39] Manufacturers who imported toxic substances for use in maquiladora production were supposed to ship the waste back to the United States for proper disposal, but few have complied. Records of the Texas Water Commission showed that only 143 tons of toxic waste were returned to Texas in 1987, although an estimated 5,000 tons were produced that year in Juarez alone. The rest was apparently poured into sewers or dumped on the land. It would have cost producers as much as $200 a barrel to comply with the waste-disposal regulations.[40] Water samples taken at Nogales revealed "widespread contamination by the kind of chemicals that are normally found in industrial solvents," according to a *New York Times* article. This carcinogenic contamination was spreading through the aquifer.[41]

In addition to industrial pollution, severe population density combined with a lack of sanitary facilities in the maquiladora towns has turned nearby rivers and streams into open sewers. The *New York Times* article described the type of waste-disposal system used in the workers' shantytowns outside Nogales: "Behind Mr. Ramos' home was one of the communal outhouses used by residents of the shantytown. A little ditch from the outhouse led to a bigger ditch that flowed to a creek in the bottom of a ravine that flowed into the Nogales Wash, a stream that grows in size with the seasons. Like virtually every other Mexican border town, Nogales does not have any sewage treatment plants." Across from Laredo, Texas, the Mexican town of Neuva Laredo dumps 25 million gallons of raw sewage into the Rio Grande each day. Ciudad Juarez dumps its raw sewage into a canal which runs parallel to the Rio Grande, contaminating well water. A recent study found that in the nearby town of San Elizario, Texas, everyone had been exposed to hepatitis at least once before reaching 20 years of age. In Nogales, Arizona, a public-health emergency had been in effect for six months because the rate of hepatitis was twenty times the national average. Health officials speculated that people might have contracted the disease through recreational activities in or near the contaminated water, or else in "eating establishments and supermarkets along the wash where flies carried the disease from the water to food." This last possibility was of concern because the area has several large warehouses where fruits and vegetables imported from Mexico are "iced down and prepared for shipment throughout the world."[42]

Another health hazard along the U.S.-Mexico border is poor air quality. Many shantytown residents regularly burn firewood for heating and cooking. Some kilns burn discarded tires to make bricks or decorative tiles. A lack of paved roads and prevalence of older-model cars that use leaded gasoline and lack pollution-control devices on the Mexican side of the border also contributes to the air-pollution problem. The *Wall Street Journal* described the situation: "Road building and repair can't keep up with the galloping population. Traffic is gridlocked in the cities. Old cars on dirt paths raise huge clouds of dust that mingle with exhaust fumes and industrial pollution to cast a poisonous pall of smog over the border towns — and their American neighbors." The city of El Paso, Texas, is out of compliance with federal air-quality standards despite millions of dollars spent for such purposes. The reason is a big yellow-gray cloud hanging over Juarez which envelops both cities, causing frequent temperature inversions.[43] *U.S. News & World Report* reported that "(m)assive discharges of toxic fumes have occurred in chemical plants and other factories. In the Matamoros-Reynosa region alone, seven major accidents since 1986 have sent more than 350 people to hospitals and forced thousands to flee their homes."[44] When the City of Los Angeles passed a tough ordinance to curb air-pollution emissions, forty furniture manufacturers in the area who could not meet the standards simply relocated in Tijuana and continued the same practices as before. Some of the pollutants blew right back into southern California. Los Angeles lost jobs and tax base without commensurately improving its air quality.[45]

What This Bodes for Free Trade

To keep things in perspective, one should understand that the Mexican maquiladoras do not yet represent a major factor in the total scheme of North American production. They presently represent about 20% of Mexico's manufacturing volume; and Mexico is the smallest industrial producer of the three North American countries. Even so, the maquiladora program in Mexico has become a prime focus of interest and controversy in regard to a Free-Trade Agreement between Mexico, Canada, and the United States. Why is that? Its spectacular growth rate merits attention beyond considerations of present size. Management-consultant types are busy talking up the advantages of maquiladora production in cities across Canada and the United States. Some are claiming, for instance, that each manufacturing job shifted from the United States to a maquiladora factory in Mexico saves the employer about $30,000 a year, including benefits. In addition, a handout at a seminar promoting such relocation pointed out that "operators of maquila plants do not have to carry expensive insurance to cover workers against work-related hazards."[46]

On the other hand, the congested living conditions and ecological damage already inflicted upon the U.S.-Mexico border region may limit future industrial growth in that area. Mexico has therefore changed its laws to allow maquiladoras to operate farther inside the country. As yet, few foreign employers have taken advantage of that option; they feel safer close to the United States. The next logical step, then, is the Free-Trade Agreement. Not only does Mexico open up its entire country to duty-free production, but it agrees to various other conditions that will make business feel more comfortable. Salinas' entire program aims to convince business that the Mexican government is, indeed, totally and irrevocably, 100% pro-business, and that any business investments made in Mexico are entirely and completely safe.

Opponents, of course, are looking at the maquiladora experience as an indication of what might take place on a larger scale with free trade. "Maquiladoras are a paradigm for free trade", exclaimed Bill Cavitt, a U.S. Department of Commerce official.[47] "In the long term," said Catalina Denman, a public-health specialist quoted in the *New York Times*, "what happened in Nogales could happen all over Mexico if a free trade agreement produces the same kind of fast development with no real attention to human needs."[48] There would be no geographical restriction upon maquiladora-type enterprises if a Free-Trade Agreement went through. All Mexico could become engulfed in such operations. All the pollution, poverty wages, foreign domination, inadequate housing and lack of public services could engulf a nation of 90 million people. Conversely, the prospective agreement suggests to U.S. and Canadian production workers that the damage done to their livelihoods by the border-confined maquiladora plants could be multiplied several times over if their pattern is extended to the rest of Mexico. Maquiladoras, though presently manageable in size, may well become the wave of the future if the present philosophy that drives the current U.S., Canadian, and Mexican political and business elites continues unabated. Those companies now have a track record. The maquiladoras, seeking export production, are an arrangement made to please the International Monetary Fund and Wall Street bankers, but squeeze everyone else.

Employment Concerns in Canada

When the proposal for a Free-Trade Agreement between Canada and the United States was first brought to the attention of the Canadian Parliament in November 1987, an economic historian named John Ralson Saul stunned a parliamentary committee by referring to a "gaping hole" in the proposed agreement. Did the committee members realize, he asked, that by "removing our tariffs and severely limiting Ottawa's economic planning powers, we will be integrating into an American economy which is increasingly reliant upon an industrial tandem of half-price labor in the southern U.S. and ten-percent assemblage labor in the neighboring maquiladora zone"?[49] As Saul then recognized, Canada was staring down the end of a double-barreled economic shotgun. While the Canadian per-capita G.D.P. is about the same as that of the United States, the standards of social protection are higher. Canada stands, one might say, roughly in the same relationship to the United States as the United States stands in relation to Mexico regarding such protections. Inasmuch as free trade tends to put economic concerns above "quality of life" issues, Canada was facing a threat from both the United States and Mexico in preserving an important aspect of its national character.

From a U.S. perspective , the Canadian experience with the U.S.-Canada FTA should give advance warning of what we Americans might expect from a free-trade agreement with Mexico. A sort of political Gresham's Law applies in both situations. Governmental jurisdictions which cut corners on social protections to gain reduced costs for business will tend, in a free-trade environment, to reap an economic reward. Granted, the United States posed a greater threat to Canada than Mexico now does for it because the U.S. economy is so much larger. Nevertheless, the same kinds of pressures apply in both cases. Jobs will be lost to the region with the lower wages and a more relaxed attitude toward polluting the natural environment. If the U.S.-Canada FTA sent industrial employment southward to us because we offered business a better deal, so a U.S.-Mexico FTA will continue the job flight south in response to Salinas' superior offer. Therefore, we in the United States need to look at the Canadian experience during the last two years to see what free trade might have in store for us if a North American agreement is signed.

On February 5, 1991, simultaneous announcements were made in Washington by President Bush, in Mexico City by President Salinas, and in Ottawa by Prime Minister Mulroney that trilateral talks would begin that summer to create a free-trade zone covering the three North American countries. "A successful conclusion of the free-trade agreement will expand market opportunities, increase prosperity and help our three countries meet the economic challenges of the future," said President Bush.[50] For some, his cheery words must have seemed a case of deja vu. When the U.S.-Canada free-trade pact was concluded, there were similar rosy predictions of increased prosperity. President Reagan issued a statement to the effect that "the agreement would open markets and create jobs in both countries".[51] While meeting with President Salinas in Houston in April 1991, President Bush similarly announced that free trade would "create jobs and provide opportunities for the citizens of both our countries," adding that "the credibility of the United States as a trading partner is on the line."[52] The President's own credibility as an economic prophet was also, however, in question as Canadians then were experiencing their worst recession since the 1930s. With a national unemployment rate of 9.7% in January 1991, there were 1.32 million Canadians out of work. A record 42,782 Canadians declared personal bankruptcy in 1990, up 46% from the previous year. Business bankruptcies were up by 34%. Housing sales had slipped to an 8-year low.[53]

In the five years prior to signing a Free-Trade Agreement with the United States, the Canadian economy generated an average of 326,000 net new jobs each year. This figure declined to 152,000 net jobs in 1989. By November and December 1990, Canada was running a deficit in job creation. About 82,000 more jobs were being destroyed than created. How many Canadian jobs were lost in the

1990–91 recession? The Canadian Labour Congress estimated that 226,000 jobs were lost through November, 1990; however this estimate covers employment only in the goods-producing sector and at the larger firms. Most Canadians work for firms with 20 or fewer employees.[54] According to figures supplied by Statistics Canada, total employment in Canadian manufacturing industries declined by 435,000 positions between June 1989 and March 1991, or by 21.7%.[55] Some suggest that this situation reflects a period of temporary discomfort as Canada pays for its past protectionist policies and becomes integrated with the international economy. As soon as Canadian industry restructures itself to become more efficient and the Canadian dollar and interest rates come down, Canada will be back on a course of sustained economic growth. However, an article in the *Los Angeles Times* reported: "Instead of investing in modern new equipment or pumping dollars into research and development, Canadian manufacturers are closing or moving to the United States, Mexico and the Caribbean." The same article quoted Cedric Ritchie, chairman of the Bank of Nova Scotia: "Manufacturing jobs are disappearing fast — at least 150,000 in the past year. Many of these jobs are ending up south of the border and will not return with the cyclical recovery."[56]

Figure 2.4 reveals that job losses have occurred in all sectors of Canadian manufacturing. Most of the jobs were exported from Canada to the United States, and some even to Mexico. Figure 2.5 reports job relocations at selected firms. According to an article in *Canadian Dimension* magazine, the two main effects of relaxing government restrictions on U.S.-controlled firms under the Free-Trade Agreement have been "an increase in takeovers of Canadian companies and the shutting down of U.S. branch plant operations." Statistics Canada has reported that 460 Canadian-controlled companies with combined assets of $24 billion were taken over by foreign investors in 1988–89, compared with 136 foreign-owned companies with combined assets of $3 billion that were acquired by Canadian investors. As a result, foreign control of Canadian industry jumped by a full percentage point. The closing of Canadian branch plants has involved such firms as Sunbeam Corp., Clairol Canada Inc., Black & Decker, and Star Kist Tuna. Almost 75% of the closures were in Ontario, and 20% were in Quebec. While most operations were consolidated with the firm's other operations in the United States, a few

Figure 2.4

Job Losses in Canadian Manufacturing
Industries, June 1989 to March 1991

Change in Employment

Industry	numbers employed	percent change
food and beverages	(58,000)	−22.6%
rubber	(4,200)	−16.6%
plastic	(10,600)	−17.7%
leather	(6,700)	−37.2%
textiles	(17,800)	−27.1%
clothing	(21,100)	−22.9%
wood	(41,000)	−33.3%
furniture and fixtures	(19,500)	−29.4%
paper and allied	(17,100)	−13.0%
printing & publishing	(28,400)	−19.3%
primary metal	(22,500)	−21.5%
fabricated metal prod.	(44,900)	−27.5%
machinery	(24,700)	−23.2%
aircraft equipment	700	1.6%
auto & truck equip.	(12,500)	−16.6%
auto parts	(15,600)	−21.0%
electrical	(29,200)	−22.5%
nonmetal mineral prod	(17,800)	−30.6%
petroleum & coal prod.	(2,500)	−12.2%
chemicals	(13,700)	−13.3%
other	(27,900)	
total manufacturing	(435,000)	−21.7%

Source: Action Canada Dossier

Canadian manufacturers went straight to Mexico. Bruce Campbell, author of the *Canadian Dimension* article, has documented cases of forty Canadian firms "that have collectively shed 14,000 jobs in Canada under free trade and . . . have invested heavily in the Maquiladoras."[57]

Employers move production operations out of a country for a variety of reasons having to do mostly with cost. Besides the cost of labor, one should consider transportation costs, land-acquisition

Figure 2.5

Where Canadian Manufacturing Jobs Went — —

A Partial List of Recent Plant Closures

company	products	production transferred		jobs lost
		from	to	
Inglis	appliances	Toronto	Clyde OH	650
Gillette	shaving prod.	Montreal	U.S. locations	530
Bendix	auto parts	Collingwood ON	Mexico, Alabama	400
Croydon	furniture	Cambridge ON	Chicago	360
Sheller Globe	auto parts	Kingsville ON	Mexico	350
Thermodisc	thermostats	St. Thomas ON	U.S. & Mexico	300
Sunar – Hauseman	auto parts	Waterloo ON	Holland MI	280
General Motors	auto parts	Windsor ON	Findlay OH	255
Star Kist Tuna	fish proc.	Bayside NB	U.S. locations	250
Cobi Foods	food proc.	Whitby ON	U.S. locations	250
Unisys	computers	Montreal	Mexico, Calif.	230
Clairol Canada	shampoo, etc.	Knowlton PQ	Stamford CT	228
General Electric	lamps	Montreal	Mexico	200
Leviton Mfg.	electrical	Montreal	U.S. locations	175
Ford Motor	auto parts	St. Thomas ON	Mexico	140
Amerlock	hardware	Meaford ON	Chicago	140

Source: Canadian Dimension

costs, energy costs, the cost of raw materials, parts, and supplies, as well as costs relating to the regulatory and tax environment. Ferdinand Fontaine, testifying on behalf of Canadian furniture manufacturers, told a parliamentary committee in Ottawa that plant locations in the United States would have the advantage of lower interest rates, state training subsidies of up to $2,000 per job, $4.50 an hour wages, and right-to-work laws. For Maples Dimensional Wood Products, Ltd., the cost benefits in moving from Ontario to Mead-ville, Pennsylvania, included $4.50-an-hour wages, a state-guaran-teed loan for $1 million at 3% interest, and wage-and-training subsi-dies from the state.[58] Peraflex Hose, Inc., shifted most of its production from Toronto to Buffalo citing lower transportation and land-acquisition costs. One should also consider the taxes and other personal expenses of the business managers who would be making relocation decisions. The *Wall Street Journal* reported: "A $100,000-a-year executive can boost his after-tax income by as much as $20,000 just by moving to New York City from heavily taxed Toronto, ac-cording to a Price Waterhouse study. Other U.S. cities are even more attractive. Buffalo house prices averaged $90,500 last year, com-pared with $209,225 in Toronto."[59]

As one would expect, many firms that were formerly protected by tariffs and other trade barriers left Canada for various southern loca-tions once the U.S.-Canadian Free-Trade Agreement went into effect. The experiences differ by industry. In the printing industry, for example, elimination of print-in-Canada requirements, tariff protec-tion, and postal subsidies for Canadian magazines were among the reasons given for closing businesses in Canada. The dairy industry, which used to benefit from Canadian supply-management programs, now has to compete with low-priced milk from the United States. The Canadian auto-parts industry is no longer protected by import restrictions imposed by the 1965 U.S.-Canada Auto Pact. Canadian producers of various fruits and vegetables have lowered their prices as tariffs came down, forcing some growers to relocate in lower-cost areas south of the border. Likewise, the removal of domestic fish-processing requirements has caused Canadian fisheries to relocate in the United States. The Canadian timber industry is afflicted with a unique problem brought on by the Free-Trade Agreement — a special 15% tax on lumber exports which Canadian negotiators conceded under pressure from the U.S. Senate Finance Committee.[60]

Economic Pressures and Threats

Some Canadian manufacturers have used the threat of relocation un-der the U.S.-Canada FTA to force their employees to accept lower wages and benefits or abandon strikes. There was nothing subtle about this letter from Hartz Canada to 26 striking production workers at its plant in St. Thomas, Ontario: "As a result of the passage of the free trade agreement, we now have the opportunity of sourcing products produced in the U.S. without incurring duty. Our parent company produces many of these same goods manufactured or packaged in St. Thomas and with labour rates significantly lower than Hartz Canada. Competition continues to be keen and will become even more so as U.S. competitors find easier access to Canada. We must ensure that our costs are in line . . . In the event of a work stoppage, Hartz will continue to provide goods to our customers and . . . replenishment stock will be provided by Hartz U.S. and/or outside suppliers. Once products are sourced outside our St. Thomas facility the likelihood of these products returning here after the work stoppage is very remote." The workers did continue to strike and, true to its word, Hartz Canada moved operations to the United States.[61]

Employers are not always so crude in expressing the advantages that a Free-Trade Agreement would give them in dealing with employees. Indeed, the economic picture is complicated by other factors. A study by the Royal Bank of Canada attributed Canada's deteriorating trade and investment position primarily to high labor costs, taxes, and interest rates, and the strong Canadian dollar, ranking the impact of the U.S.-Canada FTA last in importance among eight factors considered.[62] On the other hand, many Canadians believe that the strong Canadian dollar is a consequence of concessions made to the United States in order to obtain the 1988 trade agreement. Former Canadian Industry Minister, Sinclair Stevens, has acknowledged, for instance, that his U.S. counterpart, Secretary of Commerce Malcolm Baldridge, told him in late 1985 that the key to obtaining an agreement on free trade was to strengthen the Canadian dollar. Whatever the case, the Bank of Canada began pushing up Canadian interest rates to the point that in June 1990 they were 7 points higher than the comparable U.S. rate. The price of the Canadian dollar rose against the U.S. dollar from $.71 in 1985 to $.75 in 1987, and to $.84 in 1988. Since 1989, it has fluctuated in the $.85 to $.87 range. In the meanwhile, Canada's merchandise trade surplus fell from $17.6 billion in late 1987 to $13.6 billion a year later, and to $10.4 billion by 1989.[63]

Some Canadians who have analyzed the U.S.-Canada FTA believe that the agreement works consistently to the detriment of the Canadian national interest as well as to the detriment of efforts to control wasteful use of natural resources and protect the environment. In part, they say, that was because the U.S. negotiators drove a harder bargain than their less experienced and more eager Canadian counterparts. In part, it was due to the anti-regulatory tendencies of free trade. Basically, the FTA allows interested commercial parties to challenge any and all sorts of government subsidies or regulations that restrict or alter the flow of trade, whether designed to promote regional development, stabilize commodity prices, encourage conservation, or limit environmental damage. Unless specifically permitted in the agreement, such measures may be deemed an "unfair trade practice" and become subject to penalties. The Canadian government has historically used subsidies or protective regulations to encourage regional development. It expected to cut a deal with the United States to continue this practice in exchange for recognizing the U.S. right to subsidize military production. The deal never materialized. "In a series of legal actions beginning in the early 1970s," wrote Scott Sinclair, "the U.S. has clearly demonstrated that it rejects the legitimacy of Canadian regional development programs. In a single countervailing duty case against fresh Atlantic groundfish, over 50 federal and provincial government programs to assist the Atlantic fishery were subject to trade penalties. Monies spent under virtually every major Canadian regional development program have been judged illegal subsidies under U.S. trade law."[64]

Canada was interested in negotiating a FTA with the United States in the belief that such an agreement would bring to an end, in Prime Minister Mulroney's words, "the threat to Canadian industry from U.S. protectionists who harass and restrict exports through the misuse of trade laws." U.S. trade laws allow retaliatory actions to be taken in the form of countervailing duties and subsidies against nations found to have engaged in unfair trade practices. The U.S.-Canada FTA allows each country to continue to apply its own trade laws against the other country's exports and to change those laws without the other's consent. According to Scott Sinclair, that provision has made it possible for U.S. firms to continue to block Canadian products through trade-dispute procedures. The Baucus-Danforth amendment, the FTA's implementing legislation, made it easier for them "to harass successful Canadian exports. A U.S. company, trade association, or union that believes a successful Canadian exporter may be subsidized can get the U.S. Trade Representative to investigate without first proving that the so-called subsidies injured U.S. industry," he observed. Between 1980 and 1988, the United States filed 264 countervailing duty cases against its trading partners, while Canada filed only one. "The American economy is being fundamentally altered through both the growing competitiveness of Europe and Japan and the globalization of U.S.-based multinationals," Sinclair wrote. "Trade remedy laws are a way to channel and control the resulting protectionism. By blaming adjustment problems on unfair foreign competition, trade remedy laws preserve the ideology of free trade and the prerogatives of U.S. investment capital, while giving American workers and domestic businesses a small measure of control over the economic upheaval threatening their jobs and communities."[65]

Some Environmental Consequences of the U.S.-Canada FTA

Although Canadian government officials at the time of its signing insisted that the U.S.-Canada FTA was "not an environmental agreement" but merely a "commercial accord", Canadian environmentalists contend that it has a "varied, wide-ranging, and overwhelmingly adverse" effect upon efforts to protect the natural environment. Such efforts are also related to other policy objects including conservation of non-renewable natural resources and Canada's supply-management program for agricultural production. Article 904 of the U.S.-Canada FTA , for instance, forbids either government to restrict energy exports for any reason other than "national security", unless it rations its domestic energy supplies to the same extent. This provision encourages wide-open production of Canadian energy for export to U.S. markets. Accordingly, two huge projects have been undertaken in northern Canada which will have a major impact on the environment: the development of natural-gas production facilities in the Mackenzie Delta area of the Canadian Arctic, including a 1200-mile pipeline across the tundra, and dam construction in James Bay to furnish 26,000 megawatts of hydroelectric power. Pressed by

FTA requirements, Canada's National Energy Board has given the oil companies permission to export 87% of their natural-gas production during the next 20 years. Besides the adverse environmental impact of such projects, the continuing production of large amounts of cheap energy will perpetuate wasteful habits of consumption and make it economically less urgent to develop alternative sources of energy.[66]

In the area of agriculture, the U.S.-Canada FTA has served to undermine the Canadian supply-management program which balances domestic supplies with demand in order to assure stable commodity markets. It was essential to this program that the marketing boards be able to restrict agricultural imports when excessive supplies drove prices down. GATT disallows quantitative restrictions on traded farm commodities. The U.S.-Canada FTA requires elimination of tariffs. Thus, when Canadian authorities attempted to limit imports of yogurt and ice cream, the United States successfully challenged this policy under GATT as an unfair trade practice. Because of the FTA, the Canadians were unable to restrict imports by raising tariffs. Canadian farmers are therefore forced to compete in a world market marked by chronic oversupply and low prices. The effect will be to hasten soil erosion by forcing family farmers off the land, to encourage large-scale farm production characterized by increased use of pesticides and chemical fertilizers, and to develop a system of specialized global production that requires more elaborate packaging and shipment of products over much longer distances. That, in turn, will increase energy expenditures related to agriculture, since it takes three times as much energy to process, package, and transport food as produce it. Faster global warming will be a likely consequence.[67]

Environmental regulations have come under attack both in Canada and the United States as industrial and government groups have challenged them as violations of the U.S.-Canada FTA:

• The Canadian pulp and paper industry has challenged U.S. recycling laws that require a certain percentage of recycled fiber in newsprint. The Conference Board of Canada, a business think tank, called such requirements "a disguised non-tariff barrier to trade because Canada does not have the supply needed of recycled fiber to maintain market share in the United States." A similar argument has been made regarding possible requirements for recycled metals.[68]

• When the U.S. Environmental Protection Agency introduced regulations to phase out the production, importation, and use of asbestos over a seven-year period, the Quebec asbestos-mining industry and the Canadian government filed a brief in the U.S. Court of Appeals arguing that such regulations violated U.S. trade obligations under both the FTA and GATT. Even through the trade laws permitted regulations that served "a legitimate domestic objective", the Canadian plaintiffs argued that a total ban on asbestos did not meet that requirement in cases where controlled asbestos use might not pose "unreasonable risks to life or health."[69]

• U.S. nonferrous metal producers have argued that governmental loans and investment credits given to Canadian lead, zinc, and copper smelters for the purpose of installing devices to control gas emissions were an unfair trade practice. The U.S. Trade Representative thought that there was sufficient merit in this argument to warrant investigating Canada's pollution-control program. If the Canadian government cuts back on such programs to reduce sulfur-dioxide emissions, acid rain will likely increase.[70]

• In the first case decided under the FTA dispute-resolution procedure, the binational panel found that Canadian requirements to land herring and salmon in Canada for inspection were "incompatible with the requirements of Article 407 of the FTA." The landing requirements were designed to help Canadian wildlife authorities ascertain that sufficient stocks of herring and salmon were maintained in its Pacific coastal waters and to deter false reporting. Although the trade panel acknowledged that such procedures did not violate FTA requirements where they were "primarily aimed at conservation", it decided in this case that the Canadian regulations were intended "to make exports more amenable to data collection" and so were an impermissible trade restriction.[71]

• The British Columbia provincial government undertook an extensive tree-planting program to halt deforestation and improve air quality. The U.S. timber industry claimed that the government-subsidized program unfairly benefited Canadian loggers and threatened to challenge it in court. The British Columbia government decided to abandon the program to avoid this expected lawsuit under the U.S.-Canada FTA.[72]

• The U.S.-Canada FTA requires the two countries to "work toward equivalent guidelines, technical regulations, standards and test methods" to regulate pesticides. It instructs the Canadian government to work toward equivalency in adopting a "risk/benefit" or partially economic approach to pesticide regulation, conforming to U.S. practice, which is less restrictive than one based on evaluation of safety alone. Environmentalists point out that the U.S. government has registered products containing 20% more active pesticide ingredients, and seven times as many pesticide products, as those registered by the Canadian government. Pesticide regulations are being "harmonized downward" in this case.[73]

Stephen Shrybman of the Canadian Environmental Law Association has observed that not only are existing environmental regulations being challenged as unfair trade practices under the U.S.-Canada FTA but the agreement has also had a chilling effect upon regulatory agencies when issuing new rules. Canada's Department of Consumer and Corporate Affairs refused to impose stricter labelling requirements upon irradiated food, noting that such "requirements of Canada and the U.S.A. may need to be further coordinated to avoid a potential non-tariff trade barrier." Health and Welfare Canada, for similar reasons, has rejected proposals that it impose tighter controls upon food containers with lead-soldered seams. Business groups have been quick to use the FTA's new trade-liberalizing provisions to challenge various kinds of conservation or environmental regulations. The Ontario Chamber of Commerce has argued, for instance, that air-pollution standards ought to be "relaxed" in that province to allow its businesses to compete more effectively under free trade. The Canadian Chemical Producers Association summarized the issue quite well in pointing out that "if unnecessary or excessive (regulatory) costs are introduced unilaterally any any country, innovation and development will simply cease or be transferred to jurisdictions with a more favorable business climate."[74] By "unnecessary or excessive" is meant what does not drop to the lowest common denominator of public tolerance. Thus, attempts by environmentalists to set higher standards of protection for the earth's environment and resources will run into a barely visible stone wall imposed by a supposedly nonenvironmental "commercial accord".

Talking with our Continental Neighbors

The bottom line in the free-trade discussion is that production and jobs will flow from the higher-cost to the lower-cost areas, and with them hopes of material well-being. Higher-cost areas are usually associated with higher social standards, more government spending for community services, more humane treatment of workers, higher wages, tougher environmental standards, and so on. Since consumer markets tend to follow the level of wages, these, too, would be located mostly in the higher-cost areas. The Free-Trade Agreement would allow cost-cutting employers to unbundle production from markets or cease to treat social and economic systems as a package. People would be relegated to becoming production factors judged mainly on the basis of cost. Economic growth would flow in the direction of lower social and environmental standards. In the case of the U.S.-Canada Free-Trade Agreement, this means that that the growth has slid away from Canada and toward the United States. In the case of a U.S.-Mexico agreement, it will mean sliding away from the United States toward Mexico. The socially less responsible employers will lead the charge to the labor hellholes south of the border, and be handsomely rewarded for it. Citing theoretical arguments for free trade, they will say that the process was inevitable, being economically ordained by forces of the free market. They will suggest that opponents of free trade are backward sorts of persons who will soon be swept into history's dustbin.

There is just one thing which might hold up this invincible parade: The North American Free-Trade Agreement has not yet gotten past Congress. The U.S. Congress might get cold feet about throwing U.S. taxpayers out on the street to increase corporate efficiency. The members of Congress might start to worry about further deindustrialization accompanying free trade. They might view business aspirations to escape government regulation and avoid taxes with less than enthusiastic support. They might be reluctant to hook up with an authoritarian Mexican state that routinely violates labor and human rights. Seeing through the "racist" argument, they might begin to listen to those "other" voices in Mexico and Canada which, for good reason, are against a free-trade agreement with the United States.

People from the two countries which are our neighbors have been talking to each other about this impending North American Free-Trade Agreement. We should listen to what they say. Maude Barlow, chair of the Council of Canadians, told a gathering in Mexico City in October 1990: "The United States-Canada Free-Trade Agreement is a corporate bill of rights and also a blueprint for other such deals to follow . . . The United States is trying to get around the GATT process and set up a series of multilateral or bilateral free trade agreements in which it is the central power and its corporate elite is dominant. Now, these corporations talk very enthusiastically about what they call a 'world without borders.' In fact, what they are seeking is a tightly controlled system in which there is no power strong enough to protect the needs and rights of people. Those in control can play workers in one country off against workers in another. And governments will not be sufficiently strong to regulate on behalf of their populations . . . The transnational conglomerates are co-opting the world's nations. And in each country they have to find corporate and government sponsors to deliver the country and its people to them. In Canada our corporate elite and our government became a willing participant."[75]

Cuauhtemoc Cardenas of the Mexican opposition P.R.D. party told a gathering of Canadians in November 1990: "The apparent opening of the Mexican economy to the rest of the world has, in fact, resulted in the Mexican people being shut in behind a wall of political intolerance, human rights abuse, electoral fraud and growing social inequality . . . In the name of free trade, the Mexican government and its allies in Washington want the world to ignore that other Mexico. Their free trade agenda is narrow and simple: Mexico will sell its cheap labor to attract foreign capital, which in turn will guarantee the survival of one of the last remaining authoritarian political systems in Latin America. Low wages, anti-democratic union practices, the disgraceful lack of environmental regulation, dangerous working conditions, and unprotected consumers are proudly presented by the Mexican government as assets in the struggle for international competitiveness. At the same time, the government disguises the way in which Mexico's real assets, particularly oil, would be sold out in the free trade package . . . We are not opposed to a continental trade and development pact with Canada and the United States. We maintain that trade must be seen as an instrument of development and that a new kind of development model must be at the core of any continental trade negotiations."[76]

It is time that we in the United States be brought into these discussions with people in the two neighboring countries, not just to stave off anti-American feelings but also to expand our own consciousness and concern beyond narrowly defined national limits. This new hemispheric awareness, if extended from the corporate and political elite to ordinary people, would become a beneficial outcome of the current discussions concerning a U.S.-Mexico-Canada FTA. And so, the negativity in opposing such an agreement could, in a dialectical way, be transformed into a new positive force that would push the American people into new forms of political cooperation with the Canadians, Mexicans, and other peoples and nations. Already a network has been established between trade unionists in the three countries opposed to free trade, creating a structure of personal contact and communications upon which to build future cooperative actions. The challenge now is to develop and promote a positive transnational alternative to the free-trade approach which will instead champion the human interest. In partnership with our like-minded Mexican and Canadian neighbors, we Americans would then be building a moral and political movement of sufficient scope to match that of the giant corporations.

PART THREE
Against Business Totalitarianism

Evolution of Divided Power in Western Society

When civilization (being that culture based on writing) began in Iraq and Egypt six thousand years ago, society was organized by a single power structure located in the temple. Priest-kings ruled human communities in the name of their local god. Peasant farmers tilled the surrounding fields fertilized by overflowing rivers and watered by communal irrigation works. The knowledge of seasons to plant crops and of bookkeeping techniques to record grain storage and trade was possessed by temple functionaries trained in the arts of writing, arithmetic, and astronomy. From those rude beginnings, civilization spread from the temple center into the larger community. There has been a fracturing of power in society as its functions became differentiated and developed in separate institutions. Government was the first institution to detach. Separating themselves from the temple cults, monarchs waged war on neighboring city-states and built territorial empires. The first Pharaoh was a king from upper Egypt who conquered the northern peoples of the Delta around 3000 B.C. The conquering kings established royal courts which became centers of government. These governments promulgated laws, settled disputes, communicated with foreigners, and collected taxes. Starting with the Persian empire, they also coined money and maintained a system of roads.

During the 6th and 5th centuries B.C., a philosophical revolution took place in the Old World which gave rise to a new order of religion; for this was the time of Buddha, Confucius, Zoroaster, Isaiah, Pythagoras, and Socrates. Infused with philosophy, religion ad-

vanced beyond the practice of sacrificial rituals to formulate creeds
and promote ethical conduct. Its attention became focused upon a
body of sacred literature. Thus transformed, religion came in conflict
with the practice of civic rites. It later detached from the state to form
a second power center. During that period of conflict, Christians living in the Roman empire were martyred for refusing to worship the
emperor's spirit. Centuries of persecution failed, however, to destroy
their community of faith. Acknowledging the Roman government's
inability to suppress independent religion, Constantine I took the
Christian church into a power-sharing arrangement with the state.
A century later the church survived the disintegration of the western
Roman state, while in the Byzantine east the church-state partnership
continued intact.

As surviving partner and heir to the fallen western empire, the Roman church had political and cultural as well as religious authority.
The barbarian tribes that overran the empire had military power, but
they hungered for civilization. The Popes, bishops of Rome, be-
stowed moral and political legitimacy upon those kings who supported the catholic faith against Christian heresies and heathen cults.
Frankish kings became their principal allies. In 800 A.D., Pope Leo
III crowned Charlemagne Emperor of Rome and created a new political office. Although the "Holy Roman Emperor" was theoretically
subordinate to the Pope in Christian society , he became the Pope's
rival in a struggle for real political power. Emperors claimed the right
to appoint church officials serving within their territorial domain.
Popes responded by excommunicating unsubmissive Emperors.
Later the fight between these two rivals degenerated into wars and assassination attempts. The Popes made a further bid for political
power by organizing crusades against Moslem rulers of the Holy
Land. They envisioned a universal Christian realm in which both religious and political authority would be vested in the Roman see. In
the end, Luther's Protestant movement destroyed European religious
unity. Powerful monarchs emerged in several nations to challenge the
Holy Roman Emperors. So western society escaped the creation of
a religiously based totalitarianism to match the earlier political one
of the Caesars.

About this time, a third type of institution appeared in western
Europe to challenge the power of the other two. Commercial institutions began to develop apart from those of feudal society. Sloughing

off serfdom, people went into the towns to work for wages. Guilds were formed to train and regulate labor. Trading companies were established to carry on commerce with foreign lands. Universities arose as centers of theoretical learning. Such events came into cultural focus with the Italian Renaissance of the 14th and 15th centuries. The new-made wealth gave rise to innovation in architecture and the visual arts. Humanist scholars rediscovered ancient Greek and Roman texts. In pursuit of riches, Portuguese and Spanish navigators explored distant places on earth, discovering a second hemisphere. Silver and gold poured into Europe from Spain's American colonies. The English monarch chartered commercial companies to develop land along North America's eastern seaboard. Louis XIV set an example of royal extravagance that nearly impoverished the French nation. Portuguese, Dutch, and English merchants trafficked in African slaves.

In a later phase, western society experienced a reaction against absolute monarchy and colonial rule. First the Dutch rebelled against Spanish Hapsburg rule. English Puritans, acting in the name of Parliament, then rebelled against the authoritarian ways of Charles I. Parliament, which had traditionally represented the commercial classes, was being asked to approve royal requests to levy new taxes. England's North American colonies, asked to pay more taxes, fought a successful war for independence from the mother country. When, a decade later, the French king was forced to summon an Etats-General to raise additional revenues to support his bankrupt government, that event precipitated a violent political and social upheaval in which the commercially based "third estate" disinherited the aristocratic and religious classes. The U.S. Civil War of the mid 19th century dealt with the consequences of Negro slavery. The Russian Marxist revolution of the early 20th century brought internal violence and war. In the meanwhile, nonwestern peoples have struggled to win political independence from various European colonial powers.

A different type of revolution took place in the cities of north-central England during the late 18th century as scientific learning was applied to commercial life. Watt's invention of a steam engine, signalling the start of this "Industrial Revolution", led to steam-powered textile mills, steamboats, and locomotives. Advances in metallurgy produced better grades of iron and steel. Experiments with electricity brought telegraph and telephone networks, Edison's light bulb, and other electrical appliances. Gasoline-powered engines made it possible to travel by airplane and automobile. These technological inventions spawned various new kinds of commercial products. A business class emerged to manage their manufacturing and commercial operations. A class of production workers, recruited initially from the farms, supplied the raw labor. Additionally, bankers, engineers, bookkeepers, salesmen, and other such employees were needed in administrative capacities, and had to be trained. In all, these various functions and activities and the people involved in them constituted a third social sector, the economic or commercial, which, though it did not receive serious attention until the last half millennium, has since become the most energetic and, perhaps, the most powerful one of the three.

Government, religion, and business, then, are the principal sectors of society. They each emerged and developed at different times in world history. As spheres of human activity, they remain fundamentally distinct and separate from each other. The more advanced types of societies seem to require that their functions be placed in separate institutions, even as higher forms of life contain a multitude of specialized cells. Western society has developed such a tradition of divided power. Religion and government have been separate centers of power since the days of the Roman empire, while the business or commercial sector grew apart from the other two. Moreover, each of the three sectors contains an internal division of power. Western Christianity became split between the Roman Catholic and Protestant denominations, while Jews, Quakers, Unitarians, and other minorities also have found a place within the religious spectrum. Instead of forming a universal empire, the several nations of Europe have kept each other at bay politically with "balance of power" diplomacy. The framers of the U.S. Constitution, fearing abuse of government power, split governmental functions between the executive, legislative, and judicial branches, and divided the legislature into two separate houses. The First Amendment prescribes separation between church and state.

This scheme of society, while at first seeming to be weak, has proved safest and best in the long run. Lord Acton's principle that "power corrupts and absolute power corrupts absolutely" has come to haunt totalitarian systems. Fascist totalitarianism shocked the world by its wartime brutality and use of concentration camps. Because no person or group was able to oppose him, Adolf Hitler single-handedly pulled a powerful nation into his mad scheme of world domination. In the case of Marxist-Leninist socialism, the peoples of Asia and eastern Europe have been put through a lengthy period of terror and police-state oppression. The socialist economic system, characterized by central planning, has been shown to be less dynamic, innovative, and productive than western capitalism. In head-to-head military competition with the West, the Soviet Union found that it lacked the economic wherewithal to continue the contest. The combination of government with business enterprise, which is the essence of socialism, succeeded mainly in creating lethargic bureaucracies in which party loyalty counted more than work effort. There was no competition among productive entities to spur better performance. There was no government dealing with business at arm's length, able and ready to punish abuse. The only means of correction was self-correction by the ruling political party. Therefore, while the checks-and-balances system may appear less efficient than a scheme of unified power, events of the 20th century have shown the wisdom of its approach.

Rise and Fall of Political Totalitarianism in the Soviet Union

Marxist-Leninist totalitarianism is historically interesting because its scheme of power can be traced back to origins in the Byzantine Roman empire. Unlike the situation in western Europe after Rome's fall, church and state here remained together in the same structure. The Orthodox church functioned almost like a department of government. When Constantinople fell to the Ottoman Turks in 1453 A.D., the Byzantine state came to an end but its church continued. The political center of gravity for this religion shifted from Constantinople to Moscow where a powerful duke became its patron. Moscow, monk Theophilus claimed, was the "Third Rome", since Constantinople (the Second Rome) had fallen to infidels and Rome itself to heretics. A century later, the Muscovite Grand Duke took the title of Czar (Caesar). So the unified structure of church and state, characteristic of the eastern Roman empire, was transferred to

Czarist Russia.[1] The Bolsheviks inherited the totalitarian tradition of the Czars while adding to it a quasi-religious ideology that prescribed state ownership of the means of production. In this way, the three sectors of organized society—government, religion, and commerce—were fused together in a tight cultural and structural bond.

In our time the Soviet Union has faced the same challenge from western culture which Czarist Russia faced in the days of Peter the Great. Totalitarian states are apt to be technologically less advanced because they lack social pluralism and stifle free thought. Because a nation must keep up with technology to remain militarily strong, both Czar Peter and Mikhail Gorbachev chose to pursue an opening to the West. Breaking with its totalitarian past, Gorbachev announced at the 1986 Party Congress that "(s)ocialism fosters the diversity of people's interests, requirements and abilities . . . "[2] Perestroika, or decentralized power, would be the new order of the day. A spirit of glasnost, or openness of expression, would henceforth prevail. Letting this new light into the dark house of Soviet totalitarianism, Gorbachev was seeming to risk the state's very existence upon a type of reform antithetical to its nature. Soon the socialist planners were talking of promoting free-market economies. Soon communists were surrendering their monopoly of political power. Soon, one by one, the satellite nation of eastern Europe were slipping out of the socialist orbit and joining the West. Soon the Soviet Union itself was dissolved. It seemed that Marxist-Leninist socialism, if not quite dead, was at least writhing on the "dustbin of history." Western capitalists were elated to see history confirm that their system was superior to socialism in endurance and strength.

The Soviet economy fell prey to government's total control of business. While for a time ideological fervor was able to sustain increased production, stagnation eventually set in as political privilege brought corruption and the sense of individual initiative was lost. The internal decay of socialist society was accompanied by increased external pressures from the west. Under President Reagan, the U.S. Government turned itself into an instrument of combat against enemies of the capitalist system. Its foreign policy included a combination of military and economic moves against leftist governments, supplemented by cultural subversion delivered through the communications media. The United States engaged the Soviet Union militarily in an accelerated arms race. U.S. military expenditures rose from

$134.0 billion, or 5.0 % of GNP, in 1980 to $273.4 billion, or 6.6% of GNP in 1986.[3] Whatever its cost to the U.S. economy, this approach made good sense as a strategy for winning the Cold War. It forced the Soviet Union, with an economy half the size of the U.S. economy, to maintain rough parity with the United States in the level of military expenditures, while starving other sectors of the Soviet society. The intensified financial pressure exposed more quickly the inherent weakness of an economic system based on totalitarian control.

Socialism's weakness lay more in its totalitarian structure than in its ideological opposition to private business. The effective merger of government with productive enterprise was found to create stagnant bureaucracies rather than a stronger and more efficient economy. It would be a mistake, however, to conclude that government cannot play a useful role in regulating business activities. On the contrary, business checked by government can be as or more productive of good results as business left to do as it pleases. That is because the institutions of business are no less prone to the sort of corruption that comes with absolute power than government is. The healthy model of society is one which embodies a system of divided power. The unhealthy model is one of concentrated and unchecked power. If, therefore, free-enterprise zealots succeed in extinguishing or minimizing government power, they could create their own kind of totalitarianism that would be as damaging to society as the totalitarian system created by those who sought to extinguish private business. Business and government need each other to remain healthy and strong. Society must retain this scheme of divided power.

How Global Debt Subverted Government Power

A little-recognized facet of Cold War competition had to do with the crisis of Third World debt. During the 1960s and 1970s, bankers from the First World sold developing countries on the idea of obtaining loans to build infrastructure so they could achieve more rapid economic growth. To become major players in the global economy, these nations would need to build roads and airports, docks, power plants, steel mills, and other facilities allowing industry to operate efficiently. Governments in Latin America and other less developed parts of the world went ahead with these loans, expecting to repay them from revenues generated by their faster-growing economies. Those expectations somehow miscarried. Jude Wanniski, a supply-side economist, has suggested that the heavy tax burden to pay for the development killed business initiative. Another explanation would be that the expected return on investment never materialized because of weak markets for the products which these nations planned to produce. With so many developing nations each developing their resources, commodity production increased and prices fell. Interest rates meanwhile soared. The borrowing nations were stuck with a massive foreign debt which they could not service. Wanniski described the situation: "Imagine buying a television set in 1955 and paying for it over 30 years and you have a picture of the fix the Third World is in. The TV set (the original development project) has long ago been scrapped, but the finance charges go on and on."[4]

Two international lending institutions, the World Bank and the International Monetary Fund, coordinated the borrowing and repayment activities of developing nations. "The IMF and the World Bank are run by and for the money-center banks, the aim being the aversion of international financial collapse and their own bankrupt-cies," Wanniski observed. "The World Bank's objective is to squeeze the U.S. taxpayer for resources to send to the Third World, with the avowed aim of helping nations develop so their expanding tax bases can support their debt service. The IMF's pattern is to squeeze the taxpayers of the recipient nations via IMF imposed 'austerity plans' to collect the revenues needed to meet international debt obligations. The net result of this one-two punch has been the exact opposite of the intended aim, pushing developing nations up the Laffer Curve and inviting civil strife, revolutions, terrorism and authoritarian takeovers of one kind or another."[5]

In fact, the mounting Third World debt created a boon for mili-tant capitalism. In the name of "austerity plans", the debt obligation gave the IMF the right to dictate to foreign governments what their economic policies should be. In other words, an institution con-trolled by western bankers was able to tell Brazil, Mexico, or, for that matter, a communist nation such as Poland that it had to control wages, ease government restrictions on foreign investment, and liberalize trade in order to obtain further loans to keep the nation from defaulting on its debt payments. Once national sovereignty was violated in this way, any and all sorts of further capitalistic "reforms" became possible. In short, without resorting to military force or conventional diplomatic pressures, the international bankers could reach down into a country and undo socialism.

The full extent of the international debt crisis became evident during 1981–82 when a combination of higher interest rates and falling commodity prices (including oil) exposed the perilous financial condition of borrowing nations. By 1986, this Third World debt had reached $1 trillion. The loans of the ten largest U.S. commercial banks to just six countries—Brazil, Mexico, Argentina, Venezuela, Chile, and the Philippines—represented 150% of their stockholders' equity.[6] When the banks made their imprudent loans to foreign governments, such loans were believed to be of high quality because a nation's "full faith and credit" stood behind them. Later, the bankers realized that they would have difficulty collecting from governments if the loans turned sour. They responded by charging the borrowers a higher interest rate to cover the greater risks. The governments went along with those arrangements, as borrowers generally do when they feel dependent upon banks for further credit. Gradually the idea took hold that, in a practical sense, the governments did not have to make interest payments to the banks, or pay the principal either, for that matter. They could simply default on the loans, walking away from their debt problems by unilateral decision, and there was little the banks could do about it. Everyone realized, though, that such a decision would involve great risks. Having defaulted, the governments might never again obtain credit from western lending institutions.

Nevertheless, this situation posed a political challenge to western capitalism. During those dark days of the early to mid 1980s, the possibility that Third World nations might form a "debtors' cartel" to cancel their foreign debt was often discussed in U.S. financial circles. If the debtor nations took such a step, they would, of course, face retaliation from the banks, but the banks themselves would also be perilously weakened. Furthermore, if western creditors actually carried through on their threat to impose a credit boycott upon the defaulting nations, they could drive those nations out of the western camp and into the waiting arms of the Second World. What trade and aid the United States was no longer willing to provide the Third

World countries could perhaps be picked up, in other words, by the Soviet Union and its allies. Such an opportunity this offered the cause of international socialism — to capture in its orbit numerous grateful Third World nations, all authentic victims of capitalism, without firing a shot! First, however, the Third World governments had to initiate the process by declaring a default. Holding them back was national pride combined with unrelenting appeals from western bankers and political leaders and the sobering realization that the Soviet bloc, especially in its economically weakened state, was no substitute for the West.

The U.S. Government meanwhile made every effort to keep the debtor nations financially afloat. We opened our trade doors generously to their imports while tolerating a drastic reduction in U.S. exports, which had an especially harsh impact on farmers in the midwestern states. The United States took 90% of the increased exports from Latin America between 1983 and 1984. Japan and the European Community nations took relatively little.[7] U.S. diplomats meanwhile redrew the political map of Latin America through a combination of guns and dollars. The elected communist government in Chile was forcibly replaced with a military regime which brought in economists trained at the University of Chicago to convert the Chilean economy to principles of the free market. Another Marxist government, in Nicaragua, was squeezed by a trade embargo and Contra military pressures. Eventually it, too, fell. In Mexico, a Harvard-trained economist, Carlos Salinas de Gortari, spearheaded the conversion from nationalistic protectionism to an economy wide open to foreign investment and trade.

Smith, Keynes, and their Heirs

In the 1980s, conservative governments came to power in several large western industrialized nations. The capitalist system went on the attack both at home and abroad. A massive U.S. arms build-up checked Soviet military might around the world. The large debt owed to western banks, combined with weak commodity prices, kept Third World countries politically docile and financially strapped. The domestic agenda in the United States included tax cuts, control of inflation, privatization of public services, industrial deregulation, and union-busting. On the other hand, the traditional conservative goal of a balanced national budget was spectacularly ignored. As government increased its use of force against foreign enemies and lower-class criminals, average real wages dropped and work hours rose. More manufacturing jobs were lost through outsourcing to low-wage countries abroad. Such policies work to the advantage of business interests, but against the interests of government and working people. Workers are hurt by the drop in real wages, the increase in work time, the loss of jobs in deregulated industries, and the weakening of unions. Government as an institution is reduced by privatization and the cut in taxes. A smaller government presence in economic life means greater opportunity for private operators. Lower inflation rates preserve the value of money for its present owners. Free trade gives multinational corporations license to send products and funds across national borders with minimal government interference.

As the situation now stands, the political pendulum has swung quite far in the direction of favoring business. Conversely, the fortunes of imperial government have receded. Ideological conservatives keep pushing for government to withdraw from economic affairs. Embellishing upon the ideas of Adam Smith, some are questioning the basic legitimacy of government in today's world, beyond, of course, its use of military and police force to quell popular uprisings. Writing in the *Wall Street Journal*, Kenichi Ohmae, managing director of McKinsey & Co. in Japan, has questioned the need for most government services: "The two traditional 'products' of governments — military protection and access to natural resources — are losing their value. Commodities can be arbitraged across producing countries, and if you have the wealth to buy these commodities you certainly have access to them . . . Thus, there is diminishing need for military power to protect a country's 'scarce' resources . . . Besides military forces, another benefit governments offer their people is ideology. With their taxes, people pay for the 'truth'. But Cable News Network and the tales of the good life it spreads throughout the world have made standards of living, not political dogma, the criteria by which governments are judged." In fact, he declared: "The role of national governments is much less important than (people) think; governments are little more than spoilers who disrupt markets with their interference and announcements."[8]

Such a pronouncement goes well beyond what Adam Smith might

have said. Smith was not a "free enterprise" fanatic, but a level-headed, scholarly type of person who gave government as well as business a needed place in society. A true scientist, he observed how the economy actually worked. While governments have always been involved in economic affairs, the primary mechanism of economic control, he wrote, rested more upon natural or unregulated incentives of the market. The more advanced industries became more productive of wealth because of a system of progressively specialized labor which required that goods be freely and fairly exchanged. Smith's best-known concept, however, had to do with proclaiming that "invisible" forces coordinate transactions in the marketplace to produce an optimal result. The capitalist, Smith wrote, "generally neither intends to promote the public interest, nor knows how much he is promoting it. He intends only his own security, only his own gain. And he is in this led by an invisible hand to promote an end which was no part of his intention. By pursuing his own interest he frequently promotes that of society more effectually than when he really intends to promote it."[9]

The idea that an "invisible hand" will coordinate economic activities, each freely willed by adversarially inclined individuals, to produce the best result for society has bolstered businessmen's demands that they be left alone to do as they please no matter how socially destructive or selfish their deeds may seem on the surface. It also suggests that government, labor, and other well-intentioned groups, who are purporting to serve the public interest, may actually hurt it when they oppose or restrict business. As ideological godfather of capitalism, Adam Smith's writings have therefore been read to give license to business owners and managers in their self-interested pursuits, while restraining political efforts to help working people. So minimum-wage laws are bad while leveraged buyouts which force mass layoffs show progress toward a more efficient production system. In Smith's name, inhumane business decisions have been rationalized as decisions of the free market. The free market—i.e., business managers deciding alone—determines everything correctly. If the managers decide to raise their own salaries , it must be to satisfy some deeper marketplace need. All is dictated by hard laws of economics, and politics must be kept out of the picture.

Of course that is nonsense. Politics, and not just economic requirements, enters into most business situations. Within large business firms, for instance, top management becomes a force with virtually absolute power over the organization. True, management reports to a board of directors who are elected by the corporate shareholders. However, this theoretical subordination of management to a group of owners has little practical effect when ownership is complacent or diffuse. The board members are likely to be hand-picked by upper management, and they certainly depend on it for essential information. Management will have unchallenged control of a business organization unless the operating results are conspicuously poor or a financial raid is taking place. Under normal circumstances, then, the political aspect is dominant. Whoever is in favor with the top boss, and with the chain of bosses down the line, will receive the lion's share of benefits resulting from the corporation's economic, or free-market, activities. Business managers often distinguish between the private and public sectors, implying that the one is competitively disciplined while the other is political. To persons down in the ranks, that sort of distinction is meaningless. A large business organization is not so different than the government. Both are bureaucracies, and bureaucracies are politically driven.

Adam Smith himself was not enamored of business behavior. He noted that businessmen conspired to fix prices through monopolistic agreements with their competitors and "combined" as employers to drive down the level of wages. Anticipating Karl Marx, he proposed a "labor theory of value". He upheld the legitimacy of government in its various functions. The first duty of the sovereign (the government) was to protect society from external violence, he observed in *Wealth of Nations*. The sovereign's second duty was to protect "every member of the society from the injustice or oppression of every other member of it" through a system of justice and laws. The third duty was to maintain public works needed for commerce and to carry out education of the young. Finally, the sovereign had a duty to himself to incur "a certain expense . . . for the support of his dignity", which can be interpreted to mean that heads of state have a right to live in opulence and style.[10] One can argue that governments have performed their last duty best, and have also fulfilled the first and third duties with varying degrees of success. It is the second duty which causes problems for laissez-faire capitalists. Does government have a right to protect citizens from their own or another's rapacity and greed? Adam Smith believed so.

Smith had written that a division of labor and free-market exchange of products would create a capital surplus that might cause
the level of wealth to rise. If wages rose along with the demand for
skilled labor, that might eat up profits and consume the accumulated
capital. However, the supply of labor had a way of increasing, too,
as increased prosperity enabled more working-class children to survive. Conversely, the labor supply would decrease as employment
opportunities softened and more children starved. Such faith that a
capitalistic economy could maintain an adequate level of employment through capital investment received a jolting setback during the
Great Depression. Casting about for ways to restore employment,
the Roosevelt administration settled upon a program of fiscal stimulus derived from the ideas of John Maynard Keynes. Keynes' basic argument was that it was indeed possible for private business investment to fall short and remain at a level insufficient to sustain full
employment. In that case, government needed to spend more money
than usual to supplement private spending. During ebbs in the business cycle, he proposed that the federal government should run a
budget deficit to pour funds into the economy. Those deficits could
be recovered by running budget surpluses in prosperous years. With
"built-in stabilizers", government could prevent excessive swings in
the business cycle, and so the "economic problem" would be solved.

Borrowed funds to finance World War II allowed a powerful
demonstration of Keynes' scheme. After the war, accumulated personal savings were used to purchase consumer goods, and the economy was back with a roar. In the post-war period, the federal government has taken an active role in managing the economy through
monetary and fiscal techniques. Western capitalism has thus switched
to a semi-socialist or mixed economy. Unfortunately, the U.S.
Government ran budget deficits in prosperous as well as hard times,
so that the national debt kept steadily climbing. Another product of
the New Deal era, Social Security, has accumulated a large actuarial
deficit as politicians dipped into its fund to pay medical, disability,
and survivor's benefits along with generous pensions for the initial
group of retirees. That shortfall precipitated an increase in the regres-
sive FICA tax. Still another New Deal creation, federal deposit insurance for personal savings accounts, has become a multibillion-dollar
headache. It will cost the U.S. taxpayer as much as $500 billion to bail
out failed savings-and-loan banks in the aftermath of their deregula-

tion and lending binge. Further billions may be required to replenish the deposit-insurance fund for the regular commercial banks.

At the present time, the financial affairs of the U.S. Government are in a more or less continual state of crisis. Repeated emergency resolutions are required from Congress to raise the debt ceiling so that the government can pay its bills. We are, in other words, about at the end of the line with Keynes and his ideas of public borrowing to revive prosperity. Further progress appears to be blocked along the lines of "tax, spend, elect" or, in the Reagan variation, "do not tax, borrow, spend, and elect". The Federal Reserve Board, too, can do only so much by way of manipulating the money supply. Pyramids of money are spurious wealth. We need to refocus instead on the non-financial, "real world" aspect of economic life. Real wealth does not consist of government-printed money or Treasury bills but of productive enterprises, homes, clothing, food, automobiles, and such things, and the related markets. In the private-sector, the purely financial approach to economic life is counterproductive. Such an approach destroys communities of productive people in order to give nonproductive predators a succulent killing. It is a myth that this strengthens America's economic base.

Figure 3.1

Reprinted with permission of the *St. Paul Pioneer Press*

What we have, therefore, is not a government that is too hard on private-sector players, but one not quite hard enough. We have the seeming paradox of "big government" combined with governmental regulatory weakness. The paradox is explained by the fact that government and business are not sufficiently distant from one another in their institutional dealings. The politicians and capitalistic bureaucrats are "in bed together" at the highest levels. Therefore, we in America are not so far as we have supposed from having our own totalitarian system. The separation which ought to exist between business and government has somehow disappeared. It may have started out as a case of government expanding into and encroaching upon the domain of business; but now business feels quite comfortable with enlarged public-sector activity. The New Deal created the phenomenon of "big government" in the sense that large sums of money were run through the government's coffers. Government was substantially entering the realm of commerce, where it did not properly belong. The cost of this move was that government became corrupted by business. The politicians, with their sights set upon short-term re-election needs, could not handle the long-term financial responsibilities. Money as well as power corrupted them.

Today the U.S. public has the impression that their elected officials are in it mostly for the money. Even if top government salaries are low in relation to comparable positions in private industry, the perks and post-government career opportunities more than make up for that deficiency. The regulators and regulated ones are occupationally too close. To help business interests gain access to important politicians has become a valuable commercial service. Michael Deaver, once a top adviser to President Reagan, built up an $18 million-a-year consulting business within one year of leaving government employment, representing such clients as Canada and South Korea. The U.S. ambassador to the Soviet Union, Robert B. Strauss, traded upon his connections as former chairman of the Democratic National Committee and former U.S. Trade Representative to make a personal fortune in part by helping Japanese corporations acquire properties in the United States. The current U.S. Trade Representative, Carla Hills, formerly represented Japanese business interests, as have her two top deputies.[11]

According to Pat Choate, Japan spends $100 million each year to hire "1,000 Washington, D.C. lobbyists, superlawyers, former high-ranking public officials, public relations specialists, political advisers—even former presidents" to help persuade the U.S. Government to adopt policies favorable to Japanese business interests. It spends another $300 million for local activities, including contributions to U.S. political campaigns. The United States, on the other hand, has a negligible lobbying presence in Toyko, largely because the Japanese public would not tolerate such behavior on the part of its current or former government officials. "It is, after all," wrote Choate," the greed and self-interest in Washington, D.C., that makes it all possible, the 'revolving door' of government at the highest levels that confuses 'public service' with 'personal advancement' and mistakes 'legal' for 'ethical'. For many, a top job in the cabinet is merely a sabbatical from a more permanent career as a registered agent lobbying for a foreign corporation."[12] Is it any wonder, then, that many Americans, no matter how personally well off they may be, feel betrayed by their leaders and cynical about the system?

The Nature of Business Totalitarianism

Adam Smith saw a need for government, among other things, to protect "every member of the society from the injustice or oppression of every other member of it." The state would be a referee in that process. In order to fulfill its role, government would have to keep itself separate from the individuals, institutions, or interests being judged. Firm walls of separation should stand especially between government and business , as economic pursuits touch people's lives more urgently than others. Injustices are perceived through humanity's sense of morality. Moral concerns can be expressed through religious and cultural institutions. These, in turn, can have an impact on the political process. To a lesser degree, they can also be directed at the economic sector through appeals for ethical investment or humane employment practices. Democratically elected trade unions can become active centers of power working on behalf of human needs and rights.

In general, the matter of protecting the human interest against economic exploitation boils down to maintaining healthy conflict between the separate power centers of business and government. In a democracy, government represents, ideally, the needs and wants of people who are citizens of the community. The power resides in official representatives elected according to the principle of an equal vote per person. Business, on the other hand, reflects the commercial aspirations of its owners and managers, and is focused on profit. The ownership of money or a position of authority within a money-based organization determines the distribution of power. So we can see that two quite different kinds of organizations share power in an industrialized society and that, if the human interest is to be fully protected, government must maintain its strength and independence vis-a-vis business groups. This requirement becomes difficult to meet in a society of weakening religious or moral values, where a vision of community interest is lacking. In such situations, money supplies the organizing force in society and controls public policy.

A further problem arises when business expands its operation beyond the jurisdiction of any government. Then the business entity can play governments off against each other to win inordinate concessions for itself. As we move to a global economy, parochial governments have been outflanked in this way by worldwide business groups seeking maximum profits, and have been forced to compromise on protection of basic human needs. Conversely, as businesses around the world have become accustomed to appeasement by government, popular discontent is inflamed. The social and political tension mounts. The stage is set for a showdown between the institutions of government and business — an epic struggle between two centers of power, reminiscent of the struggle between Pope and Emperor a thousand years ago. Government slaps taxes and restrictive regulations upon business. Business threatens to move production and jobs to another political locality. These are like brothers become worst enemies. The one sees greed in the other; the other barely tolerates that one's existence.

Flush with money, business ventures forth into the society, breaking down barriers that separate it from other institutions. A kind of business totalitarianism is created as business's financial muscle overcomes the other power centers. A spreading slick of commercialism settles over the culture. Ironically, though government created money, politicians are chronically short of this commodity. It is estimated that the average U.S. Senator needs to raise $4 million to wage a successful re-election campaign. Business, on the other hand, has plenty of money. Elected officials therefore depend on financial contributions from business and other such groups. Former Senator William Proxmire has described the current system of campaign financing as "a system of thinly concealed bribery that not only buys (lawmakers') attention but frequently buys their votes." It is a clean swap of money for "access" to lawmakers which can be expected to ripen into favoritism.[13] The large number of business lobbyists in Washington, D.C., and at the state capitals testifies to the fact that few business managers still believe in laissez-faire capitalism but are themselves lining up at the trough to obtain their fair share of the public largesse, and perhaps even more.

Regarding the other two branches of government, one might suppose that the judicial system, too, is swayed by moneyed interests. The high hourly rates charged by private attorneys serve as a stiff entry fee to the courts, screening out the concerns of economically marginal persons. As for the third branch of government, President Bush is an "old shoe" business supporter whom *U.S. News & World Report* has called "a free-market conservative at heart", with a "minimalist approach" to domestic affairs.[14] One of the President's pet projects is to reform education by making it more responsive to the needs of business. He has appointed a commission of corporate leaders to look into the problem of graduates inadequately prepared for careers. He has promoted the privatization of elementary and secondary education to introduce marketplace competition to this area. So another of government's traditional functions is falling into business hands. Prison management may be yet another. The "public-private partnership" runs deep. Business and government have ceased to deal with each other at arm's length. A mutual interest in money cuts across their institutional boundaries.

The barrier between business and the cultural-spiritual sector has been breached as commercial television has become our dominant form of culture. Its images have won people's souls by capturing their attention for long periods of time. Although the commercial message cannot be too heavy-handed, it fosters a definite set of values. Serious thinking about political or social issues is discouraged in favor of escapist entertainment. Opulent lifestyles are everywhere on display. And, when push comes to shove, the programming cannot offend the commercial sponsors, the media owners, or the affluent entertainers and "behind the scenes" managers. Money is always the bottom line in this or any other business. Organized religion is relatively safe from the financially corrupting influence of this medium, although a televangelist such as Jim Bakker will occasionally succumb. Education, on the other hand, has permitted itself to become a mere appendage to the career system. No longer can an aspiring young man or woman start out with nothing and, through sheer ability and hard work, climb the ladder of corporate or professional success. Nowadays, to enter the starting gate of the chase after lucrative careers, the would-be laborer must invest big money in a college education and put in years of unpaid classroom work while postponing income from a career job.

In summary, U.S. society is dominated by an interlocking set of commercially centered interests that have largely broken down the institutional barriers separating business, government, and culture. In a healthier type of society, government would provide a check upon abusive power in the business sector. The seemingly powerless spiritual communities, in turn, would provide a check on abusive government power. Lacking external or self-imposed discipline, top corporate managers have become plunderers of their own organizations. Able to set their own salaries, they have set salary levels high. Between 1977 and 1987, chief executives' salaries and bonuses grew twice as fast as hourly workers' wages.[15] When businesses lost money, underperforming management typically responded by laying off production workers. Faced with takeover threats, corporations equipped themselves with "poison pill" and other defenses, and offered senior managers "golden parachutes". The name of the game, however, was for managers to become owners. Through leveraged buyouts, the corporate managers have arranged sometimes to buy the very firms that they managed, presumably negotiating for the current owners a fair price. Managers of financial institutions who assisted in this process settled for multimillion-dollar fees.

The standard argument is that free-market forces determine executive pay and that to attract high-caliber managerial talent corporations must pay astronomically high salaries. One should recognize, however, that quality or complexity of personal workmanship is only one of several factors that decide who will be promoted or hired for high corporate positions. Regarding promotion criteria, a front-page column in the *Wall Street Journal* disclosed: "Chief executives look most for loyalty and a sense of humor when choosing subordinates

. . . Hard work and integrity are also-rans."[16] Loyalty and humor are not economic qualities: they are qualities that help to cement a personal relationship with one's superiors. If, therefore, many or most top-level executives were chosen more for their political skills than for qualities of work performance, then political restraints upon private-sector pay become entirely appropriate.

While public attention has tended to focus upon compensation for corporate executives, an equally abusive situation exists with respect to professional fees. Private attorneys, in particular, have prospered greatly from their exclusive access to the courts. The root of the problem is the merger of private interests with public power. The legal profession, like others, is controlled by state licensing boards, dominated by the professions themselves, which restrict entrance to the occupation and so drive up the level of fees. One finds a similar arrangement in other unusually lucrative opportunities such as those in the savings-and-loan and insurance industries. Because of government's lax regulation, the financial system has often been used to gamble with other people's money and take the profits at hand while sticking someone else (usually the general taxpayer) with the downside risk. Government looked the other way as financial managers and assorted professionals have thus looted the public.

The essence of business totalitarianism is not that government withers away leaving business in total control. It is that government becomes too close to business, puts itself at the service of business, and uses the state's power of coercion to further private interests. "Big government" is part of this process. Not content with impartial regulation, government has become an active participant in economic functions, appropriating huge sums of money. The legitimate need to defeat Hitler in World War II produced a permanent war economy which is not so easily dissolved even when our principal adversary has vacated the battlefield. The legitimate goal of redistributing wealth from the rich to the poor has given government, in effect, the power to redistribute wealth any way it chooses. And so, the revenues pouring into government coffers have allowed lawmakers to spend money on pet projects and build monuments to themselves. The walls of separation between government and private-sector or not-for-profit enterprise have decayed and fallen away.

As socialist governments abroad seized totalitarian power and created a miserable type of society, so we in the United States must be concerned about a similar concentration of power in the hands of business. Business should not be permitted to breach the boundaries that separate it from government and cultural institutions. We Americans are not so entirely different from the peoples who suffered from communist rule. Absolute political power created what might be called "hard-core" totalitarianism. Some of its characteristics would include the use of state-affiliated police or military power to repress political expression and control thought. Under unchecked capitalism, we have, instead, "soft-core" totalitarianism; this squeezes people economically and spiritually. While such a system may seem easier to bear because the oppression is less intense, it is real oppression nonetheless. The remedy in both cases is to create a pluralistic structure of power which offers internal resistance to abuse. In a socialist society, this means building up the private sector of business so that it can take its place alongside government as an effective power center. Under capitalist totalitarianism, this means strengthening and reforming government so it can restrain the worst tendencies of business.

Swing toward a more Balanced Position

In late 1989, the socialist order in eastern Europe began collapsing like a set of dominos. That event accomplished what needed initially to be done for the victims of hard-core totalitarianism. While business zealots saw this as a sign of capitalism's complete triumph, it, in fact, represented a swing of the historical pendulum to another phase. The next event is not to freeze the pendulum forever in one place but move back to a more balanced position. That corrective activity may well take place in western societies; it is our turn now for political correction. Prospectively, we in the West may do what the peoples of eastern Europe have already done: fight the totalitarianism of our kind. Personal freedom is the goal in both cases, though the roles of institutions are reversed. We must reacquaint ourselves with the positive uses of government, while they in the east relearn free markets. So contemporary history may bring forth a pattern of events resembling Hegelian dialectics. The thesis, government-centered totalitarianism, brings forth upon its collapse an antithetical business-centered development, exhibiting a lack of governmental regulation. The third movement, creating synthesis, would stake out an intermediate position between the two previous extremes. Of necessity its structure would be more moderate and complex than the previous ones, or essentially pluralistic. It is possible that the opening shot in the anti-totalitarian battle against business domination of our hemisphere and world will be the unexpected defeat of the U.S.-Mexico-Canada free trade proposal.

Seen from that perspective, the fight against a North American FTA represents an attempt to cut short the period of antithetical development, nipping business totalitarianism in the bud as it attempts to spread beyond the borders of the United States into the two neighboring countries. The Canadians, enjoying a relatively advanced social-welfare system, were shocked by their nation's quick conversion to international business values when the Mulroney administration signed a Free-Trade Agreement with the United States. It is possible that Canadian voters will repudiate the 1988 agreement at their first available opportunity. The Mexicans, on the other hand, have a tradition of totalitarian rule inherited from Spanish colonial times. The President of Mexico, head of state, is also the head of the ruling political party, which controls the major trade unions. The Mexican government retains a number of state-owned businesses. There is also an anti-clerical tradition in Mexican politics. In short, its political system, which proceeds from the Constitution of 1917, rather resembles that established in the Soviet Union during the same year. Starting in 1985, however, the government of Mexico abruptly changed course and formed an alliance with foreign banks and corporations. As a result, the totalitarian structure of the Mexican state has been placed at the service of private commercial interests—an ominous combination given the ideological aspirations of the proponents of free trade.

In the Mexican maquiladoras we have a glimpse of a possible type of future society if the business-centered totalitarianism is allowed to proceed to term. This is a picture of human degradation approaching the conditions endured in soviet Russia. The positive alternative is not a reversion to government-centered totalitarianism but a scheme of social moderation. Such a scheme might involve less government and more private enterprise than socialism but more government and less business control than what is found in the United States. The key to achieving that situation would be to develop alternative centers of power which can resist totalitarian pressures. The two most important institutions in that regard are those of organized labor and religion. Such institutions build communities of people apart from business and government. Within their structures individuals are able to express their human concerns, communicate with a sympathetic audience, and build the broadened consensus of opinion needed to resist abusive economic or political power.

The Pope's View of an Economically Just Society

Historically it would seem that religion was better suited for the struggle against political totalitarianism, and organized labor for the fight against totalitarian abuse by business groups. The Christian church has a history of resisting state oppression that goes back to Roman times. The church has also itself participated in oppressing people, when it exercised political power. At the present time, though, organized religion represents more an anti-totalitarian force in society than a powerful oppressor. While we Americans tend to think of religion as being irrelevant to political struggles, we also know that Christian groups became active cells of opposition to Nazi and communist tyranny. We have seen how a dissident Moslem cleric, the Ayatollah Khomeini, led a political movement which overthrew the Shah of Iran. Another example of religious influence in political affairs would be the career of Pope John Paul II. The Pope played a key role in the collapse of East Bloc socialism through the support he gave the Polish Solidarity union in 1981. That trade-union movement, inspired in part by the election of a Polish national as Pope, was the first successful challenge to socialist totalitarian power in eastern Europe. Its ripening fruit a decade later gave eloquent response to Stalin's sarcastic question: "How many divisions does he (the Pope) have?"

John Paul II has also issued two papal encyclicals offering a moral critique of economic and political affairs. In his latest encyclical, which is entitled "Centesimus Annus", he recommended that human societies assume a moderate position between the extremes of unlimited state or business power. Noting the collapse of socialism in eastern Europe, the Pope posed this question: "Can it perhaps be said

that, after the failure of Communism, capitalism is the victorious social system, and that capitalism should be the goal of the countries
now making efforts to rebuild their economy and society? Is this the
model which ought to be proposed to the countries of the third world
which are searching for the path to true economic and civil progress?
The answer is obviously complex. If by 'capitalism' is meant an economic system which recognizes the fundamental and positive role of
business, the market, private property and the resulting responsibility for the means of production, as well as free human creativity in
the economic sector, then the answer is certainly in the affirma-
tive . . . But if by 'capitalism' is meant a system in which freedom
in the economic sector is not circumscribed within a strong juridical
framework which places it at the service of human freedom in its totality, and which sees it as a particular aspect of that freedom, the
core of which is ethical and religious, then the reply is certainly
negative."[17]

While acknowledging "the legitimate role of profit as an indication that a business is functioning well," the Pope also observed that
"it is possible for the financial accounts to be in order, and yet for the
people—who make up the firm's most valuable asset—to be hu-
miliated and their dignity offended." The state has a duty, he said,
"to provide for the defense and preservation of common goods such
as the natural and human environment." In that regard, John Paul II
found " a new limit on the market: there are collective and qualitative
needs which cannot be satisfied by market mechanisms . . . There
are goods which by their very nature cannot and must not be bought
or sold. Certainly the mechanisms of the market offer secure advantages . . . Nevertheless, these mechanisms carry the risk of an
'idolatry' of the market . . . The Marxist solution has failed, but
the realities of marginalization and exploitation remain in the world,
especially the third world, as does the reality of human alienation, especially in the more advanced countries . . . The collapse of the
Communist system in so many countries certainly removes an obstacle to facing these problems in an appropriate and realistic way, but
it is not enough to bring about their solution. Indeed, there is a risk
that a radical capitalistic ideology could spread which refuses even
to consider these problems, in the a priori belief that any attempt to
solve them is doomed to failure, and which blindly entrusts their solution to the free development of market forces."[18]

Trade Unions as an Anti-totalitarian Force

The Pope might well have been speaking of the situation in the Mexican maquiladoras whose pattern would be extended with free trade. Mexico has one of the world's largest populations of Roman Catholics. The church in Latin America has effectively contributed to human-rights and social-justice campaigns. When we look at such struggles in an industrializing Third World country such as Mexico, though, our attention must also be drawn to the other great center of resistance to totalitarian power: the trade unions. Mexico has both state-run or bureaucratic trade unions, which are part of the totalitarian structure, and independent or democratic trade unions. The democratic trade unions have borne the brunt of totalitarian might in that land. Their members have engaged in heroic opposition to powerful economic forces and, against great odds, upheld the human interest. For ordinary working people, they represent the main hope of gaining improvements in wages and working conditions and of restoring dignity to the work place. Even in a land of powerless people, these make-shift organizations have power. They are tough nuts which the totalitarian economic machinery cannot quite crack.

In the United States, there is a similar split between bureaucratic and democratic tendencies within the labor movement. Union membership has been declining for quite some time, and management has learned over the years to outflank labor organizations. It has learned specifically how to move production out of unionized plants and into nonunion facilities or low-wage areas abroad. Such developments have created a paradox for labor. The more successful a union is in increasing wages and benefits for its members, the more likely it is that management will close down the facility and move to a place where unions are weak or nonexistent. Professors Peter Linneman and Michael Wachter of the University of Pennsylvania have studied the so-called "de-industrialization of America" and found that job loss in the U.S. economy was closely correlated with the degree of unionization. Employment declined in those industrial sectors dominated by unions, but not in others. If labor costs increased through successful contract negotiations, the employer moved.[19] At least, that was true of private-sector employers. In the public sector, employers are more tied down to particular locations and so cannot escape their union contracts geographically. As a result, union gains have lately tended to be confined to the public sector. Even so, government officials have adopted the new strategy of "privatization" to circumvent collective-bargaining contracts for public employees. They farm out work to lower-paying enterprises in the private sector and shrink the size of government services so that the same union-busting result is accomplished.

The bottom line is that U.S. trade unions will have to change in order to survive. They cannot remain strictly a local operation; otherwise, their most impressive victories will become defeats. U.S. unions have tended to shun ideological discussions and political struggles and stick to "bread and butter" issues benefiting their local members. Such parochialism has become a luxury in today's world. The trade-union movement must develop a broader perspective, both in terms of geography and its functional mission. The solidarity upon which union strength depends must be extended to workers in other cities and states, and even foreign countries. Labor must also broaden its view to seek strategic alliances with other groups. This means abandoning xenophobic attitudes with respect to outside persons or groups, participating in ad hoc coalitions, and developing a scheme of improvement for the community as a whole. The unions cannot avoid becoming more political, more ideological, and even more "spiritual" if they are to become effective centers of resistance to abuse by totalitarian business power.

In today's world, labor organizations in different countries need to form networks for mutual aid and intelligence matching those of the business organizations. Through correspondence, conferences, and personal travel they must accomplish the difficult tasks of breaking down old animosities based on nationalistic pride, overcoming language barriers, conquering racial and ethnic prejudices, and developing coordinated programs of action despite their limited resources for communication and transportation. Those efforts, if successful, will eventually spill over into political areas, so that parallel programs of government to advance labor interests will simultaneously emerge in several parts of the world. Already the prospect of a Free-Trade Agreement between Mexico, Canada, and the United States has brought trade unionists in those three countries closer together. A MEXUSCAN "Solidarity Network" has been formed to cement personal relationships between Mexican, U.S., and Canadian labor activists at a local level. Auto workers, textile workers, agricultural producers, and other such groups have met with their counterparts in the other two countries to discuss trade and other questions.[20] At the grassroots level, labor is indeed breaking out of its nationalistic shell and attacking cultural barriers. From a business perspective, the prospective North American FTA is accomplishing that unintended result.

Ultimately, totalitarian society will come to an end when the power in society is more evenly shared by its three major types of institutions: the political, cultural or spiritual, and economic. Each sector will keep abuse from the others in check, like the children's hand game of paper, scissors, and rock. The political sector will prevail over the economic, the spiritual over the political, and the economic over the spiritual. It will be, anyhow, a three-cornered contest between these power groups to shape the future. The political sector is immediately the most powerful; for it holds a monopoly of physical force. Political totalitarianism is therefore the most dangerous kind of totalitarian power. The economic sector, which can withhold materials essential for life, also has great coercive power. Its form of totalitarianism is the second worst kind. To the extent, therefore, that the spiritual-cultural sector of society — comprising its religious, educational, artistic, and communicative functions — can carve out a larger space for itself in areas once controlled by economic or political power, the two worst kinds of totalitarianism can perhaps be broken down, and humanity's period of suffering under such regimes be brought to a speedier conclusion.

Some Functions of Government in the Approaching Age

The crux of the current phase of the anti-totalitarian struggle has to do with determining the proper relationship between government and business. In particular, it would have to do with defining the role of government in regulating the economy. Government does, after all, have the upper hand in dealings with business. Yet, some would deny that government has much of an economic role to play. It behooves us, then, to speculate upon its various functions in this post-Keynesian age:

(1) All are agreed that government legitimately possesses a monopoly of force in organized society, both to repel foreign enemies and to exercise domestic police powers. Government makes laws and enforces them. Government creates rules for civilized conduct and punishes infractions. Generally it is better that the society maintain order through voluntary consent rather than by exercising force as a first resort.

The flip side of government's monopoly of force is its moral responsibility to behave in a civilized way, or, in other words, to observe internationally recognized standards of human rights. This is apparently something new in human history. Only since the 1970s has the human-rights agenda been aggressively applied to national governments. First ridiculed when President Carter raised the issue in a conspicuous manner, we have seen how the awareness of human-rights violations has been critical to events that have taken place in the Soviet Union and eastern Europe. The Chinese government has become vulnerable as well to this kind of criticism through the linkage of human rights to U.S. trade policy. Now that Amnesty International has formally charged the Government of Mexico with "flagrant human-rights abuses" related to use of torture by its military forces and police, such considerations may also tip the scales against approval of NAFTA if the Bush administration continues to ignore social criteria in discussions of trade policy.[21]

(2) There are functions which government has assumed as a convenience for society. They would include coining money, building and maintaining roads, operating a post office, constructing harbors and airports, disposing of sewage and waste, supervising public health, providing fire protection, running a municipal bus system, and educating the young. These public undertakings fall under the category of maintaining community infrastructure. Society must have some systems in place for the other parts to function. What is not clear, in some cases, is whether government or private industry should be responsible for providing the services. Much lies in a gray area. Government, it seems, should provide the bedrock services that are necessary for society regardless of demand, while business should provide other kinds of services and goods up to the level of demand. Even this distinction is often unclear. Should government or business remove trash? Which should operate the local bus system? What about schools? What about health-insurance coverage?

In reality, a dual system of public services has emerged in many areas, with both government and business involved. That would seem to make good sense. Since neither sector would then have a monopoly, some measure of competition could be introduced. Industries that are now being privatized lend themselves to both private- and public-sector enterprise. The public sector, for instance, might operate the core bus routes in a city while private-sector operators take the peripheral traffic. Public schools might be available for everyone while private schools met special educational needs. The same concept could be applied, in reverse, to high-cost service in the private sector. As privatization has been pursued to circumvent the high-cost labor associated with unionized public employees, so "publicization" might counter high-cost labor associated with the private professions. The practice of law, for instance, could as easily be handled by salaried government bureaucrats as by expensive legal entrepreneurs. Medical care could be dispensed by trained personnel on public payrolls as well as by private practitioners. Government financial inspectors could practice "public accounting" alongside the licensed CPA's. In these and other areas, government might become the low-cost provider of professional services while customers wanting "higher quality" could continue to contract in the private sector.

(3) Has government a legitimate role in regulating the private economy? Several functions come to mind.

(a) The federal government employs techniques of fiscal and monetary manipulation to overcome destructive swings in the business cycle. Those techniques should continue to be used if helpful. After Reagan, however, government's ability to use countercyclical spending to cure recessions has been greatly diminished. The federal budget does not have much slack for discretionary expenditures after paying all the interest.

(b) Some people want government to control private-sector "looting". Rep. Martin Sabo has introduced a bill in Congress which would deny corporations a business-expense tax deduction for executive salaries that exceeded 25 times the salary received by the lowest-paid corporate employee.[22] A federal law that went into effect in January 1991 requires a one-year waiting period for ex-federal employees to engage in lobbying or advising clients on trade matters. Pat Choate argues that this period should be extended to five or ten years, and that top federal officeholders be permanently barred from selling trade-related services.[23]

(c) Although the free market is able to coordinate the manufacturing and distribution of most economically valuable products by Adam Smith's "invisible hand", some results of free-market activity are socially unacceptable. For example, society cannot afford to let the price of labor drop below a certain level. Likewise, the mechanisms of the free market cannot properly deal with distributing finite quantities of natural resources. It cannot deal with industrial pollution which sticks neighboring communities with the cost of discharging toxic wastes while the polluters become rich. These inequities are problems for government to solve. Government needs to take action supplementing free-market activities in order to obtain a satisfactory result overall.

A type of problem insoluble by free-market forces alone is the problem of production oversupply. For example, millions of farmers all producing the same agricultural products with increased efficiency will ultimately drive each other out of business unless the market expands to the same degree. Perhaps society thinks it can afford to let some farmers go bankrupt and leave the farm if they can find other lines of work? Society cannot afford, however, to put everyone in that situation. The alternative would be to employ what is called "supply-management techniques" for limiting production. The Canadian government long protected farm prices in this way. The government estimated internal demand for agricultural commodities, established domestic supply levels, and then issued marketing certificates to prospective producers. It also set import quotas for those products. Such a system , while raising the price to consumers, stabilized farm production, gave farmers a fair price, and avoided expensive subsidies.

Many other types of products besides farm commodities are in chronic oversupply. There is production overcapacity in industries ranging from automobiles to consumer electronics to clothing and computers. Even if the current recession should end, the OECD predicts that joblessness in the First World will remain at high levels for some time to come. It sees a risk of people "drifting into long-term unemployment and losing skills, motivation, good work habits and the capacity to learn new skills."[24] What should be done about this situation? Perhaps supply-management techniques can be applied to industrial labor. Specifically, those techniques could be applied by reducing the scheduled hours of work for broad segments of the work force. Thus government could support the price of labor—i.e. bring stable or rising wage levels—without overturning decisions of the free market. Its intervention would directly address labor supply, not price.

Reduced Work Time as a Way of Managing the Labor Supply

As it is usually measured, the quantity of labor is a product of the number of persons employed and the average hours worked in a given period of time. One worker-hour of labor is an hour worked by one person. The supply of labor can therefore be reduced either by limiting employment or average hours. To limit the number of people employed might be to condemn the superfluous workers to unemployment. Assuming that annual incomes did not drop, the approach of controlling hours of work would seem preferable. Leisure is considered to be a positive condition so long as there are adequate income levels. Because human labor is an essential ingredient in most commercial products, its supply tends to correlate with production supply in general. Given the relative inability of government to control employment levels, the level of work hours becomes the principal means by which government can deal with production oversupply and stagnant markets.

Government can control the average hours worked within its jurisdiction by enacting legislation. The U.S. Government, for instance, could reduce work time in the United States by cutting the standard hours established under the Fair Labor Standards Act (FLSA) or by raising the penalty-pay rate for overtime. The FLSA requires that U.S. employers pay eligible employees one-and-one-half times their normal hourly rate for time worked beyond forty hours in a week. Longer hours are not legally prohibited but are made more expensive. In 1983, Rep. John Conyers introduced a bill in Congress to reduce the standard workweek from forty to thirty-two hours over an eight-year period, increase the rate of overtime pay to double time, and abolish mandatory overtime. This and other such bills have failed to pass. Alternatively, working hours in the United States might be reduced by enacting minimum-vacation laws similar to those in Europe. In 1970, the International Labor Organization adopted a convention calling for employers to grant at least three weeks of paid vacation to employees with one or more years of service. The United States did not ratify that particular convention. At the outset of the Great Depression, there was considerable interest in cutting hours of work. Both Roosevelt and Hoover made that proposal during the 1932 campaign. After Roosevelt's election, however, his "brain trust" soured on the idea. Those New Deal advisors hoped to achieve full employment through state-run programs instead of pessimistically "sharing the work." A 30-hour workweek bill sponsored by Senator Hugo Black of Alabama passed the U.S. Senate in 1933, but was tied up in the House Rules Committee after the President's opposition became known. Nevertheless, the Roosevelt Administration supported reduced work hours as a component of the National Recovery Administration's industrial codes. The U.S. Supreme Court struck down this approach in 1935. Later, the Administration drafted two pieces of court-proof legislation, the Walsh-Healey Act of 1936, which created a 40-hour standard for firms that had contracts with the federal government, and the Fair Labor Standards Act of 1938. Although the political tide was moving away from this approach in favor of Keynesian stimulus, the New Deal left some sound legal machinery for reducing hours.

Reduced work time today makes sense from a number of standpoints. First, U.S. workers are experiencing conflict between work and family life because of inadequate free time. A *New York Times* poll conducted in the summer of 1989 found that "women who work outside the home report that their children and their marriages are being shortchanged, and they lament having too little time for themselves."[25] A national survey conducted for a major life-insurance company reported that "Americans believe the greatest threat to the family is the inability of parents to spend enough time with their children."[26] A second reason to reduce work time would be to relieve the unemployment problem. Employment and average hours are inversely related if productivity and production output remain constant. A corollary to this argument would be that shorter work hours might reduce the amount of wasteful production. A third reason, which will be discussed in the next chapter, has to do with regulating world development and trade.

The Alternative to Reduced Hours:
Economic Waste

The economic argument relating to the alleged tradeoff between employment and work hours remains controversial. It will require additional explanation. As a starting point, consider the displacement of human labor by machines. This process, which is associated with "increased productivity", has been taking place in all industries cumulatively over a long period of time. What is its ultimate effect? Initially workers and their union spokesmen feared that labor displacement would throw people out of work and unemployment would rise proportionately as a result. That dire prediction has not yet come to pass. While discharging workers does immediately create unemployment, the discharged workers usually find employment in other lines of work. The cumulative result is not a steadily rising level of unemployment but a progressive change in the nature of employment, shifting away from "productive" and toward what might be called "nonproductive" kinds of work.

Figure 3.2 shows the percentage of U.S. workers employed in various types of industries in years between 1930 and 1990. The percentage of employment has been declining in agriculture and in the "goods-producing" industries — manufacturing, mining, and contract construction — since 1930. On the other hand, employment has increased in wholesale and retail trade, civilian government, and "services & other". This last-named category includes transportation and public utilities, finance, real estate, and "services" — a mixed group of professional or subprofessional functions. Now an observation can be made of these various kinds of employment. Workers in agriculture furnish tangible products which we all need and want. Mining, manufacturing, and construction also provide useful and needed products. Employment is therefore declining in those industries associated with the production of useful goods; and it is declining most in agriculture, whose products are most useful. On the other side of the ledger, we find that the percentage of workers employed in the services-providing industries of sales, government, and services has increased. One is never sure how useful those products are, or even what they are, but the service-related products seem not to

Figure 3.2

Percent Employed in U.S. Civilian Economy
by Type of Industry, 1930 to 1990

Percentage of Workers Employed in – –

	agric= culture	goods– producing industries	wholesale & retail trade	civilian government	services & other	total
1930	25.1	30.4	14.7	8.1	21.7	100.0
1935	26.3	29.7	14.8	9.5	19.7	100.0
1940	22.0	31.9	16.3	10.1	19.7	100.0
1945	16.9	36.0	15.1	12.2	19.8	100.0
1950	13.7	35.4	17.9	11.5	21.5	100.0
1955	11.3	35.9	18.5	12.1	22.2	100.0
1960	9.2	34.2	19.1	14.0	23.5	100.0
1965	6.7	33.7	19.5	15.5	24.6	100.0
1970	4.7	31.7	20.2	16.9	26.5	100.0
1975	4.4	28.1	21.2	18.2	28.1	100.0
1980	3.6	27.4	21.7	17.3	30.0	100.0
1985	3.1	24.7	22.9	16.3	33.0	100.0
1990	2.8	22.0	23.1	16.1	36.0	100.0

Source: Bureau of Labor Statistics

be as useful, by and large, as agricultural or manufactured products are. If, therefore, the trend is for employment to decline in the more productive areas and to increase in the less productive areas, will there not be a deterioration in the basket of product, considered from the standpoint of utility? Economists do not often raise this type of question; it is considered too subjective.

One who did raise the question, though, was Adam Smith. He wrote in *Wealth of Nations*: "Whatever be the actual state of the skill, dexterity, and judgment with which labor is applied in any nation, the abundance or scantiness of its annual supply must depend . . . upon the proportion between the number of those who are annually employed in useful labor, and that of those who are not so employed . . . The labor of some of the most respectable orders in the society is, like that of menial servants, unproductive of any value . . . The sovereign, for example, with all the officers both of justice and war who serve under him, the whole army and navy, are unproductive laborers . . . In the same class must be ranked, some both of the gravest and most important, and some of the most frivolous professions: churchmen, lawyers, physicians, men of letters of all kinds, players, buffoons, musicians, opera-singers, opera-dancers, etc. . . . Both productive and unproductive laborers, and those who do not labor at all, are all equally maintained by the annual produce of the land and labor of the country. This produce, how great soever, can never be infinite, but must have certain limits. Accordingly, therefore, as a smaller or greater proportion of it is in any one year employed in maintaining unproductive hands, the more in the one case and the less in the other will remain for the productive, and the next year's produce will be greater or smaller accordingly."[27]

Does one dare judge the usefulness of products when a firm dollar value has been attached? Financially oriented economists probably would not. A dollar is a dollar, and, so long as the financial pie keeps growing, economic opportunities abound for the sharpies and the tax collector is satisfied. Yet, there are some things which may have a monetary value but which, most people might agree, society would be better off without. Cocaine is an example. What are some others?

• A type of useless expense increasingly incurred by this society would be the incarceration of criminals. An international study found that 1,057,875 persons were locked up in the U.S. prisons and jails in 1989. That number represents a five-fold increase since 1970, when the prison population numbered 196,429. The incarceration rate in the United States is now the highest in the world. We keep 426 persons per 100,000 population imprisoned, compared with 333 persons per 100,000 in South Africa, 268 persons per 100,000 in the Soviet Union, and 45 per 100,000 in Japan.[28]

• Private security firms in the United States employ 1.5 million persons and spend $52 billion annually. Public law-enforcement agencies employ 600,000 persons and spend $30 billion each year. The National Institute of Justice estimates that by the year 2000 annual spending by private security firms will double.[29]

• Advertising expenditures in the United States rose from $73.8 billion in 1983 to $130.0 billion in 1990—a 71% increase in seven years.[30] The *Wall Street Journal* reported that in the 1980s marketers "blitzed the U.S. consumer with sales pitches, collectively spending more than $6 a week on every man, woman and child in the U.S. — almost 50% more per capita than in any other nation."[31] Telemarketing by prison inmates would seem to be the next logical step, and is, in fact, now being carried out in sixteen states.[32]

• There is an assortment of other activities which have dollars attached but do not seem to benefit people very much. Some kinds of financially weighty but otherwise dubious products would include peacetime expenditures for armaments, harassing lawsuits, megabuck lotteries, relentless campaigns to sell merchandise at Christmas, the escalating need to acquire academic credentials — the list goes on.

Is there an alternative to this economic nonsense? While living in France in 1784, Benjamin Franklin wrote to a friend in America: "What occasions then so much want and misery? It is the employment of men and women in works that produce neither the necessaries nor conveniences of life, who, with those who do nothing, consume the necessaries raised by the laborious . . . Look round the world and see the millions employed in doing nothing or in something that amounts to nothing . . . Could all these people, now employed in raising, making, or carrying superfluities, be subsisted in raising necessaries? I think they might . . . It has been computed by some political arithmetician that if every man and woman would work for four hours each day on something useful, that labor would procure all the necessaries and comforts of life, want and misery would be banished out of the world, and the rest of the 24 hours might be leisure and pleasure."[33]

The average workweek in the United States has declined by 11% during the past 50 years, while labor productivity has increased by more than three times. That combination of events has forced the displacement of labor into nonproductive industries and occupations to the detriment of real national wealth. The spurious growth of output has kept employment levels high and government solvent, but sacrificed various opportunities that might otherwise have been possible for workers in their human aspect. In insisting upon viewing economic activity through a lens of dollars, we do not see what actually is happening to people in their lives. The financial mechanisms are useful as a distributive device. Shorter work hours would, however, gain a better price for labor to the extent that labor is an economic commodity subject to laws of supply and demand. Thus the financial arrangement would tend to follow the real correction brought to the labor market as work hours were reduced by government action.

A Need for Political Self-Reform

This ability to regulate hours of work illustrates the type of economic function which governments might usefully undertake. The free market does not automatically solve all our problems. Government has a necessary regulatory role to play. Yet, if government is to participate more actively in economic affairs, this fact must be faced: the American people do not want more government. And why should they? Government has not helped them very much. Its general approach has been to take resources away from everyone and give back to the politically favored few. Once it was that government redistributed wealth from the rich to the poor; and that was accepted because it seemed fair. But having established in principle its right to redistribute wealth, government proceeded to redistribute wealth to anyone, poor or rich, in accordance with its own desire. Political advantage rather than need became the basis of the wealth redistribution. So government policy degenerated into special-interest politics. The community was torn apart at various levels.

The American public resents the transformation of politics into financial opportunities for the politicians. Too often "public service" has been a prelude to a more lucrative private-sector career. People expect that government officials should not use their positions just to make money; for there is an honor in holding public office which ought to be its own reward. Therefore, the idea of public service ought to include something of personal sacrifice. As the Roman Catholic church reformed itself by requiring priests to remain celibate, so U.S. elected officials today need to accept some measure of abstinence with respect to acquiring wealth. The institution of government needs to assume a more disciplined nature to ward off corruption and retain public confidence.

If, however, the society is spiritually so poor that money is its main object, it can hardly avoid having a venal and corrupt government. Nothing cannot beat something, and money is something. If the elected official were personally religious, that might be enough to keep money in check. A nonreligious person, too, can be ethically disciplined if he or she has a higher purpose of some sort. Therefore, political ideals are important. They used to say that the Italian communists ran honest municipal governments; those communists apparently still believed in their ideas. But if the idea is not communism, it must still involve a purpose larger than oneself. Therefore government, if it is to reclaim its proper place in society, should renounce self-indulgence and instead develop some well-developed programs of community improvement. That broad focus, more than the personalities involved, will keep government honest.

There is no inconsistency between the conservative ideal of smaller government and government's seeking a more active regulatory function. Government as regulator of the free market does not need to expend large amounts of resources; it can be lean and efficient in its regulatory role. Government needs, however, to regain people's confidence both in the legitimacy of its functions and in its quality of performance. Ironically, for some people the Republican-led war in the Persian Gulf helped to restore confidence in the competence of government. Even some conservatives looked upon government with renewed hope.[34] Ultimately, however, the political left should be the main beneficiary of this new confidence in government. The conservatives, allied with business, are less able to criticize and condemn this horrible new vision of man, the production factor. Basically, then, it is a question of whether people exist for the sake of more efficient production or whether production exists for the sake of people. This is a political struggle for the control of government to determine whether or not government will exercise its regulatory powers with respect to business in order to put the human interest first.

While some contend that global trade competition and rising levels of debt tie government's hands in this matter, the plain fact is that national governments have the power to decide those things any way they wish. Governments can open or close their borders to trade. Governments can create money, or they can make money and debt disappear. Those alleged powers of government are fact: Adam Smith's theory was only an argument addressed to government to use its powers in a certain way. If, therefore, international business persists in promoting its degrading view of man the producer, then western capitalism may well receive its comeuppance at the hands of the political left, even as East Bloc socialism was recently rebuffed by proponents of the free market. With the decline of totalitarian social-ism in the East, the political left in the West is made stronger, not weaker. For, under the shadow of communism, leftist politics seemed a sinister force. Its ideology had denied that private business had a right to existence, being supposedly founded upon theft. But now the leftist position has moderated to the point of accepting the right of business managers to manage business and of property owners to own property. The political right, on the other hand, is currently trespassing upon government's domain. This is the ideolog-ical posture that puts business salaries and profits ahead of food for malnourished children and lets the rivers and air be fouled with in-dustrial wastes.

Therefore, the good fight, the one deserving public support, will likely come from the political left rather than from the political right. But the left should first move beyond its "big government" inclina-tions inherited from the New Deal, beyond its reliance on financial mechanisms, and beyond its preoccupation with demographic conflict, to become a force for anti-totalitarian change. The political left should drop its legacy of arrogant hatred, whether directed against bourgeois capitalists or white males, along with the violent baggage of the underclass. Upholding an all-inclusive national com-munity, the left should also, however, seek to regain the internation-alist perspective of its own past. The effort to defeat the prospective U.S.-Mexico-Canada Free-Trade Agreement could become a major event in that process. It is not that the three North American coun-tries should not some day form some kind of more permanent combi-nation, but that the political conservatives now in power in those countries should not be the ones to pour the concrete.

PART FOUR

Speculations Concerning a Positive Alternative to Free Trade

The Battle over "Fast Track"

The political battle over adoption of a North American Free-Trade Agreement has aroused public interest and debate in the United States as no other trade-related proposal has in many a year. "We've never had a trade issue that has been this hot," said Harry Freeman, a business lobbyist. "It's quite a donnybrook." Ralph Nader's group, Public Citizen, opposed the prospective FTA because it would weaken pesticide and other health regulations. The Child Labor Coalition was opposed to the potentially increased exploitation of Mexican children. The AFL-CIO was concerned about loss of U.S. jobs due to cheap labor. Environmental groups such as Greenpeace and the National Wildlife Federation focused upon environmental degradation in the maquiladora border region. The popular ground swell of opposition to the free-trade proposal stunned many observers. In March 1991, Rep. Dan Rostenkowski, chairman of the House Ways and Means Committee, warned a meeting of business leaders that labor unions, environmentalists, and other such groups were mobilizing against free trade. "If you want to win this thing, move your ass," he said.[1]

Move it they did. The *Wall Street Journal* reported that "corporate America (has) assembled a virtual lobbying Who's Who, including corporate chiefs from American Express Co., Procter & Gamble Co. and many other blue-chip concerns. The business forces have now regained strong footing and have set up a practically non-stop schedule of meetings with lawmakers. In a show of bipartisan might, a business delegation led by two former U.S. trade representatives, Democrat Robert Strauss and Republican William Brock, met with President Bush on the issue last week . . . Mexico, which had not previously employed Washington lobbyists, has suddenly upstaged Japan as the foreign government with the most visible lobbying muscle. Beginning in January, the Mexican government began hiring an A-team of lobbyists and lawyers, including such GOP heavyhitters as Charls Walker and such politically connected Democrats as Joseph O'Neill, a former top aide to Senate Finance Committee Chairman Lloyd Bentsen and Robert Keefe, a former strategist for the late Sen. Henry Jackson . . . Mexican business interests, meanwhile, have formed their own version of the Business Roundtable and have hired the Washington law firm of Steptoe & Johnson. 'When in Rome do as the Romans do,' says one Mexican government official. 'When in Washington, do as people inside the beltway do.' "[2]

The battle over free trade has actually consisted of two sets of battles. The first took place in the spring of 1991 when the U.S. Congress considered President Bush's request to extend "fast-track" negotiating authority for another two years. Such authority, given to the President in the Omnibus Trade and Competitiveness Act of 1988, would have expired on June 1, 1991, had Congress not granted the extension. The "fast-track" provision allows the President to negotiate trade agreements with other countries and submit them to Congress without the possibility of modification. Congress simply votes the agreement up or down, word-for-word as delivered to it by the President. The rationale for this procedure is that foreign governments will refuse to negotiate trade agreements with the United States if Congress is allowed to whittle them away by attaching "special-interest" amendments. Therefore, a "go-slow approach is tantamount to a no-go approach," one supporter warned.[3] Opponents, on the other hand, charged that fast-track authority limited public discussion of such proposals and required Congress to relinquish to the President its Constitutional authority to set trade policy. In the end, Congress approved the extension of fast-track authority, although the vote was close. On May 23, 1991, the U.S. House of Representatives voted to defeat a motion to deny such authority by a margin of

231 to 192. The Senate approved fast-track by a 59-to-36 vote on the following day.

So ended the first set of battles, or so it seemed. The process was ready to move on to the main event, which was negotiation and approval or rejection of the agreement itself. In fact, however, the U.S. Congress was not quite ready to accept the decision that it had just reached. The House vote approving Presidential fast-track authority was followed by another vote on a non-binding resolution proposed by Rep. Richard Gephardt of Missouri which conditioned Congressional approval of fast track on the President's living up to his commitments with respect to labor, environmental, and health standards. This resolution passed by a 329-to-85 vote. In the U.S. Senate, Donald Riegle of Michigan sponsored a resolution to modify fast-track authority by allowing Congress to amend a North American FTA in five areas including enforcement of labor and environmental standards. It also proposed to eliminate the 20-hour time limit on permissible debate of the Agreement and reduce the period of fast-track extension from two years to one year. Meanwhile, a Fair Trade Caucus was formed in the House under the leadership of Reps. Marcy Kaptur of Ohio and Byron Dorgan of North Dakota to coordinate the continuing Congressional fight against the prospective FTA.

Alignment of Forces since the "Fast Track" Vote

Since the vote on fast-track extension in late May 1991, trade representatives from the three North American countries have begun their negotiations. The first set of general meetings took place in Toronto in June, followed by another in Seattle in August and a third round in Zacatecas, Mexico, in late October, 1991. The U.S. Trade Representative also scheduled a series of public hearings on the prospective agreement in six U.S. cities during August and September of that year. These various events have become focal points of opposition as well as support. Besides the general meetings, representatives of the three North American countries have engaged in a series of sector-specific discussions such as those involving the dairy or timber industries. They have reached agreement on such issues as establishing a code for marketing infant formula. The more precise the topic of negotiation, the easier it usually has been to reach an agreement. Since the Bush-Salinas meeting on December 14, 1991, at Camp David, there has been intense pressure to wrap up the entire negotiations by the early spring so that an agreement can be presented to Congress and be decided before it can become an issue in the 1992 national-election campaign.

Many expect a battle royal to take place between supporters and opponents of NAFTA in the United States. The pro-FTA forces can be expected to support whatever agreement the Bush administration delivers to Congress, flexing their political and financial muscles through a powerful network of business lobbyists, lawyers, and public-relations consultants. In addition, this side can count on strong support from the communications media and from academic experts. The Mexican government reportedly has a $100 million war chest of money to distribute to academic institutions and other U.S. groups that might support its position on free trade. For instance, the University of Minnesota received a sizable grant from that government to establish a free-trade study program at its Humphrey Institute following Minnesota Governor Arne Carlson's visit to Mexico in November 1991.[4] The anti-FTA position is a bit more complicated. One phase of the "fair trade" battle, focused uponCongress, might be described as an extended fight against fast track. Another phase is to develop an alternative set of trade proposals to address labor, environmental, and other concerns, which, if its provisions were excluded from NAFTA, would presumably make it unacceptable. In that event, the anti-FTA forces would move to a third phase, which would be to seek Congressional rejection of the agreement.

Another way of looking at the anti-FTA forces in the United States is to see the various groups arranged in concentric circles around the center of power, which would be the U.S. Congress. In the innermost circle would be the Senators and Representatives themselves, along with Congressional staff. Groups in the next, surrounding ring would consist of national labor, farm, consumer, and environmental organizations working closely with members of Congress to monitor the trade negotiations. Some are organized in an umbrella group called "Citizen Trade Watch", which is staffed by researchers and attorneys from Ralph Nader's Public Citizen. Another Washington-based coalition of more than 200 regional and national groups called "Mobilization on Development, Trade, Labor, and the Environment" (MODTLE), involving many of the same organizations as Citizen Trade Watch, has developed an alternative agenda for the trade negotiations in dialogue with Mexican and Canadian counterparts. Finally, there is a third ring of anti-FTA forces located outside Washington, D.C.. Some organizations of national scope that are involved with this issue would include the Minneapolis-based Fair Trade Campaign, the Chicago-based Federation for Industrial Retention and Renewal (FIRR), and the New York City-based Coalition for Justice in the Maquiladoras. Numerous other groups are also fighting free trade at the local level. Minnesota Fair Trade Coalition would be an example.

Inside the Washington, D.C. beltway, opponents of the prospective agreement are focusing their efforts upon bills to rescind or modify fast-track authority and upon alternative trade agendas. The object is to open up room for Congressional amendment so that the agreement can be reshaped to reflect various interests and concerns or, if that fails, to defeat it. The "endgame", according to one participant, is either to reject the FTA or else to enact a heavily amended version. If one or the other house of Congress refuses to pass fast-tracked enabling legislation, the agreement is defeated. Alternatively, if the Riegle resolution or a similar measure passes, FTA opponents can amend the negotiated agreement to include provisions creating a "baseline" for future action. The President could be put in the position of vetoing a free-trade bill that makes concessions to labor or environmental groups. In any event, such amendments would create an agenda to reject the terms of a free-trade pact dictated by business interests alone. Outside the beltway, the range of options is broader. Some opponents are interested less in the NAFTA itself than in building coalitions and networking with similar groups across the country as well as in Mexico and Canada to script a different future. Then there are some who want to see the agreement defeated because of political antipathy to President Bush or their perception of the damage it would do to their community or the environment.

Alternative Agendas

MODTLE's alternative agenda was developed in consultation with many different groups of people, in Mexico and Canada as well as in the United States. A Mexican group called Red Mexicana de Accion Frente al Libre Comercial (RMALC) was formed on April 11, 1991, by about fifty labor and social-service organizations in Mexico to study the impact of free trade and suggest alternatives. In Canada, the Action Canada Network (ACN) has continued its opposition to free trade since the Canadian agreement with the United States became effective. Anti-FTA forces from the three North American countries met in Chicago in late April to compare notes and seek to develop common interests. The Canadian approach has tended to be outright rejectionist. MODTLE and RMALC, on the other hand, have produced documents outlining features which they say ought to be included in any agreement to make it acceptable to their constituencies. Representatives of the three national groups held an international forum on free trade at Zacatecas, Mexico, on October 25–27, while the trinational negotiators were conducting official discussions in the same city. They issued a "final declaration" which expressed points of agreement between them. The declaration said—

"Our governments must respond to the following proposals in order to make a viable continental development agreement:

(1) The (Mexican) external debt continues to be a heavy burden; its cancellation or substantial reduction is an indispensable condition for acquiring the financial resources necessary for continental development. The reduction of military budgets and subsidies for business would allow the reorientation of substantial sums to meet social needs.

(2) The implementation of compensatory mechanism that counter the inequalities and displacement of productive sectors that are being generated by the progress of economic integration and which assure a just and sane new order.

(3) The establishment of a process of equalization of work conditions, health, education, salaries, and other conditions of living to the highest levels and standards.

(4) The promotion of a new continental alliance in the framework of a new development pact.

(5) The creation of a trilateral social mechanism that guarantees the fulfillment of human rights based on the existing Universal Declaration of Human Rights, and guarantees a commercial and economic opening that is necessarily linked to greater social participation and genuine democracy.

(6) Culture, education and communication are essential parts of development model that respects the special characteristics and

self determination of peoples. Relationships and interdependence should be determined on the basis of national needs and strategies. Culture, education and communication should be excluded from any trade agreement.

(7) The trade agreement should guarantee food security and national sovereignty over natural resources. Basic grains, dairy products, and meat should not be included in any trade agreement whenever national demand has not been satisfied. Unprocessed forest products should not be included in any trade agreement.

(8) Our vision of development recognizes the social role of women and therefore considers it necessary to improve the level of protection of women's rights, using the highest existing standards in our societies as a base for further improvement.

(9) In regard to the environment, we reject the cross-border dumping of toxic wastes. Environmental regulations should be improved and social control mechanisms should be established to ensure their enforcement. In the same way, fiscal policies should be developed to prevent environmental harm and to regenerate the environment where it has been damaged by existing economic practices.

(10) The trade agreement should respect the collective rights of workers, including freedom of association, collective bargaining and the right to strike. Democratic, autonomous and representative unionism is the guarantee of a just distribution of productivity. Company controlled unionism should not be allowed to function as an incentive to investment. Cheap labor must not be used as a competitive advantage.

(11) Free trade should not be a pretext or means to modify our constitution.

(12) There must be an immediate implementation of a plan to increase minimum wages in Mexico with the purpose of advancing a common regional minimum salary in the medium term, without affecting negatively the level of wages of Canadian and U.S. workers.

(13) The establishment of a code of conduct for transnational companies to prevent monopolistic practices and violations of existing laws.

(14) Social security programs oriented toward preserving a minimum basic level of well-being must not be considered unfair trade subsidies. Social security systems and the insurance industry should be exempt from negotiations.

(15) Migrant workers should be included in the trade agreement in order to protect their rights. A framework agreement

should be negotiated to ensure the legal rights of migrants and to advance labor mobility.

(16) The Forum is in solidarity with (a) Canadian workers who demand the abrogation of the existing free trade agreement between Canada and the United States as a precondition for a continental development pact, (b) University students, in particular the National Autonomous University Workers Union of Mexico (STUNAM), (c) the boycott of Levi Strauss products by the women workers of Fuerza Unida of San Antonio, Texas."[5]

The above points of agreement incorporate most of what was contained in a position statement issued by the Mexican anti-FTA organization, RMALC, in August 1991. This statement, "Points for Consideration in the Other Agenda of the Treaty", also included demands for a more open and public discussion of NAFTA, protection of the Mexican fishing industry, exclusion of oil from the treaty, and an explicit condemnation of low wages as a form of "social dumping." MODTLE has produced a more extensive and detailed statement of principles which paralleled the international declaration while expanding on certain themes. Its document, "Development and Trade Strategies for North America", was the product of study groups in six areas. Space here prevents more than an outline of the principal conclusions:

I. Agreement Objectives—trinational economic and social development consistent with internationally recognized human rights, which also recognizes the three nations' different levels of development and seeks to narrow the differences in an upward direction.

II. Environmental and Consumer Protection

(A) Full assessment of NAFTA's environmental impact.

(B) Preserve strong local standards to protect public health and the environment.

(C) Prevent environmental dumping across national borders.

(D) Compensatory taxes or tariffs to help pay for environmental damage.

(E) Recognize legitimacy of environmental concerns in trade policy.

(F) Informed public participation.

(G) Eliminate trade in hazardous waste.

III. Labor Rights and Standards

(A) Commit the three governments to respecting workers' rights of free association and collective bargaining, etc.

(B) Create enforcement mechanism to punish infractions of labor standards and rights.

(C) Include the goal of paying "a living wage".

(D) Create a realistic program to enforce workplace health and safety standards.

(E) Provide more funds for investment in social infrastructure — medical care, education, unemployment protection.

(F) Develop a program to eradicate child labor.

(G) Re-examine programs to protect the rights of migrant workers.

IV. Human Rights

(A) Reaffirm commitment to internationally-recognized human rights.

(B) Strengthen procedures to challenge human-rights violations.

(C) Improve the rights of immigrant workers.

V. Agriculture

(A) Encourage national self-reliance with respect to food production.

(B) Enforce inspection procedures in shipping food across national borders.

(C) Include anti-dumping penalties for food exports in the agreement.

(D) Make foreign-debt repayment secondary to feeding people.

(E) Provide a mechanism for resolving agricultural disputes.

VI. Funding Mechanisms to Raise Labor and Environmental Standards

(A) Provide sufficient funds to enforce labor, health, and environmental standards.

(B) Establish a trinational commission to monitor progress in raising the standards.

(C) Provide enough funds to raise social standards and to improve infrastructure.

(D) Apply funds to help communities adversely affected by
free trade.

VII. Enforcement Mechanisms to Ensure Compliance with Labor,
Environmental and Human Rights Standards
(A) Encourage local solutions for rights violations.
(B) Allow any interested citizen to challenge violations.
(C) Allow complaints to be aired in public.
(D) Link compliance with labor, environmental, and human
rights to trade concessions for governments and corpo-
rations.
(E) Apply trade sanctions and penalties to individual corpo-
rations rather than to entire nations.
(F) Subscribe to a code of conduct for multinational corpo-
rations.[6]

The Rejectionist Alternative

MODTLE representatives envisioned that the above principles
would "become the basis for our advocacy in Congress for changes
in the NAFTA (or for its rejection)."[7] The document includes additional provisions for environmental or human-rights agreements to
be negotiated in parallel with NAFTA. It is clear, however, that this
approach is on a collision course with the approach taken by the
trinational trade negotiators who have said that their negotiations
are limited to a discussion of trade issues and will therefore exclude
social and other concerns. The U.S. Trade Representative, Carla
Hills, told the press gathered in Seattle for the trinational talks in late
August that, according to the *Seattle Post-Intelligencer*, "the proposed free trade agreement with Canada and Mexico doesn't need a
'social charter' covering wage disparities, labor rights or environmental standards. She said a free trade zone running from Alaska to
the Yucatan Peninsula couldn't be compared to the European Community, which has such a charter. 'The European Community is a
common market,' she told a news conference . . . 'It deals with far
more than reducing barriers so trade can expand. We're negotiating
a trade agreement.' "[8] On the same day (August 21) that this report
was published, the Trade Representative's office in Washington,
D.C. released, without explanation, a bulletin noting that a petition

challenging Mexico's eligibility to receive trade benefits under the Generalized System of Preferences because of worker-rights violations had been rejected.[9] Hills later denied that she made the statement quoted in the Seattle newspaper, but took no steps to expand the negotiating agenda.

Timothy Kehoe, a University of Minnesota economist, defends the decision to restrict the NAFTA negotiations to "trade" issues alone. When asked why the business community opposed inclusion of labor standards in the agreement, he replied: "Mexican labor law provides more protection for workers than the comparable U.S. laws. Criticism is made of the level of enforcement in Mexico, and certainly there's a problem here. But enforcement of this type of law is what we economists call a 'luxury good.' We're very wealthy; we can enforce those kinds of laws. The Mexicans have more difficulty with them. But there's something quite delicate about this situation. The United States, if it negotiated a treaty with the Soviet Union, would not want the Soviets talking every day about problems with the U.S. judicial system or with U.S. police. Likewise, the Mexicans take offense at paternalistic attitudes in the United States toward them." Calman Cohen, representing the Emergency Committee for American Trade, added: "We're not talking about an EC type of arrangement (or) a merging of the political apparatus of Mexico and the United States . . . It is an objective, however, of U.S. industry to see continued improvement in the protections that are available in Mexico. One of the best assurances that we in America have that there will be continued progress on enforcement of social standards in Mexico is a more prosperous Mexico."[10]

A different sort of objection was expressed by Laurell Ritchie of the Canadian anti-FTA group, Common Frontiers. She and other Canadians have held the opinion that free trade provided a cover for the conservative agenda of deregulating business and gutting the social protections of government. "One of the reasons that Mulroney entered into the negotiations for the FTA was that, given the lack of a domestic mandate to make those incredible changes in our economy, there had to be an external force that caused them to occur, and indeed free-trade negotiations became Mulroney's excuse for introducing those things. And the same is true of Salinas. He had to find external reasons to continue the transformations," she said. In that context, Ritchie expressed skepticism that a "social charter" could be successfully mixed with an agreement for free trade. "This may be the route that has to be taken in the United States," she observed. "But I would like to take a devil's advocate's position on whether piggybacking the social charter on the body of an agreement which is fundamentally flawed will work — whether, in other words, you can put a piggyback of regulation on something which is fundamentally about deregulation."[11]

For a time, following Sen. Harris Wofford's upset victory, it appeared that the Bush administration had put NAFTA on the back burner in order to prevent this from becoming an issue during the 1992 election campaign. Instead, the Administration appeared to be advancing the timetable for concluding the "Uruguay Round" of the GATT negotiations, a less controversial trade initiative than NAFTA though perhaps more dangerous from a social or environmental standpoint. Some FTA supporters such as Rep. Bill Richardson of New Mexico expressed concern at the signal that such a politically motivated strategy would send to Mexico and the rest of Latin America about U.S. trustworthiness and resolve. Accordingly, the Administration changed course and again pushed for the quick disposition of NAFTA. "We want to get it soon," said President Bush after his meeting with President Salinas. "We want to get it just as soon as we possibly can."[12] This new demonstration of "political will" flew in the face of mounting evidence that a free-trade program would encounter opposition from Pat Buchanan and David Duke on the Republican right as well as from Congressional Democrats and the various groups that opposed fast-track extension, not to mention ordinary voters.

Washington-based critics of NAFTA have continued to push for weakened application of the fast-track rules. Besides the Riegle Amendment, a resolution introduced in late November, 1991, in the U.S. House of Representatives by Rep. Henry Waxman of California and House Majority Leader Richard Gephardt would put the President on notice of Congressional intent to reject trade agreements which weaken various kinds of legislated standards. "The Congress," it said, "will not approve legislation to implement any trade agreement (including the Uruguay Round of the GATT and the United States-Mexico Free Trade Agreement) if such agreement jeopardizes United States health, safety, labor, or environmental laws."[13] In the meanwhile, a significant rift appeared to be developing among the nations of the European Community which met at Maastricht in the Netherlands in December 1991. The United Kingdom, represented by Conservative prime minister John Majors, staunchly opposed including labor standards and other social criteria in the EC pact. The remaining eleven nations went ahead on their own with an agreement including such features.

These events suggest that the fate of NAFTA is linked with the broader historical question of the importance of worker and human rights in international trade policy. Try as they might, the trinational negotiators cannot avoid that linkage. For opponents, a basic point of decision is whether to follow the beltway insiders' "yes but" approach or, as outsiders, to move to outright rejection. It may be that the insiders have refused so far to take the latter position for fear of seeming to be unreasonable in rejecting an agreement in advance of its public unveiling. It may be that, after more than a decade of conservative ascendancy in the national administration, U.S. critics of NAFTA are too demoralized to mount an immediate, full-scale attack. Finally, it is possible that those preferring the more "responsible" approach are drawn to that position by their role as political insiders, needing to maintain good relations with various power groups. We in the political hinterland are, of course, less constrained by those concerns, as our views already carry less weight. It is therefore likely that the battle against free trade that occurs around the country will be fought on the basis of either accepting or rejecting the agreement itself. At the same time, a strictly negative campaign against free trade does not leave one in a position worth defending unless one prefers the status quo. Those who would criticize the NAFTA in its likely form owe it to others as well as themselves to say what is the better alternative.

Therefore, this book will devote its remaining space to a broad discussion of alternatives to free trade, assuming that NAFTA deserves rejection. (In that respect, its position is closer to that of the Canadian than to those of the U.S. or Mexican anti-FTA groups.) The lack of a developed alternative trade program dealt a blow to Canadian opponents of free trade in 1988 and continues to be a problem. Although the alternative expressed in this book represents primarily one person's opinions, it does at least show that the free-trade approach is not our only option. As Susan Spratt points out in her afterword, the Canadian fight against the U.S.-Canada FTA began in Ottawa, but it spread to grassroots action in cities and towns clear across Canada. The Canadian people were mobilized, and almost won. Now we in the United States, having still some time to become mobilized and organized, can attempt to shift the scene of the battle to the more favorable terrain outside the beltway. Here it does not matter so much what the pundits and editorial writers think. What counts is sheer energy.

Breakdown into Regional Trading Blocs

We also need, however, a clear picture of the end that we seek. If we are not for free trade, we must therefore be in favor of some form of regulated trade. The alternative to a world economic order that eliminates trade barriers to maximize global business is a world order regulated to protect the human interest. Instead of unrestricted economic competition, this scheme assumes cooperation between nations. Without cooperation, workers in developed countries such as the United States will become subject to punishing wage competition from the low-wage countries which will bring rising unemployment and drive living standards down. Such a cooperative order already exists, of course, in various forms. The United Nations and its specialized agencies, the World Bank and International Monetary Fund, the Group of Seven, Organization for Economic Cooperation and Development, and the GATT are among the institutions that encourage cooperative rather than competitive arrangements in the world community.

The GATT, or the General Agreement on Tariffs and Trade, is a multinational agreement setting rules for international trade. As an evolving body of rules, GATT has come under attack for its relative lack of enforcement and its exclusion of key industries such as agriculture and textiles manufacturing. The latest series of talks, the "Uruguay Round", broke down in December 1990 over the refusal of European Community nations to reduce agricultural subsidies. A year later, the impasse was still unresolved. Meanwhile, the multinational approach to trade relations has been overshadowed by the formation of three regional trading blocs which are located in North America, western Europe, and the Far East. Together, the nations included in these blocs control 65% of the world's Gross Domestic Product. Those in the European and North American blocs each control about 25% of world GDP while the faster-growing Asian bloc controls about 15%. The North American FTA is a product of the new thinking.[14] Some see it as a move to strengthen the U.S. bargaining position at GATT as the European economic union is established in 1992. Thus, "Fortress North America" must be erected to challenge "Fortress Europe." Both must be prepared to repel the onslaught of Asian products.

This model of the world economy assumes cut-throat trade competition between the three regional blocs. The survival of business requires close attention to production costs. As wages rise in the industrialized nations, their firms search elsewhere for pools of cheap labor to keep costs in line. Each bloc therefore has a leading nation, which provides the capital and managerial skills, and a group of less developed nations, which supply cheap labor and mineral resources. So the United States is intending to hook up with Mexico to obtain low-cost labor and oil. Canada's role is to be primarily "an energy and resource hinterland" according to Action Canada Network's Tony Clarke.[15] Eventually the rest of Latin America might be added to this pool of available resources. A similar arrangement also exists in the other two trading blocs. Presumably, the European bloc will be led by Germany, although the leadership role here is not so clearly established. Its resource hinterland, which in the past has comprised poorer neighboring countries such as Turkey, Greece, Ireland, Portugal, and Spain, has suddenly been expanded to include the newly liberated lands of eastern Europe. In east Asia, where Japan is the undisputed leader, Japanese planners are reviving the idea of an economic partnership with the poorer Asian countries. Japan wants access to cheap labor and raw materials and, in exchange, is willing to share some production with its neighbors, even to the extent of granting them a monopoly in certain industries. Thailand, Malaysia, Indonesia, and the Philippines are Japan's chief partners in its co-production scheme.[16]

Given this structure, the three regional blocs have become self-contained economic organisms, preparing to do battle with each other like giant reptiles. The collegiality of GATT has apparently given way to "survival of the fittest" in world markets. Each nation is scrambling to find protection somewhere within a trading bloc. This new scheme of regional organization represents, however, a definite step backward with respect to world peace. One must recall

Figure 4.1

Indexes of Hourly Compensation Costs
for Manufacturing Production Workers
in Several Countries, 1975 to 1990

(U.S. level = 100)

Country	1975	1985	1990
United States	100	100	100
Canada	91	83	107
Mexico	–	12	12
Japan	48	50	87
Hong Kong	12	13	22
Korea	6	10	28
Singapore	13	19	25
Taiwan	6	12	27
Australia	87	63	88
Germany	100	74	144
France	71	58	103
United Kingdom	52	48	84
Italy	73	56	110
Spain	41	37	78
Sweden	113	75	141
Finland	72	62	139
Netherlands	107	82	125
Brazil	14	12	19

Source: Bureau of Labor Statistics

that a similar competition among the European powers in the late
19th century led to two world wars. As Japan is simultaneously being
reviled and urged to rearm, a reversion to military as well as trade
competition between the three regions is not inconceivable. Top U.S.
policymakers understand this quite well. While President Bush was
pushing for an FTA with Canada and Mexico, Secretary of State
Baker warned the foreign ministers of the ASEAN countries to move

cautiously in developing new trade and security alliances that would replace "tried and tested frameworks" involving the United States. "We have had a remarkable degree of stability in this region," he said. "We ought to be careful about changing those arrangements . . . unless we're absolutely certain that the something else is better and will work."[17]

The same could be said in reference to the new trade alliance being contemplated in North America. If, frustrated by events in the GATT negotiations, the United States neglects multinational trade in favor of regional deals, an economic as well as political price would be paid. Professor Jagdish Bhagwati of Columbia University believes that U.S. firms might miss out on more important business opportunities if they focus too much on the intra-hemispheric market. "It is not credible," he wrote in *Foreign Affairs*," that the United States would shoot itself in the foot, and indeed higher up, by sidetracking her energies and her trade to a region whose fragile democracies, inflations, debts and slow growth rates offer a far less attractive market than the burgeoning Far East and the European Community, both of which are even now more substantial markets for American exports. If the United States turns foolishly away from the world to her own backyard, the European Community's likely reaction would be: fine, get buried in it."[18]

A Framework for International Cooperation

Looking at the world economy, one sees that a more significant division exists between the developed and developing nations than between the regional trading blocs. The developing nations are in a different economic situation than the developed nations. In general, people in the developing countries are afflicted by poverty, illiteracy and lack of education, poor community infrastructure, overpopulation, disease, and other such ills. Their goal must be to improve living standards and create a stable, prosperous society based on more efficient use of resources. People's material needs would be paramount, in other words. While living standards are also important in the developed countries, their type of society has moved beyond the economic problem to other challenges and opportunities relating to pursuit of a richer personal life. Japanese planners speak, for instance, of "achieving a society of comfort and wealth at a level corresponding to the strength of the national economy." The word, "comfort", is a rough translation of the Japanese word, "yutori", which means to have resources—money, space, time—to spare.[19] This idea of spaciousness and plenty represents a different goal than mere prosperity. It suggests increased opportunity for the individual soul to take root and flourish. One might say, then, that the function of the economically developed nations is to pioneer societies of the future by creating new lifestyles of affluence to which people in all nations can aspire. Their more advanced cultures would give warning or encouragement to other peoples proceeding along the same track.

International cooperation would assume that the national political authorities can agree on a particular set of goals for the world economy, recognizing the different situations of the developed and developing nations. Because the developing countries are in such urgent need of economic growth, a process should be established for transferring wealth and wealth-producing enterprise from the developed to the developing countries at a rate of speed which would be mutually tolerable. Perhaps the following points of principle could serve as a starting point for discussion. The policymakers would affirm that—

• as the world achieves a consensus favoring free-market economics, governments will continue to play a role in structuring economic activities so as to achieve community goals in such areas as employment and environmental protection.

• national governments have a responsibility to seek full employment of their citizens and, wherever possible, to encourage the development of jobs that will afford a continually rising standard of living.

• governments also have a duty to their citizens and to humanity, including future populations, to enforce policies that will protect the natural environment against unnecessarily damaging economic activities.

• great disparities of income and wealth among nations threaten to destabilize the world economic order by creating poverty, mass migrations of people, and adverse pressure on living standards and markets.

• nations which enjoy higher living standards and possess greater financial resources should pursue trade policies that will allow the escape of wealth and employment opportunities to less fortunate nations, albeit in a manner consistent with their own goal of maintaining living standards.

- reductions in work time concentrated in the developed countries would aid the developing countries in that regard in a manner consistent with principles of the free market.

- in extending economic help, the developed nations have a right to expect the developing nations to observe standards of humane treatment for workers, including adequate levels of wages and hours, as well as proper safeguards for the environment.

- international political organizations are an appropriate instrument for achieving a consensus on labor and environmental standards and for enforcing standards.

The problems posed in trade relations between the industrialized countries are not ones that cannot be solved by cooperative action. If the Europeans are "stubbornly" subsidizing their farmers and the Japanese are "irrationally" protecting their domestic rice industry, it may be that this conduct reflects legitimate social concerns. Maybe our trading partners place a higher value than we upon preserving the livelihood of persons who work in agriculture and other productive industries. Maybe they are not willing to cut those people loose to give well-heeled consumers the benefit of cheaper imports. Maybe such policies are ethically commendable and it is we, not they, who need to change our views. Maybe, too, if the interests of people are put ahead of competitive interests, it might be possible for the world's economic and political powers to sit down together and devise a cooperative program that will put false problems aside and concentrate instead on solving the real problems which they collectively face. Among them would be the problem of worldwide production overcapacity. Too much production is chasing globally too little market. The world's powers need therefore to cooperate to limit production capacity and expand markets so that a stable price and employment structure is generally created. Additional problems have to do with the scarcity of land, topsoil, water, and other raw materials, and with pollution of the natural environment. Here, too, laissez-faire economics and global free trade are powerless to find solutions, but cooperative action might succeed.

Economic Pressures Driving the NAFTA

A Free-Trade Agreement between Mexico and its two North American neighbors would also, of course, bring about a transfer of economic resources between developed and developing nations, though not in a mutually beneficial or environmentally safe manner. In that case, the three governments would allow international business to send capital and jobs to Mexico as fast as they want. While the disparities of national wealth might narrow, wages would tend to seek the lower rather than higher levels. There would be weak safeguards against environmental damage. The alternative would be a regulated trade relationship which includes protection of labor and the environment. Instead of free trade, a policy of regulated trade and investment might fit the pattern of what Cuauhtemoc Cardenas has called "a new kind of development model" for the three North American countries. To be sure, one part of this model would accommodate the free-market activities of business. Another part, though, would include regulatory actions undertaken cooperatively by the three governments. Instead of acting as the parochial champions of national interest, governments here would stand in the role of supporting an international order. Specifically they would cooperate to enforce internationally recognized labor and environmental standards, using trade restrictions as a control device.

At the present time, two pressures converge to create a need for the North American FTA. First, Mexico's huge foreign debt has forced the Mexican government to seek hard currency by becoming an export platform to penetrate U.S. and Canadian markets. Financially pressed, the government of Mexico cannot afford to pour resources into its domestic economy, but must lure foreign businesses into the country with the idea that the goods produced there will be mostly exported. Second, U.S. and Canadian firms, locked into stiff trade competition with firms in Europe and Asia, feel pressure to cut production costs in order to compete more effectively. The low wages and relative lack of environmental restrictions in Mexico offer an immediate way to cut costs and compete. While proponents of free trade suggest that those conditions are fixed, the fact is that government has the power to change them substantially. A monetary debt is only as solid as the enforcement which government chooses to pro-

vide. With bankruptcy laws, it is indeed regularly forgiving personal
and corporate debts. There is no reason why Third World debt
should not receive similar treatment. Regarding trade competition,
some of those harsh pressures might be relieved by an international
agreement to limit production. Production limitations on oil and
other commodities have had a powerful effect on prices set by the free
market. Now is the time, perhaps, for the community of nations to
embrace as a principle of cooperative action the idea of limiting
global production for a broad range of products by controlling the
supply of labor.

This gives us an agenda of an alternative trade and development
program built on removing two important obstacles to economic
growth: production overcapacity and Third World debt. Such
"growth" would not be defined in financial terms, but would occur
in the form of expanding productive and consuming activities as
financial and other impediments are removed. It would involve a
form of cooperation between the developed and developing countries
in which the developed countries help the developing countries financially but require something of them in return. The debt situation appears to be at least conceptually on its way to a partial solution. We
will describe some recent developments in the section which follows.
A solution to the problem of production overcapacity, on the other
hand, still lies in the realm of theory. It will be discussed at some
length later in this chapter.

The Debt-for-Nature Swap

Debt forgiveness is, of course, a matter of some controversy. Most
moneylenders consider this to be a supreme evil threatening society's
well-being. Yet, the principle of debt forgiveness is built into the capitalist system. Where debtors once spent time in prison, bankruptcy
laws now permit hopelessly indebted persons or groups to escape
their financial obligations. No debt is so sacred that society cannot
forgive it to meet basic human requirements. Bankers have benefited
from a deposit-insurance system which throws their debt obligations
upon the general taxpayer. How much more appropriate, then,
would it be for the international banking community to find room in
its heart to forgive Third World debt. Debts incurred by spendthrift
or corrupt government officials, which were enormously profitable

to the lending institutions, are surely forgivable as an alternative to their torturous repayment by the poor. Let those pay who took the business risks. Let government, in other words, target the financial loss of the Third World debt to banks and speculative investors who hold this odious paper rather than to the masses of impoverished people who live in developing nations or, in consequence of a North American FTA, to U.S. and Canadian production workers who stand to lose their jobs so Mexico's debt obligation to New York bankers can be met.

The developed nations took an historic step on March 15, 1991, when officials of the "Group of Seven" governments announced that each of the seven member nations would forgive at least half of the debt which Poland owed to their respective governments. The U.S. government agreed to forgive 80% of its Polish debt. In addition, western commercial banks agreed to forgive $5.8 billion of the $11.5 owed to them. Worried, however, that other debtor nations might want similar debt relief, G-7 officials stressed the "special" nature of Poland's debt situation. This preferential status, according to the *Wall Street Journal*, had to do with the fact that Poland was "struggling to enact a bold economic program after decades of central planning ruined its economy." In other words, the western bankers and government officials wanted Poland's experiment with a free-market economy to succeed, hoping that it would become a showcase for the rest of eastern Europe. In another special case, the U.S.-led group, in the aftermath of the Persian Gulf war, also found the resources to forgive part of Egypt's debt.[20] What about Mexico? In its case, debt forgiveness was apparently not under consideration, even though a study conducted by Dr. Raul Hinojosa Ojeda of the University of California at Berkeley found that "elimination of the Mexican foreign debt would have a significantly greater impact on stimulating the economies of Mexico and the United States than a Free-Trade Agreement."[21]

The Bush administration has promised to negotiate a separate agreement with Mexico to protect the environment if the North American FTA is approved. Unfortunately, environmental laws and agreements mean little if a government lacks the financial resources to enforce them. That is Mexico's problem. The need to service its huge foreign debt leaves little for environmental "luxuries". A partial solution might be to link debt forgiveness to expenditures for environmental protection. In 1987, Conservation International, a Washington-based group, paid Citicorp $100,000 to discharge a $650,000 uncollectible debt owed by Bolivia in exchange for Bolivia's promise to protect 4 million acres of tropical rain forest. This same group in 1991 agreed to retire $4 million of Mexican foreign debt in exchange for support of several environmental programs intended to preserve Mexico's ecologically diverse plant and animal species.[22] Debt forgiveness in exchange for environmental protection was also an element in the Polish deal. The Bush administration has proposed to increase the financial resources for this type of program in the "Enterprise for the Americas Initiative", which includes a provision to forgive $12 billion in Latin American debt and allow Latin governments to pay interest on the rest to local environmental projects rather than to the U.S. Treasury.[23] Sen. Christopher Dodd has introduced a bill in Congress that would encourage retirement of certain debts owed to the Export-Import Bank or the Commodity Credit Corporation by their sale to qualified purchasers who agreed to engage in debt-for-nature swaps or other approved purposes.[24]

Clearly the bulk of the loss from forgiven Third World debts should be borne by the banks themselves or by speculators who bought these assets from the banks at a discount. Considering that it is not in the foreign-policy interests of the U.S. Government that such privately held debt should continue to poison relations between the United States and peoples of the Third World, that government should take the initiative in promoting or forcing relief. At the same time, there is not reason why creative measures to share the financial pain should not be encouraged. The linkage of debt forgiveness with funding of environmental projects represents a creative way that a developing nation's burdensome debt can be retired with the creditor's consent. Environmentally conscious persons or groups in the First World will gladly purchase and cancel discounted debt securities to finance Third World environmental projects, which, in fact, benefit all humanity. Even greater sums of money could be raised for environmental protection if the U.S. government allowed special tax breaks for private contributions towards retirement of Third World debt or elicited the help of foreign investors. In any event, the developed countries have an obligation to help in this matter whether or not it involves a quid pro quo.

Limiting Production Capacity by Cutting Work Hours

First World countries also hold the key to the problem of production overcapacity. The economic problem of weak or falling prices, caused by excessive supply relative to demand, finds a political solution in cooperative efforts to limit supply. The First World countries, which possess the bulk of world consumer markets, can restrict both their own domestic production and the importation of foreign products, so that supplies entering the main world market are effectively controlled. That statement assumes, of course, that those countries are able to cooperate — again, a political rather than an economic problem. To control supply, one needs to be able to control production or the ingredients of production. In broad terms, those ingredients would include knowledge, raw materials, management, and labor. Labor, measured in worker-hours, is the ingredient most susceptible to control. Government is able to control the quantity of labor by enacting legislation which sets the standard workweek at various levels. Shorter hours equate to reduced labor supply, which, in turn, has a positive effect upon price in the labor market. Coordinated internationally, shorter work hours could stabilize the level of wages as well as employment throughout the industrialized world. Thus, supply-management techniques applied to labor would be an effective long-term method of creating jobs with adequate incomes. Government needs to take this step to counteract the continual deterioration of labor demand as capital investment systematically increases the output that employers obtain in each work hour. Otherwise, labor will be diverted to nonproductive areas or else lost.

A second purpose of shortened hours would be served in allowing a manageable escape of production and jobs to workers in developing countries. That is our primary interest in this part of the discussion. Although the economic consequences of reduced hours have been discussed with respect to the domestic economy, we need now to explain how these concepts relate to international trade. Several converging forces cause imports from developing countries to increase when the developed countries unilaterally cut their work schedules:

(1) If a national government legislates an hours reduction, the domestic supply of labor will decrease. Assuming that the demand for labor stays the same, this event will cause the price of labor to rise and, if labor markets are tight, there may be labor shortages. The result in either case would be to seek lower-cost production or to fill the void in production with increased foreign imports. (Of course, labor supply does not quite correlate with the average number of work hours since numbers of employees and levels of capital investment, employee training and motivation, knowledge, organizational efficiency, and other factors relating to the productivity of labor are also involved. Still, the level of hours worked within a closed economic system gives a rough indication of the amount of work being performed, which, in turn, correlates with volume of production.)

(2) A reduction in work hours would also give working people more leisure time. More leisure time would tend to increase the level of per-capita consumption because, as Henry Ford once observed, people "consume more in their leisure time than in their working time."[25] If the level of domestic consumption rises relative to supply, prices, again, tend to rise and more products are imported from abroad.

(3) The combination of reduced supply and increased demand for goods and services produced in the domestic economy creates an unstable condition whose equilibrium can be restored in several ways. Reductions in labor supply can be met, first, by working down the pool of unemployed workers or else by encouraging more immigration or labor-force participation by married women. Once the domestic sources are exhausted, the labor content in products can be obtained through imported products. Likewise, increased consumer demand in a national economy creates additional pressure to import foreign products. Thus national governments are able to achieve a less "favorable" merchandise-trade balance by reducing their domestic work schedules relative to work schedules in those countries which are their principal trading partners.

Why would any country want to bring upon itself a deterioration of its own trade balance? Under a mercantilist system of trade this approach makes little sense, but in the new international economic order that is now emerging it may be seen as the duty of the financially stronger, industrially more advanced nations to help the weaker, less developed nations in that way. In fact, the Japanese government has adopted the technique of reduced work hours to reduce Japan's trade surplus. This change, away from a mercantilist approach, was initiated by the centrist, pro-business government of former Prime Minister Yasuhiro Nakasone and spurred by a report of the Mayekawa committee, whose chairman was a former Bank of Japan governor. The thrust of the report was that Japanese society needed to become more oriented toward leisure and less oriented toward work in order to maintain harmonious relations with other nations.[26] Motoyuki Miyano, managing director of Japan's Leisure Development Center, was quoted in the *Wall Street Journal* to the effect that the effort to reduce hours was directed at " 'nothing less than better trade relations between the U.S. and Japan' . . . If the Japanese worked less and played more . . . Japanese competitiveness might drop just a bit, lessening trade frictions with the U.S. and Europe."[27]

While the Japanese policy change was aimed primarily at improving relations with the United States and western Europe, there is no reason why this approach should not be applied to trade relations between the developed and developing nations. The developing nations have an urgent need for more production and employment opportunities. The developed nations need to allow a better balance between work and personal life. Their people also need relief from the oppressive culture of "consumerism". The new possibility, with the potential of revolutionizing trade relations among nations, is that national practices in regulating work time can be coordinated on an international scale. Production labor is, economically, a commodity traded in the world market. Its human aspect requires, however, that this commodity be given special treatment with respect to the level of price: that price cannot be allowed to drop below humanly tolerable wage levels. Given political commitment, the community of nations can coordinate policies for regulating labor even as it presently coordinates policies of financial regulation. The technique of reduced hours, adopted unilaterally, gives national governments a means of altering its balance of trade. If, on the other hand, the world's leading industrialized nations together reduced work hours at a comparable rate, there should then be no adverse effect on trade competition or a particular nation's balance of trade. Rather, the worldwide market for labor would improve, from the labor seller's point of view, because its worldwide supply would shrink.

In the emerging international order, the developed nations as a group have an obligation to the developing nations as a group to help them achieve more rapid economic growth. That obligation is most effectively discharged by creating favorable conditions for trade. A coordinated reduction of work hours in the developed countries alone would open up their markets to greater penetration by goods and services produced in the developing countries. The natural marketplace pressure created by shorter hours to import more products would be a greater help to the developing countries in their pursuit of faster economic growth than the current approach based upon preferential tariffs. The latter approach is having less effect as tariff rates generally fall. Lower labor and waste-disposal costs offer a greater cost advantage to developing countries than the preferential treatment on tariffs which they receive, for instance, from the United States under the Generalized System of Preferences program. If the United States and other developed countries were instead to cut their work schedules unilaterally, such an event would create a powerful stimulus to exports from developing countries bound for markets in developed countries. Combined with significant debt relief, that stimulus should be enough to set the developing countries on a course of sustained economic growth, so that differences in national income would narrow and eventually a condition would be created for balanced and fair trade relations.

Attitudes in the European Community and Japan

An assumption is made, perhaps because this book is addressed primarily to U.S. readers, that the U.S. Government would take the initiative in proposing and supporting international agreements among the developed countries to help the developing countries with respect to debt relief and labor-supply management. The practicality of such measures depends less upon economic factors than the political climate in those countries which are the principal decisionmakers. We have suggested that if an agreement can be reached between the leaders of the three regional trading blocs, that would go a long way towards attaining an agreement within the international community as a whole. Political and social attitudes in the European Community, especially Germany, and in Japan would be critical to the success of such an initiative. If, for instance, the U.S. government should propose worldwide control of production through coordinated reductions in work time, might such a proposal obtain a favorable reception from our major competitors in Europe and Asia, or would we be spurned? How realistic it is politically to suggest that the developed countries can agree to put cut-throat trade competition aside and embrace some form of cooperation?

The evidence is strong that the rest of the world is quite interested in cooperation — indeed, more so than we. Our principal competitors in the other two regional trade blocs do not appear to have the same single-minded focus upon free-market competition that U.S. business and government groups have. They have instead developed a trade and development agenda that is, compared to ours, socially responsible and forward-looking. We are, in fact, the political engine that is driving others into the maelstrom of excessive competition. A German trade-union official, Reinhard Dombre, complains of "a problem that is basic and is winning more and more importance: It is the philosophy of deregulation coming to us from the U.S.A. via Great Britain. This philosophy is based on the idea that anybody can represent his interest the best by himself. It means that collective protective regulations aren't necessary and ought to be reduced. For example, employers will try to maintain production with as few employees as possible. Production shortfalls can be made up by engaging temporary workers or part-time workers or by scheduling overtime work."[28]

U.S. policymakers have an especially unprogressive attitude with respect to reducing work time. The United States has refused to ratify all ILO conventions that pertain to limiting work time including Convention #1, prescribing an 8-hour day, which was negotiated in Washington, D.C., at the end of World War I. The two weeks of annual paid vacation which U.S. workers receive on average falls short of the three-week minimum which ILO Convention No. 132 prescribes for all workers with at least one year of service. The average hours worked in the U.S. economy has slid backwards from 39.1 hours per week in 1970 to 39.4 hours per week in 1990. When the author wrote letters to more than 300 U.S. business leaders in 1989 suggesting that business form a committee to find ways that working hours in this country might be reduced, there was not a single favor-

Figure 4.2

**Average Workweek
in U.S. Civilian Economy
1947 to 1990**

year	workweek
1990	39.4
1987	39.0
1985	39.0
1982	38.0
1980	38.5
1977	38.8
1975	38.7
1972	39.4
1970	39.1
1967	40.4
1965	40.5
1962	40.5
1960	40.5
1957	41.0
1955	41.6
1952	42.4
1950	41.7
1947	43.5

Source: Bureau of Labor Statistics

able response. President Bush, at the urging of business groups, has vetoed two bills that would allow parents to take unpaid leave to care for new-born or sick children without fear of losing their jobs. These gangsterish attitudes on the part of U.S. business leaders and their allies in government make a mockery of the basic premise of this discussion, that the United States might take the lead in promoting a more cooperative and humane trading order. They do, however, suggest that, if political attitudes could somehow be turned around in this country, the rest of the world might be comparatively easy.

It will be useful to recall that in France the Socialist president, Francois Mitterrand, was swept into office in 1981 on promises to institute a 35-hour workweek. In Poland, the current president, Lech Walesa, came to prominence in the same year as leader of an independent trade union, whose principal achievement was to negotiate a 5-day workweek with the then-communist Polish government. Agitation for shorter hours has also been strong in Belgium, the Netherlands, Britain, Australia, and the Scandinavian countries. Of even greater importance, perhaps, would be the situations in Germany and Japan. While their institutions and traditions are quite different, both nations have developed types of society favoring continued social progress. Both are firmly committed to international cooperation, especially with the United States. Both are committed to further reductions in work time.

Germany has a tradition of commitment to worker rights and an active trade-union movement. The Social Democratic party, rooted in labor, has from time to time claimed majorities in the national legislature. In Germany, the social budget accounts for more than 30% of GNP. There are financial allowances to working parents with children as well as paid maternity and child-raising leave. Laid off workers receive relatively generous unemployment benefits, including the possibility of short-time compensation for workers on reduced hours. Maintenance grants are available to young people wishing to attend trade schools. A compulsory health insurance program, providing both medical and maintenance benefits, covers all employed persons and their families, university students, disabled persons, and other groups. Workers injured on the job are covered by statutory accident insurance. A state-run retirement program gives pensions to male workers who have reached 65 years of age and to female workers who have reached age 60, replacing approximately two thirds of preretirement income. German labor law protects the right of unions to engage in collective bargaining and protects individual workers against arbitrary dismissal. Most German workers receive at least 6 weeks' annual vacation, averaging 29 vacation days per year. In 1988, about half of the nation's collective-agreements called for a 40-hour workweek, and the other half called for workweeks shorter than that.[29] As the accompanying table shows, German workers have steadily been moving towards a 35-hour weekly schedule. A recently concluded collective-bargaining agreement calls for workers in the metal industry to work 35 hours a week starting April 1, 1995.[30]

For Germany as well as for other European nations, much will depend on events that occur in the context of the European Community. This group of nations, set to form an economic and social union in 1992, have adopted a Social Charter which prescribes standards

Figure 4.3

Percentage of Workers in West Germany
on Work Schedules by Level of Hours

level of contractual weekly hours

year	35	36 & 36.5	37 & 37.5	38	38.5	39 & 39.5	40 or more
1984				1.4	23.1		75.4
1985			0.2	1.3	36.3	0.1	61.9
1986			0.3	1.7	42.9	1.2	53.6
1987			23.1	2.2	24.9	5.2	45.0
1988	0.1	0.9	24.1	2.9	43.5	11.2	17.3
1989	0.1	0.9	35.7	7.3	31.8	13.0	12.7
1990	21.3	1.0	17.9	6.7	28.7	15.0	9.3

Source: Deutscher Gewerkschaftsbund
Bundesvorstand, Dusseldorf

of acceptable conduct in economic life. Known as the "Community Charter of the Fundamental Social Rights of Workers", the document is, according to Jacques Delors, "an instrument embodying European aspirations, a reflexion of our common identity (which) contains a message for all those who inside and outside the Community are looking to the progress of Europe to give them reason for hope." A passage in the Charter states: "The completion of the internal market must lead to an improvement in the living and working conditions of workers in the European Community. This process must result from an approximation of these conditions while the improvement is being maintained, as regards in particular the duration and organization of working time and forms of employment other than open-ended contracts."[31] In light of that principle, a committee of the European Parliament adopted the following amendment: "By 1992 the statutory working week under the laws of the Member States shall not exceed 38 hours. Weekly working time shall be reduced to 35 hours with effect from 1 June 1994."[32]

In contrast to Germany, Japan has risen from the ranks of the developing countries to become an industrial giant. Its tradition of corporate loyalty is strong, and the trade-union movement is of recent vintage. Average work hours still exceed those in Europe and North

America, although the situation is rapidly changing. A poll taken by the Prime Minister's office in November 1991 found that three out of five Japanese support further cuts in hours.[33] Most remarkable has been the national government's policy decision to de-emphasize the corporate culture and mercantilist trade strategies and move toward a more people-oriented economic system. With its new-found affluence, Japan has decided to pioneer the culture of affluence or, in other words, become a model of what a successful developed country ought to become once the economic requirements are met. Increased leisure is a cornerstone of the new approach. The Japanese, however, have gone about this business of leisure in a typically thoughtful and thorough way, drawing up a plan of development which focuses on people's individual lifestyles and expected patterns of consumption. The Leisure Development Center in Tokyo, which is affiliated with the Ministry of International Trade and Industry (MITI), has made plans for increased use of leisure, involving such projects as the construction of giant hotel complexes and more golf courses. The number of Japanese traveling overseas has increased by double-digit percentages during the past several years, producing a $21.3 billion deficit in Japan's trade account in the travel industry. Some projected increases in participation by Japanese in various leisure activities are shown in Figure 4.4.[34]

On July 5, 1990, MITI unveiled its trade and development strategy for the 1990s in a report entitled "International Trade and Industrial Policy in the 1990s." The report declared: "The fundamental principle guiding Japan's international trade and industrial policy has been the idea that, through economic development of Japan, we contribute to the improvement of the daily lives of the Japanese people . . . However, today this idea of 'pre-established harmony', that successful economic development is automatically reflected in people's lives, may no longer be appropriate. International trade and industrial policy must go beyond measures of people's economic well-being and production performance . . . (to) the ultimate object of these policies, namely, the improvement of the daily lives." The report continued: "More than ever, Japan must cultivate global awareness and perspective. At times, it will need to act at its own expense." Close ties would have be maintained between Japan and other nations so that "Japan can avoid becoming isolated from the global community and can enhance its trustworthiness." Japan

Figure 4.4

Forecast of Demand for Participation
by Japanese in Leisure Activities

Leisure Activity	(in 1 million persons) participation population		annual rate of increase expected
	1990	2000	
Overseas travel	9.4	12.9	3.2%
Golf	12.8	15.7	2.1%
Exposition visits	31.7	38.1	1.8%
Snow skiing	13.9	15.7	1.2%
Domestic travel	57.5	64.2	1.1%
Horticulture	34.0	37.0	0.9%
Eating out	63.2	68.2	0.8%
Driving	56.1	60.2	0.7%
Amusement park visits	38.2	40.6	0.6%
Concerts	21.1	22.4	0.6%
Picnicking	34.0	35.8	0.5%
Fishing	14.6	15.3	0.5%
Pachinko (pinball game)	28.3	28.8	0.2%
Bowling	31.9	32.4	0.1%
Moviegoing	31.2	31.5	0.1%
Sports viewing	18.9	19.0	0.0%
Swimming	22.9	22.7	−0.1%
Cycling	13.8	13.2	−0.5%
Tennis	13.8	12.8	−0.8%
Game arcade visits	14.9	13.7	−0.8%

Source: Leisure Policy Study Group,
Ministry of International Trade and Industry

should not shirk its responsibility as a wealthy nation to help less fortunate peoples, emulating "the role the United States played in world development after World War II."[35]

The report proposed, as one of the "main tasks" of the new policy, "achieving a society of comfort and wealth at a level corresponding to the strength of the national economy." That goal entailed "the establishment of a socio-economic structure that maintains a standard of comfort and wealth appropriate for an economic power of Japan's stature. In concrete terms, this means establishing standards for time, space, and commodity prices. One important element in achieving wealth and comfort in Japan is the use of time. Bringing the average number of working hours per year in line with those of other leading industrialized nations will require Japan to adopt a system in which workers work only 40 hours per week, or 1,800 hours per year. We should make efforts to achieve this goal by the first half of the 1990s." One of the most interesting concessions made to the world community was the recommendation to adopt individualism as a value. "In Japan, a 'company-oriented' way of thinking has traditionally carried great weight in people's lives. But from now on, it is desirable to realize a society that will allow every person to enjoy a 'diversified and individual lifestyle' at home and in volunteer activities and regional communities," the report proposed.[36]

Under the heading of "concrete strategies" to achieve "a diversified life", the MITI report recommended "provision of leisure opportunities (including the formation of a social consensus on the importance of leisure, expansion of leisure time, reduction of leisure cost, and establishment of leisure areas such as resorts and facilities for sports and lifelong education)." It declared that, from the perspective of improving quality of life, "positive efforts should be made to shorten working hours and provide a more relaxed working environment, even if this policy puts a burden directly on industrial activities over the short term."[37] After years of stalled progress, such efforts by the Japanese government to bring down the level of working hours have begun to pay off. In 1987, the normal hours worked by Japanese manufacturing workers were 2,138 per year, compared with 1,912 hours per year for U.S., and 1,716 hours per year for West German, manufacturing workers. The average annual hours for all Japanese workers has dropped from 2,111 hours in 1988 to 2,088 hours in 1989, and to 2,052 in 1990.[38] The goal is, again, 1,800 hours by the "first half of the 1990s", which would surpass what U.S. workers can be expected to have by that time.

Employer-Specific Tariffs: A Brake on Exports from Developing Countries

Let us assume that a political consensus can be reached among the principal developed countries that the world economy needs to move promptly to shorter hours. Let us assume that international agreements are concluded, and practical steps are taken towards that end. The result would be to generate increased pressure for the developing countries to export products to markets in the developed countries. Should nature then take its course under conditions of free trade? While the developed countries would then have done their part for the world economy, that in itself might not be enough to bring up wages and living standards in the developing countries, especially if democratic trade unions are suppressed. If their own competitive forbearance is to be a part of this new international economic order, then the developed countries have a right to expect the developing countries to cooperate with them in achieving common global objectives. Such goals would include the reduction of wage disparities between nations, more effective protection of the natural environment, and encouragement of political democracy. The developed countries have not only the right to expect such cooperation but they also are able to dictate terms in the world trading order should cooperative efforts fail. They, possessing the markets, are in the driver's seat with respect to trade relations.

The developed countries can only control trade by restricting it in some fashion. It is they who will decide which types of goods are permitted to enter their markets , in what quantities, and under what conditions. Logically, then, some mechanism must exist for restricting trade or intercepting products at the border. That mechanism already exists, of course. National governments can restrict trade by imposing tariffs, quotas, fees, etc. upon imported goods. Usually those restrictions have been imposed for the purpose of sheltering the nation's own domestic industries. Such practices have excited much ill will among nations and created diplomatic friction . We are talking, however, about a global economy shaped by cooperation as well as competition. Under those conditions it might be possible to restrict trade in a way that would serve international as well as national interests. In theory, trade restrictions designed to further a generally accepted global development plan need not arouse antagonistic reactions from one's trading partners. The developed countries could act as guardians of the global economy. They could make sure that humanity's interest is upheld by preventing importation of particular commercial products that represent violations of international policy. Still less stringently, they could impose tariffs upon those products, not forbidding importation but discouraging it by an additional financial burden.

Governments have the power either to coerce or encourage behavior. Laws usually work through coercion; certain behavior is punished as an illegal act. The other approach is for government to provide financial incentives to encourage the behavior; no moral stigma is attached to violations. For example, an additional tax on gasoline might discourage solo driving and encourage use of mass transit. The Fair Labor Standards Act requires that employers scheduling more than forty hours of work in a week pay employees an overtime premium. The employer is not forbidden to schedule longer hours, but it becomes financially disadvantageous. The same choice applies to trade regulation. Quotas and other numerical restrictions upon imports are coercive. Tariffs, on the other hand, financially encourage or discourage trade. The latter approach has the advantage of allowing greater flexibility of operation. That, in turn would tend to reduce the need for legal intervention. Unfortunately, tariffs taken in the form of countervailing duties, being punitive in nature, do involve substantial litigation. The U.S. Government relies heavily upon the use of countervailing duties to enforce whatever standards of conduct it wishes to maintain with respect to subsidies and dumping by foreign governments. To avoid this lawyer-intensive process, we may instead imagine a system of tariffs reduced to an administrative routine. Such tariffs would imply no guilt, but instead encourage (not force) producers in foreign countries to conform to certain standards of socially or environmentally beneficial modes of conduct.

Tariffs generally add an ad valorem tax to the cost of an imported item, following a published schedule of rates. We call them "protective tariffs" because they protect domestic producers against foreign competition. However, the tariff mechanism could also be used as a set of rewards and punishments to encourage certain kinds of business behavior. For instance, we might want manufacturing firms to pay higher wages, provide more benefits, schedule shorter work hours, give more encouragement to democratic unions, provide a safer and healthier work environment, and take greater steps to protect the natural environment than what they might otherwise want to offer. Tariffs could provide a financial incentive for businesses to undertake those various steps.

To create a practical mechanism, the particular social or environmental concerns would first have to be defined and evaluated according to a certain scheme of measurement. They would individually be converted into a numerical rating or index reflecting the degree of compliance with a standard or ideal. Levels of wages, for instance, are relatively easy to measure. Compliance with health and safety standards, tolerance of union activity, or protection of the environment would be more difficult. The object would be to compile a single index number to represent a traded product. Such an index should reflect all relevant factors entering into social evaluation of the business activities that created the product. It would then become the basis for setting tariff rates. The rate of the tariff would be inversely related to the degree of compliance with the standard. The better the compliance, the lower the tariff. The worse the compliance, the higher the tariff.

The purpose of this exercise would be not only to penalize employers who produce objects of trade under substandard conditions but also give them a financial incentive to improve. Sweatshop producers would still be allowed to ship goods to the United States, but they might lose their cost advantage. U.S. consumers would have pay something to the government to compensate for their decision to buy in a socially irresponsible manner. To be fair, however, the product evaluations would need to be targeted to particular employers rather than to entire countries. That is because individual employers, not countries, make the decisions concerning mode of business operations. Besides, the nationality of traded products has become increasingly confused. U.S. trade sanctions against a country such as Mexico are of dubious worth if the violators are companies operating in Mexico that are named Ford, Zenith, or General Electric.

Some may object that such a scheme would increase the paperwork associated with international trade. Traded goods and services are too diverse to be individually tracked in this way. The staffing for inspections and computations would be prohibitively expensive. However, such a system is today more practicable than it would have been in past years. In a pre-computer age, objections concerning an impossible load of paperwork connected with the gathering of facts, calculation of index numbers, and assignment to products might have been justified. Today, however, computers are able to make quickly various complex and precise calculations. They can simultaneously process thousands of different transactions. The technology of bar coding allows coded information to be attached to individual products where they can be effortlessly read and entered into data files. To make the system even more manageable, the world's major trading nations have adopted a uniform system of product codings for trade classification called the "Harmonized System". This scheme assigns a ten-digit number to each type of traded product, covering more than 5,000 different product categories. The last four digits are reserved for each nation for its own record-keeping purposes. Finally, the personnel to inspect and evaluate facilities in the countries where the exported goods are produced might be civil servants employed by international organizations. Besides allowing their expense to be shared by many nations, that arrangement would also reduce the level of resentment that people might feel toward foreign inspectors stationed upon their national soil.

It is obvious that this system of socially based trade regulation is incompatible with a scheme of free trade that envisions complete elimination of tariffs. It is also clear that U.S. policymakers will not consider such a system until the fate of the North American FTA is decided, and then only if the decision is negative. Therefore, the above scheme of selective tariffs should not be considered a definite proposal at this point in time, but merely a statement that a coherent alternative exists to free trade. What has been missing for some time has been a balanced set of incentives to stabilize trade relations between the developed and developing nations and to make sure that economic development means rising living standards and adequate environmental protection in all countries affected by international trade. The mechanisms proposed in this chapter are intended to provide regulatory balance. On one hand, we increase the flow of exports from the developing countries as the developed countries unilaterally reduce their hours of work. On the other hand, we selectively restrict the flow of trade as the developed countries apply tariffs to products from developing countries targeted to particular socially or environmentally irresponsible employers. There is, then, both an accelerator and a brake to this scheme of trade regulation. There is a way to regulate international economic development besides the customary techniques of financial control.

The GATT and Other Structures for International Cooperation

Any such scheme would require structures of international cooperation to set global policy and enforce them in a concerted manner. Currently, the world's economic community has a quasi-governmental structure to coordinate policies following Keynesian theories and enforcement techniques. This structure, called the Group of Seven (G-7), consists of finance ministers and central-bank governors from the seven leading industrial nations: Canada, France, Germany, Italy, Japan, the United Kingdom, and the United States. Acting in consultation with officials of the International Monetary Fund, these financial managers meet on a regular basis to discuss macroeconomic policies in their respective nations, compare notes, assess the world situation, reach conclusions, and so effect "economic policy coordination" within the world financial community. An IMF publication states that "the Group of Seven generally aims for high levels of employment and growth and for relative price stability. Its instruments are primarily (national) fiscal and monetary policy."[39] Unfortunately, the approach taken by the Group of Seven is based upon an incomplete economic analysis which does not do justice to the needs of a majority of the world's people. Theirs is a money-centered approach insensitive to the interests of labor. From such fora have come, for instance, calls for more free trade and for maintenance of Third World debt. Monetary and fiscal techniques, while helpful to some degree, cannot carry the entire load of economic policy.

There is, besides the financial high command, an international structure responsible for maintaining cooperative trade relations among nations, which is the GATT. Its purpose, as stated in the preamble to the 1947 agreement, is to increase living standards through "reciprocal and mutually advantageous arrangements directed to the substantial reduction of tariffs and other barriers to trade and to the elimination of discriminatory treatment in international commerce." About one hundred nations, which together account for four fifths of the world's trade, have signed this agreement. While not a formal treaty, GATT consists of a legal document drafted in 1947 to which numerous amendments, protocols, and modifications of tariff schedules have been added over the years. A secretariat headquartered in Geneva provides organizational structure. Because of its imperfect origin, GATT has a rather tenuous legal basis. When the 1944 Bretton Woods conference established the World Bank and the International Monetary Fund, a third institution known as the International Trade Organization was also created. GATT was to be a provisional document to facilitate trade negotiations while national governments were ratifying the ITO charter. The U.S. Congress, however, refused to accept the charter, so President Truman approved GATT through an executive agreement. Because GATT lacks treaty status, there remains some doubt whether the U.S. Government is legally obligated to honor its provisions. Even so, GATT enjoys broad acceptance and prestige around the world for its success in creating a relatively open trading system in the post-war era.[40]

The essence of GATT lies in its perennial series of negotiations designed to bring the international trading order in line with emerging needs of the world economy. According to a publication issued by the Congressional Budget Office, "four key principles underlie the General Agreement:

• Member countries should work to lower trade barriers in general, and to eliminate the use of quotas in particular.

• Any barrier to trade should be applied on a nondiscriminatory basis to all member countries (most-favored-nation treatment).

• Once a tariff concession is made, it cannot later be rescinded without compensating affected trade partners. Also, other forms of protection cannot be employed to circumvent the effect of the concession.

• Trade conflicts should be settled by consultation whenever possible, using as a guide a set of codified and mutually accepted rules for the conduct of trade."[41]

Nothing here is said of labor matters. In particular, the question of reduced working hours does not arise. The GATT agenda does not address the observance of fair labor standards although this topic has become an increasingly important element in trade relations. GATT does, however, deal with differences in the situation of developed and developing nations. A fourth part was added to the Agreement in

1965 which acknowledged the special needs of developing nations. Article 36, paragraph 8, states that "the developed contracting parties do not expect reciprocity for commitments made by them in trade negotiations to reduce or remove tariffs and other barriers to the trade of the less-developed contracting parties." Thus, the developing countries were given permission to protect their infant industries by erecting higher trade barriers than what the developed countries had agreed to accept. Because of their precarious economic condition, these countries were also to be penalized less severely for infractions of GATT rules. By general agreement, they were authorized to lean on the developed countries just a bit to accumulate capital for development purposes.[42]

Part IV of the Agreement, inspired by the 1964 UN Conference on Trade and Development, marked a fundamental departure from GATT's insistence upon equality of treatment among signatory nations. Previously, issues of economic development were considered outside the scope of trade agreements. The World Bank was supposed to handle this area. But, as trade became increasingly important to the world economy, developmental issues could no longer be ignored. GATT members accepted the principle of unequal or preferential treatment for the developing countries, which represented an exception to the Most-Favored-Nation concept. GATT established a Trade and Development Committee to look after the interests of developing countries. Once a year, representatives of the developed countries are summoned before this committee to explain their remaining trade barriers to imports from developing countries. In addition, several developed countries, starting with Australia in 1966, have created a preferential system of tariffs to allow goods from developing countries to enter their markets duty-free. The U.S. program, established under the Trade Act of 1974, is called the "Generalized System of Preferences". Another program which was enacted in 1983, called the "Caribbean Basin Initiative", extends preferential treatment to designated countries in the Caribbean region and Central America.[43]

GATT has also departed from its traditional free-trade position with respect to international trade in commodities. The economies of developing countries are, of course, highly dependent upon production of commodities such as coffee, sugar, cocoa, cotton, and tropical timber. Various international agreements have been concluded by commodity-producing nations which seek to stabilize the price of commodities around a long-term baseline or else raise the price above this line. "Viewed from a traditional GATT perspective," wrote Kenneth W. Dam, "such agreements resemble cartel agreements in which sellers combine to restrict sales and thereby raise the market price of a product." Yet, GATT has given its blessing to this type of arrangement, embodying the principle of production supply management. Article 38, paragraph 2, states that the contracting parties "shall . . . take action . . . to provide improved and acceptable conditions of access to world markets for primary products of particular interest to less-developed contracting parties and to devise measures designed to stabilize and improve conditions of world markets in these products including measures designed to attain stable, equitable and remunerative prices for exports of such products."[44]

The significance of this provision, from our standpoint, is that once the international trading community has accepted the principle that a particular group of nations can employ techniques of supply management to obtain fair prices on the world market for a particular group of commodities, there is no reason why the same principle should not be extended to other commodities which may benefit still other nations. Article 11, in fact, allows supply-management systems such as the one protecting Canadian agriculture to be exempted from the general provisions of GATT.[45] Labor, too, is an international commodity that needs a fair price. Therefore, the concept of labor supply management, achieved by a coordinated reduction in work hours, seems generally consistent with GATT's purposes and provisions. The idea that developing countries are poor, and therefore in need of assistance, while the developed countries are rich must be reconciled with the reality of class-based differences in all countries. The leaders of both the developing and developed nations are apt to be wealthy oligarchs or otherwise members of privileged classes, while working people everywhere are reduced to labor commodities traded in the market. A moral dimension should be added to the system arguing for the preferential treatment of labor. The Mexican Action Network on Free Trade has moved in that direction with its proposal for upward harmonization of North American wages. In the language of GATT, its spokesmen have argued: "Cheap labor should be considered as a form of 'dumping', like a subsidy to capital, and should be penalized in exchanges."[46]

Prodded by labor groups in the 1980s, the U.S. Government adopted the respect for internationally recognized worker rights as an element of its trade policy. The United States has attempted to introduce this concept into the GATT negotiations, starting with the Uruguay Round. The U.S. delegation sought to form a working group to discuss worker rights at the GATT ministerial conference held in September 1986, but encountered opposition from other delegations, primarily those representing developing countries. Such opponents reportedly "view the efforts of the United States and other developed countries to infuse international labor standards into GATT as a 'Trojan horse for protectionism.' "[47] Again, in the autumn of 1990, the United States proposed that a working party be formed at GATT to "examine the relationship of internationally recognized labour standards to international trade," according to a report in *GATT Focus*. Its particular proposal focused on three types of labor standards: freedom of association, freedom to organize and bargain collectively, and freedom from forced or compulsory labor. Brazil, Mexico, the ASEAN countries, Tanzania, Chile, India, Bolivia, Nigeria, Egypt, Peru, Nicaragua, Yugoslavia, Morocco and Cuba expressed opposition to the U.S. request. They said that this subject belonged to the ILO rather than to the GATT. The European Community, the Nordic countries, Switzerland, Canada, Czechoslovakia, Poland, Hungary, and Japan supported the U.S. proposal. The Council agreed to reconsider the matter at a future meeting.[48]

The developing countries' fear that including worker rights in the trade discussions might be directed against them is not without justification. The particular kinds of rights that the U.S. delegation chose to discuss are ones most often violated in their societies. Nations such as South Korea and Mexico have cut corners, for instance, in preserving the right of industrial workers to associate in democratic trade unions. Squeezing the worker has been a traditional means by which developing countries have accumulated capital more quickly. The developed countries, on the other hand, can afford high standards of labor protection. Therefore, to place worker rights on the GATT agenda as a factor permitting an exception to its Most-Favored-Nation rule could work to the disadvantage of developing countries. A possible way around this obstacle might be to include some other kinds of worker rights in the package which, hopefully, would lean in the developing countries' favor. Such a "right" might be that of industrial workers to receive a fair share of the gains achieved in labor productivity within their national economies to be taken in the form of reduced work hours. Since larger gains in labor productivity are achieved in the developed countries, the cost of meeting this new standard would be borne primarily by them.[49] If that approach fails, GATT negotiators might consider including language in the proposal, specifically exempting the developing countries from this requirement.

The argument that the question of worker rights belongs to the ILO also has considerable merit. The ILO, or International Labor Organization, is a specialized agency of the United Nations which handles labor matters. Unlike GATT and the United Nations itself, the ILO dates back to the period following World War I, having originally been part of the League of Nations. Its primary function is to set international labor standards. These are codes recommended to national governments for voluntary adoption. The ILO has issued standards relating to weekly hours of work, workers' freedom of association, prohibition of child labor, minimum paid vacations, unemployment insurance, paid educational leave, seafarers' pensions, and so on. Like GATT, it maintains a secretariat, sponsors studies, holds conferences, distributes publications, and generally acts as a clearinghouse for information in its area. Admittedly, the activities of GATT and the ILO need to be coordinated more closely. A blue-ribbon panel of the Economic Policy Council of the United Nations Association of the U.S.A., chaired by former U.S. Secretary of Labor Ray Marshall, has recently recommended: "The U.S. government should convene a working group in the United States to assess the possibility of linking the ILO and GATT in a way that both promotes the raising of living standards and protects the fundamental human rights of workers in all corners of the world. Furthermore . . . the U.S. government should lead efforts within both the GATT and the ILO to develop cooperative measures . . . for strengthening the linkage between workers' rights and international trade."[50]

The MITI report, "International Trade and Industrial Policy in the 1990s", also proposed to improve international cooperation by expanding the role of GATT and other bodies. "Strengthening the international economic system and promoting its vitality requires," it said, "the study for possibly expanding and using GATT and OECD in several respects including greater use for dispute settlement, mechanisms for more effective policy coordination, strengthened coordination of measures for trade, international finance, and domestic economic policy." To deal with trade imbalances, the Japanese government report called for "recognition of the importance and effectiveness of domestic measures to promote investment in infrastructure, basic research, the knowledge base, reduced working hours, etc., and international coordination of domestic policy based on a mutual understanding and cooperation since efforts of a single country working alone can have only limited success." For its own part, Japan's domestic policy should give "greater consideration . . . to the quality of human life in all policy areas," the report declared. "In other words, Japan must adopt 'human-oriented international trade and industrial policies.' "[51]

Would it be too much to expect that the U.S. Government, too, might pursue "human-oriented international trade and industrial policies"? If we had the brave spirit of Americans in previous generations, such a question might be more easily answered. Now, however, the country seems caught in a tight vise of financial "necessities" defined by economic special interests. One would think that after fifty years of the 40-hour week, with large cumulative gains in labor productivity achieved during that period, it would be time to move on to a more advanced standard. Considering that the year 1992 marks the 500th anniversary of Columbus' first voyage to America and a new millennium will be upon us in eight short years, one may perhaps be forgiven the luxury of imagining that this nation's policymakers will dare to commemorate important deeds in the past by making equally bold plans of their own. Why not project a 4-day, 32-hour workweek by the year 2000? Why not a 6-week annual paid vacation? Surely by the time of the next millennial passing America can afford to give its workers the same amount of leisure as workers in the German metal industry now enjoy. As the world economy becomes better integrated, it is time to think of improving the condition of labor on a global scale. It is time to use the existing institutions of international cooperation more boldly and creatively, whether they be the ILO, OECD, or GATT, separately or in combination. Why not negotiate, besides peace, how the various governments can improve the lives of their people?

Some Precedents in Linking Labor
Standards to Trade

The power to set trade policy continues to be held mainly by national governments. The U.S., Japanese, German, British, French, and other First World governments are the dominant players on the world economic scene. National laws have an important impact on trade relations both in their own right and as precedent-setters for international agreements. Some persons argue that labor questions ought to be kept separate from trade policy. They suggest that trade unionists who believe otherwise are attempting to insert their own special-interest agenda into an area where it does not properly belong. Such concerns will be, at best, a side issue that can be dealt with separately. To introduce a worker-rights theme into trade discussions is thus made to made to seem inappropriate. The fact is, however, that historically this is the way that labor standards often enter the realm of public policy—through trade. The trade regulations come first. Then, at a later date, worker rights are injected into the regulations as a socially stabilizing element.

Political proposals must be advanced with a sense of legitimacy in terms of the traditions and legal framework of each country. Fortunately, the U.S. Government has such a tradition of labor protection. In fact, the federal government's right to regulate trade has been the main legal springboard to protection of workers' rights in general. Article I, Section 8 of the U.S. Constitution gave Congress the power "to regulate commerce with foreign nations, and among the several states, and with the Indian tribes." In effect, a huge free-trade zone was created throughout the country. Based upon this "interstate-commerce clause", Congress later enacted the Fair Labor Standards Act of 1938, which set a national minimum wage, established a standard number of weekly hours of work, required premium pay for overtime, and prohibited child labor. Because of the weak link to interstate trade, the U.S. Supreme Court had declared an earlier version of this law unconstitutional. The Fair Labor Standards Act, being more carefully drafted, has managed to withstand such challenges. If Congress had not been authorized to regulate interstate commerce, then its power to regulate hours might have been limited to policing the work conditions of federal contractors. As it is, federal law potentially excludes from interstate commerce goods produced in violation of the hours requirement.

The power to regulate foreign trade is, if anything, even more explicitly granted to Congress under the U.S. Constitution. Here, too, subsequent legislation based on this regulatory power has included features protecting worker rights. One of the first such steps was the prohibition of imports manufactured by convict labor in the 1890 McKinley Tariff act. In 1947, the founders of the prospective International Trade Organization recognized a common interest "in the achievement and maintenance of fair labor standards." This topic was also discussed at the first GATT conference.[52] A number of U.S. trade laws enacted during the 1980s include provisions to protect worker rights. They include the Caribbean Basin Initiative of 1983, the Renewal Act of 1984, and the Omnibus Trade and Competitiveness Act of 1988. Denial of worker rights in foreign countries which receive trade benefits under programs created by those various laws has become grounds for denying the benefits to those countries.

While GATT does not recognize violations of worker rights as an unlawful trade practice that would merit retaliation, it does allow signatories to make an exception to the Most-Favored-Nation rule in regard to preferential treatment for developing countries. This feature allows worker-rights criteria to enter GATT through the back door. As previously noted, the United States extends trade preferences to certain developing nations under two separate programs. Their legal basis was the Trade Act of 1974 (whose term of application was extended until 1993 by the Renewal Act of 1984) and the Caribbean Basin Economic Recovery Act passed in 1983. Both these laws eliminate U.S. duties on a broad range of products imported from the beneficiary developing nations, but also allow the President to revoke the trade privileges when a nation violates internationally recognized worker rights. Those rights, as defined by Section 503 of the Renewal Act, would include:

"(A) the right of association;
(B) the right to organize and bargain collectively;
(C) a prohibition on the use of any form of forced or compulsory labor;
(D) a minimum age for the employment of children; and
(E) acceptable conditions of work with respect to minimum

wages, hours of work, and occupational safety and health."[53]

The Caribbean Basin Initiative and the Generalized System of Preferences (which was established by Section 502 of the Trade Act of 1974) were both designed to help certain developing nations achieve faster economic growth. Therefore, the United States limits participation in these programs to nations whose economies are in the developing stage and which do not offend U.S. sensibilities by nationalizing foreign-owned businesses, belonging to OPEC, or abusing labor. The Caribbean Basin Initiative is strictly a regional program whose participants include all the Central American and most Caribbean island nations. Cuba and Mexico are notable exceptions. The Generalized System of Preferences involves a larger group of nations. Currently the United States allows approximately 3,000 different types of products to be admitted duty-free from 136 "beneficiary developing nations." For many years, until President Reagan "graduated" them out of the program, the four "Pacific tigers" — Hong Kong, Singapore, South Korea, and Taiwan — took the lion's share of its benefits. Currently, the program's chief beneficiaries include Mexico, Brazil, Thailand, Israel, Malaysia, and the Philippines.[54]

Once a nation has been admitted as a beneficiary to the Caribbean Basin Initiative program, it stays for the duration. There is no procedure for challenging the eligibility status. The Generalized System of Preferences, on the other hand, includes several types of reviews by the President which may result in eviction from the program if the beneficiary nation is found to have violated eligibility criteria such as protection of worker rights. The law provides for an interagency review board called the Trade Policy Staff Committee to review charges that a nation has violated the program requirements. Any person can bring a petition before this committee alleging violations The committee is obliged to investigate the matter and report its findings and recommendations to the President. So far, four nations — Nicaragua, Paraguay, Romania, and Chile — have been terminated as beneficiaries under the Generalized System of Preferences because of violations of internationally recognized worker rights.[55] Mexico's eligibility to receive trade preferences as a "beneficiary developing country" under the Generalized System of Preferences was unsuccessfully challenged last year.

Two other legal provisions allow the President to impose trade sanctions against an even broader group of nations if they are found to be violating worker rights. The provisions are Section 301 of the Trade Act of 1974, as amended by the Omnibus Trade and Competitive Act of 1988, and the International Emergency Economic Powers Act of 1977. Section 301 of the Trade Act was originally intended to provide a means of retaliating against foreign trade practices that violated U.S. rights under GATT and other agreements. The President was authorized to negotiate with foreign governments to end the violations and, failing relief from those efforts, to impose unilateral sanctions against offending nations including increased tariffs or other import restrictions. The Omnibus Trade and Competitive Act added the denial of internationally recognized worker rights to the types of complaint allowed under Section 301. Any interested person is allowed to petition the U.S. Trade Representative to impose sanctions. To date, the U.S. Government has focused upon the pirating of U.S. intellectual properties rather than on worker rights. Indeed, the Reagan administration opposed making denial of worker rights an unfair trade practice under Section 301.[56]

A problem with this approach is that imposing trade sanctions under Section 301 violates U.S. obligations as a signatory to GATT. No nation may unilaterally raise tariffs upon imports from other signatory nations except under authorized conditions. GATT does, for instance, allow retaliation against fellow signatories which engage in "dumping" products abroad below cost or which employ prison labor to produce goods for export . In addition, a signatory nation is allowed to take "any action which it considers necessary for the protection of its essential security interests." Seizing upon that particular loophole, Congress enacted the International Emergency Economic Powers Act of 1977, giving the President discretionary authority to retaliate against foreign governments whose actions posed an "unusual and extraordinary threat" to U.S. security. To exercise his authority, though, the President had first to declare a "national emergency". This step was taken in 1985 when President Reagan imposed trade sanctions against South Africa. International Emergency Economic Powers Act, though drafted in accordance with GATT regulations, is considered a less effective tool for enforcing worker rights because its use is limited to extreme situations.[57]

Section 301 authority, on the other hand, is extremely effective.

With it, the President of the United States has the authority to retaliate against any country deemed guilty of unfair or unreasonable trade practices, which, among other things, would include violations of worker rights. The President must retaliate if the nation has denied U.S. rights under any trade agreement or has acted in a manner that is "unjustifiable and burdens or restricts United States commerce", unless the offending nation has taken steps to correct the problem. The President may, at his discretion, retaliate if an action or policy of a foreign country is "unreasonable or discriminatory" and "burdens or restricts" U.S. commerce. The definition of "unreasonable" includes "acts, policies, and practices which . . . constitute a persistent pattern of conduct that . . . (I) denies workers the right of association, (II) denies workers the right to organize and bargain collectively, (III) permits any form of forced or compulsory labor, (IV) fails to provide a minimum age for the employment of children, or (V) fails to provide standards for minimum wages, hours of work, and occupational safety and health of workers." If the country is found to have engaged in any of these "unreasonable" practices, the President may suspend its trade benefits, impose tariffs or other import restrictions on its goods, or assess special fees. Normally, however, Section 301 authority would be used to pressure the other country into ending the offensive trade practices.[58]

Unfortunately, such actions if undertaken by the U.S. President would be illegal under the GATT. Their unauthorized retaliation restricting trade would violate its nondiscrimination clause. Therefore, if the United States chooses to exercise its Section 301 powers, it would be pushing GATT rules to the limit and risking a breakdown in the international trading system. Section 301 reflects Congressional impatience with the GATT process after U.S. negotiators had for years attempted unsuccessfully to remove trade impediments in areas such as services and intellectual-property rights. Its authority, according to Jeffrey Schott, "changed the negotiating dynamic" of GATT and put teeth back into its enforcement procedures. Other countries realized that the United States was serious about wanting trade reform.[59] On the other hand, the use of Section 301 authority casts the United States in the role of an international scofflaw which engages in "legal disobedience" to further its own interests. This is widely seen as a bully's weapon which weakens the reciprocity of trade agreements with other countries. A deputy U.S. Trade

Representative in the Reagan administration, Michael B. Smith, complained that "(u)se of the very public Section 301 procedure, with public finding of unfairness, to deal with such complaints would tend to aggravate national sensitivities in such a way as to preclude the sort of evolutionary progress that might be achieved by other, less confrontational means."[60]

The unilateral approach, while offering an immediate remedy, is flawed by its posture of passing judgment on other nations. The U.S. Government would be setting itself up as a defender of worker rights around the world, much as it assumed the role of international policeman in the Persian Gulf war. Even if the United States had the moral authority to support that role, it would still be resented by other nations as an infringement upon their national sovereignty. The practice of condemning nations proven to have violated internationally recognized worker rights will understandably be resented by the nations accused of such practices. That resentment, in turn, will hinder investigation of the alleged abuses and perhaps stiffen resistance to change. Furthermore, to tag an entire nation as a violator of worker rights seems overly broad. Some violators may be foreign-owned companies including ones headquartered in the United States. One is led by such logic away from the judgment of nations and toward the judgment of the particular enterprises where workers are employed. One is also led to the realization, from a U.S. perspective, that we can no longer go it alone in policing world trade. Logically, it is the responsibility of the world community as a whole to enforce international labor standards. All nations have a responsibility to protect worker and human rights. The world trading community has a responsibility to create a humane system of trade relations.

The U.S. Government, as an important member of the world community, can, however, help to initiate positive change by stepping up its diplomatic efforts to inject the element of international labor protection into the GATT. If successful, this would be the third such injection; the first two were enactment of the Fair Labor Standards Act of 1938 and the 1980s amendments to U.S. trade law establishing worker-rights criteria. The world trading order must become sensitive to the need for stable and adequately compensated jobs in the both developed and developing countries. Instead of free trade, humanity needs a regulated trading system which strengthens domestic economies and promotes rising standards of living. An immediate goal would be to seek to change the GATT rules so that national governments including our own can legally retaliate against nations or businesses which violate worker rights. Ultimately, the definition of worker rights should be expanded to include hours reductions, which are a free-market equivalent to rights guarantees.

The legal mandate to convert GATT to such ends is found in an amendment to the Trade Act of 1974. In a section entitled "steps to be taken toward GATT revision", the law states: "The President shall, as soon as practicable, take such action as may be necessary to bring trade agreements . . . into conformity with principles promoting the development of an open, nondiscriminatory, and fair world economic system. The actions and principles . . . include, but are not limited to, the following. . . . (4) the adoption of international fair labor standards . ·. . in the GATT." The Omnibus Trade and Competitiveness Act of 1988 includes a section which reads: "The principal negotiating objectives of the United States regarding worker rights are —

(A) to promote respect for worker rights;

(B) to secure a review of the relationship of worker rights to GATT articles, objectives, and related instruments with a view to ensuring that the benefits of the trading system are available to all workers; and

(C) to adopt, as a principle of the GATT, that the denial of worker rights should not be a means for a country or its industries to gain competitive advantage in international trade."[61]

It should be noted that the President of the United States is not just urged but required to take action regarding the "adoption of international fair labor standards" in GATT rules. Congress, which retains ultimate Constitutional authority to regulate foreign trade, has imposed this requirement upon the President. To be sure, U.S. trade negotiators at GATT have held discussions with their foreign counterparts about the possibility of incorporating labor standards. Can we, however, be sure that these negotiators have tried their best? After all, the Reagan administration originally opposed making observance of worker rights a criterion of eligibility for trade preferences. Giving the Bush team of negotiators the benefit of the doubt, one concedes that the package of proposals which they took to the GATT discussions may be inadequate to attract the support for worker-rights criteria which they need from the developing countries. The additional proposal, that the developed countries unilaterally reduce work hours, goes well beyond what an even favorably inclined President might feel authorized to discuss at those meetings. Therefore, Congress should take the initiative in proposing this negotiating objective for the President. By whatever legal instrument seems appropriate—be it law, amendment of law, or binding or nonbinding resolution—it should put something on the table for public discussion.

If domestic legislation to reduce work time is thought to be politically too difficult, the U.S. Congress should at least pursue international negotiation. It should first insist that the President and his negotiating team observe the legal mandate to negotiate improved labor standards in their existing package. It should then seek to broaden the package of standards with respect to working hours. Ultimately, this effort must be directed at creating a new definition of a GATT code; for, of all international bodies concerned with such matters, GATT has by far the sharpest teeth. Noncompliance with its rules would be actionable for retaliation by other GATT signatories. In reality, though, the GATT does not negotiate new labor standards. That function belongs to the International Labor Organization. As a competent standard-setting body, the ILO will consider proposals to create new standards in particular areas of labor practice. If approved by its tripartite deliberating body, it would promulgate a new convention which could then be incorporated into the GATT rules. By implication, violations of the most important ILO conventions ought to be cause for retaliation within GATT. Also, a nation's failure to ratify the most important ILO conventions (such as freedom of association, holidays with pay, etc.) ought to be grounds for trade retaliation. It is doubtful, however, that the U.S. Congress would soon push that particular agenda since the United States has a poor record in ratifying ILO conventions.

To Reaffirm Free Labor and Democracy

Still, we can dream, can we not? With the fall of communism in the Soviet Union and a new millennium fast approaching, we can take one small step towards improving workers' lives in the United States by giving the President legal instructions to negotiate improved labor standards in whatever international forum is considered appropriate. When, for instance, Presidential fast-track authority expires in June 1993 (or a year earlier, if the Riegle amendment passes), then the Congress can issue a new set of negotiating instructions for the President to take to GATT which, hopefully, would include a provision for reduced work hours. Although that proposal may seem unrealistic in today's political environment, it is economically far more realistic and, indeed, moderate than the idea of combining two labor markets of vastly disproportionate income levels in a North American free-trade zone. Such a far-reaching proposal cannot, however, become part of the trade agenda without an extensive debate channeled through Congress which carries a popular mandate for change. That is where the Bush administration went wrong with NAFTA. It thought it could hurry the process along without giving the public or nonbusiness groups much opportunity to be heard on the subject. It thought it could outfox potential opponents and "fast-track" the discussion.

From now on, openness and not secrecy of negotiations should enter into the practice of determining trade policy. Democratic processes need scrupulously to be maintained. The prospective North American Free-Trade Agreement, as it now appears to be, is a monument to the misguided belief that free-market economies can be combined with a lack of political democracy. Abraham Lincoln's warning that a "house divided against itself cannot stand" applies as well to the debate concerning free trade. Do we want a society based on free labor or cheap labor? The issue remains much the same now as in Lincoln's day. Building upon clear precedents in both U.S. law and in the GATT agreement, we are on solid ground in arguing that the time has come to inject labor standards into agreements on trade. The time has come to establish durable legal structures that shield people's livelihoods from unrestricted free-market competition. This is what free trade is about, not combating the ideological evils of protectionism. We are right in asserting that NAFTA is not just about "trade". This discussion is also about protecting democracy, the natural environment, the dignity of labor, and the future of our communities as a home for prosperous and free people.

AUTHOR'S
ACKNOWLEDGMENTS

This book began with a lengthy discussion of free trade and the Mexican labor situation that I had with Jose Quintana in the first week of January, 1991. Three weeks later, I attended a conference sponsored by UAW Local 879, "Competition vs. Solidarity in an Era of Free Trade", which was held at Macalester College in St. Paul thanks to Peter Rachleff, a history professor there.

This conference, allegedly first of its kind in the country, set the tone for much that has followed. We had three young labor leaders from Mexico—Raul Escobar, Jose Santos Martinez, Hector de la Cueva—who finally were given visas to enter the United States after Local 879's Tom Laney contacted most of the Minnesota Congressional delegation. They told of their struggle for union democracy at Ford of Mexico's Cuautitlan assembly plant and wore black ribbons in commemoration of their slain brother, Cleto Nigno. We had a group of Canadians from Winnipeg—Jim Silver, Bob Ages, Susan Spratt—ready to share with us their considerable knowledge and experience of free trade. We had some American labor people—Joe Fahey, Jack Hedrick, Mary McGinn, Matt Witt—attending from distant places, along with David Morris, Mark Ritchie, and many other local people.

An organization was formed as a result of this conference called Minnesota Fair Trade Coalition. Lynn Hinkle, Larry Dunham, Jim Mangan, Kristin Dawkins, Rachel Lord, Larry Weiss, and Dave Butcher, from Pequot Lakes, Minn., were some of the regulars at our steering-committee meetings. We twice met with Minnesota Attorney General Skip Humphrey at the time of his trip to Mexico with a human-rights delegation, and once with an Hispanic neighborhood group in West St. Paul. Coalition members held a press conference at the state capitol in St. Paul, featuring U.S. Senator Paul Wellstone, to express opposition to "fast-track" extension. The issue was beginning to attract public attention.

A group of us piled into a rented van and drove down to Chicago to participate in public hearings of the U.S. International Trade Commission on April 10th. Six people shared two rooms at the Knickerbocker Hotel, and, between us, gave three of the testimonies heard by the Commission that day, including Larry Dunham's stirring, impromptu narrative of his experience with unemployment and work with a temporary-help agency. Tom Laney and Ted LaValley flew directly from Chicago to Mexico City to participate in a continental meeting of free-trade opponents.

Two weeks later, some of the same people took another van and this time drove to the Hyatt Regency Hotel in Dearborn, Michigan, for the Labor Notes conference. We saw old friends from previous gatherings, including Jose Santos and Hector de la Cueva from Mexico, and heard the Teamsters' Ron Carey speak. The workshops on the U.S.-Mexico Free-Trade Agreement, at which Local 879 people made presentations, were some of the liveliest and best attended ones of the conference.

I had read in a book published by the Lawyers Committee for Human Rights that anyone could file a petition with a committee in the U.S. Trade Representative's office challenging a country's right to receive trade benefits under the Generalized System of Preferences (GSP) if the country violated internationally recognized worker rights. Tom Laney, Jose Quintana, and I decided to make the challenge in Mexico's case. We had plenty of evidence to document worker-rights violations at the Cuautitlan Ford plant. Dan LaBotz, at the Labor Notes conference, and Pharis Harvey, his publisher, gave permission to use additional materials from Dan's yet unpublished book on Mexican labor practices. A Minneapolis attorney, Dan Gerdts, helped with preparation of the petition. The lengthy petition, and the twenty required copies, were in the mail by May 15th.

A letter arrived asking for volunteers to be international observers at the court-ordered union election that would be taking place at the Cuautitlan plant on June 3rd. I answered the call as did Skip Pepin of Local 879. Equipped with camcorders, we spent 20 hours standing outside the plant gates waiting for tidbits of information about the election held inside the plant. Matt Witt translated for us. Some

2,000 police in riot gear guarded company property as supporters of COR, the challenging union, chanted slogans and made speeches. The incumbent union, CTM, won by a margin of 1,325 votes to 1,112. There was, however, evidence of fraud.

While pausing for lunch in the early afternoon, Matt Witt said something to Skip and me which left an impression. He suggested that individuals can indeed be effective in influencing political situations. Most people, he said, make the mistake of trying to change the world by petitioning large bureaucratic organizations. That approach seldom works. Instead, the important thing is action that puts pressure on those organizations. A group is defined not merely by how many members it has but what it does. Even a small group of people, through action, can create its own gravitational force that will sooner or later require the larger organizations to adjust. That is why it was important that we personally came to Mexico.

On the following day, I had a chance to visit the offices of Frente Autentico Trabajo, an independent labor federation, to meet Manuel Garcia Urrutia, Alfredo Dominguez, Bertha Lujan, and Alejandro Quiroz who were members of the Mexican committee (RMALC) opposed to free trade. We had a long and interesting conversation that carried through a late-afternoon lunch at a nearby restaurant. Wednesday morning, there was time for me to stroll through Chapultepec Park and do a quick tour of the Museo Nacional de Antropologia before heading for the airport and the return flight to the United States. Two weeks later, my lost luggage containing my only change of clothes, which had not arrived in Mexico City, was returned to the Minneapolis-St. Paul airport.

In August, I flew east for a two-week visit with family members and made side trips to see two advocates of shorter work hours, Barbara Brandt in Boston and Fred Gaboury in New York. Then I drove down to Washington, D.C., to visit some Congressional offices, the AFL-CIO, ILO, International Labor Rights Education and Research Fund, and Neil and Wendy Kotler. While in Washington, I learned that the U.S. Trade Representative had rejected the GSP petition our group had submitted in May. Having now waited over four months to receive the legally mandated statement of reasons for the rejection, we intend soon to send letters of rebuttal to all members of Congress.

The Minnesota Fair Trade Coalition hosted a national conference on free trade in the first week of September. Manuel Garcia flew up from Mexico City. Rebekah Greenwald drove in from Washington, D.C. to attend this conference and her brother's wedding. Jim Benn and Laurie Michalowski of Chicago, Craig Merrilees and Frank Martin del Campo of San Francisco, Mary McGinn and Pete Kelly of Detroit, Nelson Salinas of Miami, Jerry Tucker of Missouri, Les LaFleur of Massachusetts, Steve Hecker of Oregon, Bruce Allen of Ontario, Bob Ages of Winnipeg, Lori Wallach and Doug Hellinger of Washington, D.C., and Dan Leahy of Olympia, Washington, among others, all gathered in the Macalester College chapel to consider issues related to free trade, discuss the formation of a national network, and hear Bishop Tom Gumbleton of Detroit deliver the principal talk. This conference inspired Dan Leahy to organize fair-trade conferences of his own on the west coast.

In the fall, we became serious about local organization. The Minnesota Fair Trade Coalition established formal committees and received an infusion of fresh blood. A new group of people including Barb Kesler, Mark Thisius, Pia Sass, Faye Hamm, Joe Burns, Steve Peterson, Chris Moon, and Rocky, a Viet Nam vet, brought renewed energy and purpose to our enterprise. With the help of a spirited group of housing activists, Up and Out of Poverty St. Paul, we picketed the Minneapolis headquarters of Green Giant to protest the failure to install waste-water treatment facilities at their food-processing plant in Irapuato, Mexico, and, in the process, learned that the company planned to install the long-promised facilities in early 1992. A month later, in subzero temperatures, we attended the Christmas open-house at the Minnesota Governor's mansion and had some colorful and frank exchanges with the Governor himself that were shared with local television audiences.

In October, Raul Escobar came up from Mexico to address the Minnesota AFL-CIO state convention. He stayed with Tom and Barb Laney, and gave us an informal Spanish lesson at dinner one evening. Tom called Raul a "cine estrella" (movie star) after watching his dynamic convention performance on videotape. Tom Laney, Rod Haworth, Ted la Valley, and I attended yet another two-day conference on the North American Free-Trade Agreement at the Minneapolis convention center in late November. Contrary to earlier expectations, this one was unique in providing a good balance of views between supporters and opponents of the proposed agreement. And, finally, there was a chance to meet Pharis Harvey.

In the course of these various activities, I collected a mountain of literature, videotapes, etc., about the free-trade issue, and from these and other materials wrote a book. I am grateful to Mark Ritchie for a discussion helping to clarify some concepts, to Donna Montgomery, Pat Ricci, and other friends at Minnesota Independent Publishers Association who helped with the publishing end, and artist Dick Perlich and bookseller J.T. Stout, and, of course, to my many comrades in arms, both local and international, who have carried on the good fight during much of this past year.

Minneapolis, Minnesota
December 29, 1991

A Declaration

We, trade unionists from Mexico, Canada, and the United States, declare our solidarity with each other and against the prospective "free-trade" agreement between Mexico and the United States to which Canada may become a party. A U.S.-Mexico free-trade agreement would be bad for Mexican workers. A U.S.-Mexico free-trade agreement would be bad for U.S. workers. A U.S.-Mexico free-trade agreement would compound the damage done to Canadian workers from Canada's previous free-trade agreement with the United States.

In reality, such an agreement would further destabilize employment and living standards in all three countries. It is a pact between the economic and political elites of North America to maximize their personal privileges at the expense of their fellow citizens. It is an attack on the social contract and on the powers of government itself by a structure of financial interests that has outgrown any restraints upon itself.

We, the undersigned, continue to believe in our countries. We continue to believe in the democratic process. We believe in the power of free unions. We believe in sentiments of human decency, justice, and love that can overcome the worst sorts of corruption. While we favor closer contact between our three countries including expanded trade, we oppose the so-called "free trade" agreement between Mexico and the United States, and would urge the U.S. Congress to deny the President "fast-track" authority in this matter.

Signed in St. Paul, Minnesota, on January 27, 1991, by—

STATEMENT OF
JIM SILVER

We Canadians are getting clobbered by the (U.S.-Canada) Free-Trade Agreement. And, what the Free-Trade Agreement is doing to us I expect that the U.S.-Mexico agreement will do to you in short order. The Free-Trade Agreement is not really about trade but more about limiting the role of government, tying the hands of the state, and preventing it from doing various things. The agreement is not as much about tariff barriers as about nontariff barriers.

With respect to energy, for example, the Canada-U.S. Free-Trade Agreement says that the Canadian government cannot restrict the output or outflow of energy resources, cannot impose border taxes on the outflow, cannot set a minimum price, cannot charge Canadians a lower price than foreign buyers, and, most importantly, cannot cut off the United States in times of emergency. In other words, we could be short of energy while having to continue to sell to the United States. What Reagan and Mulroney did, then, in signing the Free-Trade Agreement was to stand at the border and turn a big wheel that opened the sluice gates allowing our resources to slush out of Canada and into the United States. And presumably that's what the U.S.-Mexico deal is about, too.

With respect to investment, American companies are now entitled to national treatment; they must be treated the same as Canadian companies. We cannot screen foreign investments to determine whether or not they benefit Canada unless the investment is in excess of $150 million. We cannot place performance requirements on foreign investments—i.e., require a certain amount of Canadian content. In these kinds of matters, the hands of our government are tied. All is turned over to the marketplace. The market is merely a euphemism for multinational corporations.

With respect to social programs, the Free-Trade Agreement severely restricts our ability to put new programs in place and, as a result of "harmonization"—creating a "level playing field" between Canada and the United States—our existing programs are also at risk. What we have in the Free-Trade Agreement has been called a "charter of rights for multinational corporations".

The impact on jobs has been catastrophic. Statistics Canada estimates that 239,000 manufacturing jobs have been lost in the past two years. The Canadian Labor Congress estimates that around 226,000 jobs have been lost. These are probably underestimates because they do not reflect the smaller companies that have been forced to close as a result of the Free-Trade Agreement.

Our economy is structured in an unusual way, being primarily a branch-plant economy. The companies located in Canada have names that you would recognize—they are your American companies. They came in initially because we had tariff barriers. Their function was to jump over those barriers. Once the tariff barriers came down, the companies left. There was no point in their existing in Canada any longer. In some cases, they have simply closed and let the Canadian market be supplied from the United States. In other cases, they have relocated—to Buffalo, to the sunbelt, to the maquiladoras—leaving behind a warehouse, a sales office, and precious few jobs.

In all things, what the Free-Trade Agreement between Canada and the United States did was to force us down to the lowest common denominator. A shift is taking place in the tax burden because Canadian corporations cannot compete against U.S. corporations which pay a lower tax. Therefore, we must lower our corporate taxes in order to compete. If the government refuses to cut corporate taxes, then we'll have to close and you'll lose jobs. So there is downward pressure. There is downward pressure on wage levels, downward pressure on benefits, downward pressure on corporate taxes, and downward pressure on social programs. In short, the Free-Trade Agreement is part of a larger economic and political package, comprising a neo-conservative agenda, which includes privatization, deregulation, contracting out, and dramatic cuts in government programs.

What is happening in Canada is that the structures that bind us as a nation—the horizontal, East-West links that made Canada—are being gutted. There are cuts to Via Rail, cuts to the Canadian Broadcasting Corporation, cuts to health spending, and cuts to education.

All these horizontal links are being loosened while at the same time the North-South ties with the United States are being tightened to accommodate the demands of the large corporations.

Jim Silver is a professor of political science at the University of Winnipeg and editor of Canadian Dimension magazine.

STATEMENT OF HECTOR DE LA CUEVA

President Salinas said in his State of the Union message that he hoped Mexico would cease to be part of the Third World but instead become a First World country. He apparently did not mean that there should be economic development that would make Mexico equal to the more developed countries, but instead was talking about integrating into the First World—the United States—through a process that will be completed in the Free-Trade Agreement. So we would be part of the First World in the same sense that Puerto Rico is part of the First World.

In any event, the Mexican government has been preparing for this agreement for the last five years. It has created a national productivity agreement, or "National Solidarity Program", which is a scheme to take away earned benefits and replace them with charity or so-called "safety net" programs. For some time now, there has been a commercial opening of this country to foreign products and investment, which has affected Mexican agriculture and industrial sectors such as textiles, shoes, electronics, and toy manufactures. It is estimated that 110,000 Mexican workers have lost their jobs because of the trade openings. Mexican companies have been taken over by U.S. companies, such as when Pepsi Cola swallowed a major cookie manufacturer.

In recent years, the number of workers in predominantly U.S.-owned maquiladora assembly plants has increased from 100,000 to about 500,000. This obviously affects U.S. and Canadian workers through plant closings. However, the maquiladora system also affects Mexican workers because, since the maquiladora workers do not have decent wages or benefits, there is pressure on other, more privileged Mexican workers to accept concessions. Meanwhile, there is a fierce attack on union contracts in the name of improving productivity. Low wages are maintained in the name of maintaining national competitiveness. So we are facing not only the traditionally lower Mexican wage but an actual drop in buying power of more than 50% in the last eight years.

Even worse is the attack upon labor rights in Mexico. While the government uses words like "modernization" to describe its plan to change labor relations, what actually has happened is increased use of the police to attack workers' movements. Last month, the government gave the Secretary of Labor more power to decide which union leaderships to recognize and which not to recognize. It would be impossible to give you a complete list of incidents during the last two years in which workers have been taken prisoner, faced police action, been fired, or where the government has ruled their strikes to be illegal. Mexican workers have occasionally experienced violence at the hands of the government and CTM, the government-affiliated labor federation. The struggle at Ford, including a whole series of manipulations by the government, would be an example.

The Free-Trade Agreement is a form of blackmail against workers in all three countries. It is a way of blackmailing U.S. and Canadian workers into accepting a lower standard of living. It is a way of blackmailing and threatening Mexican workers to continue to accept miserable working conditions in order to have jobs. So we are opposed to the signing of a Free-Trade Agreement, especially in the form being discussed.

At the same time we are confronted with a continuing process of economic integration between the three countries. We have to act in very practical ways to confront the repressive strategy of employers with programs of solidarity between workers in the three countries. I feel that the type of action taken on January 8th in connection with the Ford workers' "International Day of Justice" points the way to what is needed. In short, our task as workers is to create "solidarity without borders".

Hector de la Cueva is a researcher with Centro de Investigacion Laboral y Asesoria Sindical in Mexico City. He formerly worked at the Cuautitlan Ford assembly plant.

STATEMENT OF
JOE FAHEY

I live and work in the community of Watsonville, California, where I represent the 4,000 members of Teamsters Local 912. Watsonville is located between Monterey and Santa Cruz at the head of the great Salinas valley which has provided much of the United States with vegetables for many years. It was the setting for John Steinbeck's *In Dubious Battle*.

Our community's agricultural base has made it the home of many ethnic groups: Mexicans, Chinese, Filipinos, Italians, and Yugoslavs, among others. These people all came to work the land, and, since World War II, to work in plants that process the fruits and vegetables that don't go to fresh market. This work is now leaving. Our community is being hurt by decisions being made in corporate board rooms thousands of miles from here. Small companies are closing or being taken over by huge transnational corporations that are running away.

Green Giant was first to head to Mexico. In 1983 they were bought by Pillsbury which opened a vegetable processing facility in Irapuato and eliminated 800 jobs in Watsonville. In 1989 Pillsbury was taken over by Grand Metropolitan, a giant English holding company which decided to use broccoli and cauliflower grown in Mexico. This eliminated another 380 Watsonville workers. Other companies have followed Green Giant's example. Today, about 9,000 fewer people in the Watsonville area are working in the food and related industries.

While the private sector has benefited from running away from our town, the public is paying for it. Workers pay with their livelihoods. Taxpayers pay to retrain them and provide them with extended unemployment benefits, Medical care, food stamps, etc. More of the local tax burden is taken up by individual taxpayers as the corporations flee. The residents and the remaining food processors (who aren't big enough to move) pay an increased share of costs, for instance, for the $20 million sewage-treatment plant that was mandated by the EPA to clean waste water from Green Giant's and the other departing employers' former operations.

People in Irapuato, Mexico, pay in another way. Clean water there is in short supply. The rivers running through town are severely polluted by the untreated sewage of 500,000 inhabitants and by industrial wastes from factories and a nearby oil refinery. Green Giant, free of local regulation, is drilling more than 450 feet deep to pump out about a million gallons a day of potable water in order to clean and wash exported vegetables. They currently discharge the dirty water, untreated, back into the polluted river.

The children of Irapuato pay too. Because of their parents' declining wages, more of them are entering the work force at an early age. Indeed, the Mexican public has seen a vast reduction in standard of living since 1982 when foreign investment was liberalized. The foreign companies actually pay less in annual wages to their workers than Mexican employers do. To get around a constitutional requirement to pay their workers a share of the profits, the TNC's juggle their books to show no profitability from Mexican operations.

This story is not unique to Watsonville, Irapuato, or the food processing industry. We are seeing our communities throughout the United States and the world being degraded by private-sector decision making on a large scale. Given the diversification and resources of the corporate giants, it's difficult for isolated local struggles to be effective in combating their abuse. It is becoming increasingly clear to those of us who have fought this kind of fight, that the tactics of taking on one employer at a time will not be effective in this "New World Order". To have some control over our communities, we must be able to change laws.

Now, just as this realization is being made, the transnational corporations with the help of their friends in government want to change the rules of the game. This is what Free Trade with Mexico is about. This is what GATT is about. Corporations want governments to make it even easier for them to run away from environmental standards, worker protections, and any but the lowest standards of community responsibility. By virtue of trade agreements, they want the right to ignore the rules of fair conduct established by local, state and even national governments. They want a system, for instance, that would overrule Californians who pass tougher environmental initiatives.

I would suggest that anyone who is interested in maintaining or improving our standard of living or protecting the planet needs to understand what we're up against. To fight this "free trade" menace, we need a broad vision of community improvement that involves workers, environmentalists, human-rights activists, and other public-spirited persons in the United States, Mexico, Canada, and everywhere else. The globalization of Capital makes necessary a corresponding globalization of Labor, whose "solidarity", however, must now include almost everyone. The transnational corporations are in a better position than before to take advantage of narrow self-interests and play us off against each other. We must resist these manipulations in concert with our brothers and sisters throughout the world. Economic forces seem to be creating a situation where, in order to change our own communities, we now have to change the entire world!

Joe Fahey is president of Teamsters Local 912 in Watsonville, Calif., which was affected by Green Giant's move of certain food-processing operations to Mexico.

STATEMENT OF
RAUL ESCOBAR

In regard to a free-trade agreement, the Mexican government is basically saying to foreign corporations that Mexico is a good place to come and do business because they can repress the workers. Therefore, they say the companies will find labor peace. I remember an incident in February 1990, when we met with Fidel Velazquez (national leader of CTM, the Confederation of Mexican Workers) during contract negotiations with the Ford plant in Chihuahua. While we were talking, the governor of Chihuahua called and said that he wanted the conflict resolved at the plant. Fidel Velazquez replied: "Don't worry about it, we'll sign the contract tonight. We've just got to give these guys their time." This illustrates how CTM handles negotiations.

We think that having unelected union leadership is going to cause a lot of problems, when those leaders negotiate away the rights and benefits of the workers. The workers will not be satisfied with this kind of negotiation, and there will not be labor peace. So, if the companies are looking for worldwide competitiveness, they are not going to find it because workers' needs will not be satisfied with a wage that pays $3.00 a day, which is the minimum wage in Mexico. The foreign companies will not find the peace or productivity they expect from Mexican workers until there is justice in terms of wages, benefits, and jobs.

That is our struggle, our two demands being union democracy and just wages for Ford workers. We are also aware that it has been the Mexican government's policy to maintain low wages because that is the way they bring in the foreign companies. The free-trade agreement will not be a treaty among equals. The only thing that Mexico can offer is its cheap labor — besides, of course, its natural resources, which the foreign companies also want to exploit.

We have had to confront many problems during the past year and a half, and have been willing to look for real solutions. However, we have found the authorities unwilling to reciprocate. In dealings with workers, they have violated the Constitution of the Mexican Republic. Those persons who killed our brother, Cleto Nigno, are now free. So justice has not come about yet.

It is important for us workers to be concerned about our union organization and about workers' living conditions when facing this kind of treaty or agreement. In our Ford plant, we have adopted a slogan: "The hands that Cleto brought together will never be separated." And we believe this is echoed by the slogan of Canadian and U.S. workers when they say: "An injury to one is an injury to all." The problem is not between countries; we are repressed and exploited in all countries. We owe it to those who have died to keep this struggle standing and alive.

Raul Escobar Briones is a member of the negotiating committee of the Ford Workers Democratic Movement at the Cuautitlan plant and its principal spokesman.

STATEMENT OF
TOM LANEY

In 1986 social activists in our local union organized a seminar on the U.S. Catholic Bishops' Pastoral Letter on the Economy because we were concerned about the lack of social justice work within the trade unions. The Pastoral presented a critical view of American corporate competitive behavior and called for a "preferential option for the poor."

At that time, what was left of the American labor movement was facing destructive forces. The trade union bureaucracy was tightening its embrace of the corporate agenda. National unions including the United Auto Workers were agreeing to contracts that placed local unions in competition with one another. They signed "sourcing" agreements that gave the companies the right to outsource auto work to plants based on "comparative advantage". These agreements reflect the same principle which drives President Bush toward "free trade" with Mexico. You could call it a "preferential option for the wealthy."

This "preferential option for the wealthy" means that the division between rich and poor will widen as business continues to seek the weakest social situations in our cities, states, countries and world. That is what our Canadian friends have experienced with free trade. That is what we ourselves can expect if the Bush trade agenda is approved.

I have known Bill McGaughey for about 10 years. We met because he is a proponent for a shorter work-week, an issue that engaged many U.S. trade unionists before we were sucked up in retreat. But I did not know Bill well until the emergence of the North American Free Trade issue. Now the prospect of the NAFTA has given me the opportunity to become a friend of Bill McGaughey. He's one of those intellectuals with an activist heart. This book will help to understand who wins and who loses if Bush, Salinas and Mulroney have their way with North American trade.

In the past year, I have met dozens of farmers, workers, environmentalists, and even some union bureaucrats who are working their hardest to build Solidarity in North America. Activists in Mexico, Canada and the United States are crisscrossing the continent building networks and coalitions to promote fair legislation, better communications and, most importantly, friendship. As my friend Jim Benn puts it, we have in "some weird way" come together with workers in other cities and countries who are being hurt by the same transnational corporations who have damaged so many U.S. workers. Burned-out rank and filers in the U.S. are being revitalized by the courage, determination and strategies of democratic unionists in Mexico. Only Solidarity can bring us trade agreements that provide real human development.

Tom Laney is recording secretary of U.A.W. Local 879 in St. Paul, Minn., and a representative of the MEXUSCAN Solidarity Network committee.

STATEMENT OF
SUSAN SPRATT

We began our movement in 1985 when we learned that the Canadian government was holding discussions with the United States concerning free trade. The leaders of several large organizations assembled that year in Ottawa, including the Council of Canadians, the Canadian Labor Congress, and several churches, to talk about its problems.

What came of this was that coalitions sprang up around the country—coalitions of labor, church organizations, educators, antipoverty groups, social-justice organizations, and individual unions in each city—not just the large umbrella groups. The Canadian Auto Workers played an instrumental part in all of them, though. It was the first time, I believe, since the Depression that we have had such a coalition in Canada. The large groups in Ottawa made the political decisions and plotted strategy, but it was the grass-roots coalitions in the various cities that did the mobilization, turned out the people, and educated them on the free-trade deal.

People in Canada wanted information about the agreement. We had to research it and come up with statistics to support our case, because everywhere we went the supporters of free trade told us that we were hysterical, we were emotional, and we were trying to mislead the Canadian public. As a trade unionist, I remember that workers on the shop floor were skeptical. OK, they said, you're telling us this is a bad deal and telling us why it's a bad deal. But we also want to know what our churches think of it, we want to know what other organizations think of it—because labor is always against this stuff. That was the importance of forming coalitions.

I want to explain how the media approached this issue and treated the various segments of the community. Basically, labor was treated as a narrow special interest which was taking care of its members' narrow concerns, and that only. When our leaders addressed the broader social questions or anything that went beyond what the media calls "bread-and-butter issues", they received little coverage. Employers, on the other hand, were making a concerted effort to promote free trade. They were bringing workers into lunchrooms and telling them that if they did not vote for free trade they would be voting against their jobs.

Day after day, business leaders were paraded before us in the media explaining how they would be forced to rethink their investment plans if the free-trade agreement were not approved. We were told that the stock market would crash. Instead of being presented for what they were — men who were demanding that their personal and business interests be considered paramount — these business leaders were treated as guardians of the national interest. And they appeared to have almost unlimited access to the media.

In Manitoba, the province I come from, twelve economists put out a press release saying they were opposed to free trade and explaining why. It received no mention in the newspaper. But when one right-wing economist came out and said what a great deal free trade was, his comments received front-page coverage. This is not to say that the press did not run some articles in which critics of the free trade were allowed to voice their concerns. In such cases, though, the paper usually included comments and rebuttals from free-trade boosters. On the other hand, the newspapers made little effort to achieve a balance of opinion in the pro-trade articles that they frequently ran. Some playing fields, as we have seen, were simply not meant to be level.

On the positive side, I can say with some pride that the Pro-Canada Network still exists. We're still fighting and we're still taking on the people who support free trade, although they refuse to debate with us now. They wanted to debate with us during the national election, but they sure don't want to debate with us now.

Susan Spratt is an organizer for the Canadian Association of Industrial, Mechanical and Allied Workers (CAIMAW) in Winnipeg. She and her husband, Bob Ages, are active in CHOICES, the Manitoba affiliate of Action Canada Network.

STATEMENT OF JOSE QUINTANA

I regard free trade as an unjust and abusive arrangement which will destabilize national economies and impoverish the working-class people in all countries. A Free-Trade Agreement, if approved, can be expected to bring poverty, mass migrations, and greater disparities of income. It might also create an epidemic of child-labor practices in third-world countries.

Working people in Mexico, the United States, and Canada have strong feelings for their families and for their countries. They still have hope for the improvement of future generations. They must be allowed to pursue and reach their goals without the threat of losing their jobs in an international economic rat-race. Martin Luther King once said: "Injustice anywhere is a threat to justice everywhere."

A Free-Trade Agreement would not benefit the people in the three countries, but only the transnational companies. Workers in Canada and the United States would have to work harder and for longer hours while living in fear of losing their jobs. Workers in Mexico would continue to be exploited for a few pesos to support their families. Many Mexican children would have to sacrifice their educations to help supplement their already menial family incomes.

A Free-Trade Agreement would also create an atmosphere of anger and meanness as workers from different ethnic groups or different countries are pitted against each other. In the name of competitiveness, more of us would be working for a minimum wage. Organized labor would continue to take major losses. Employers would be quick to get rid of the unions, cut wages, and void contracts. If the unions went out on strike, they would close plants and move to Mexico or somewhere else. Governments would become increasingly undemocratic.

Therefore, I see the Free-Trade Agreement as being more than a commercial arrangement. It really touches the totality of our lives.

That being the case, the agreement should make provision for everything essential to our lives and not leave anything out. Congress must debate the whole range of issues affecting the peace, happiness, and prosperity of us and our families. We the people must demand that a fair and complete debate take place in Congress, as so much depends on their decision. God bless the three North American countries!

Jose Quintana is a member of UAW Local 879 and a member of its Civil Rights committee.

NOTES

Part One

1. "Accord could boost continental economy" (editorial), St. Paul *Pioneer Press* (February 6, 1991), p. 10A.

2. "The fast-track stakes" (editorial), *Wall Street Journal* (May 23, 1991), p. A14.

3. *Wall Street Journal* (May 2, 1991), p. A5. Quotes Roderick de Arment, Deputy Secretary of Labor

4. "Mexico: a new economic era", *Business Week* (November 12, 1990), p. 108.

5. U.S. International Trade Commission, *The likely impact on the United States of a free trade agreement with Mexico*, Publication 2353, report to House Ways and Means Committee and Senate Finance Committee (February 1991), p. 2–1. See also: Jeffrey J. Schott, Free Trade Areas and U.S. Trade Policy, pp. 1–58.

6. Raymond M. Hebert, "European elections show shared dream", *Winnipeg Free Press* (July 10, 1989), p. 7.

7. See booklet, *"$4 a day, no way!"*, published by American Education Labor Center, 2000 P Street N.W., suite 300, Washington, DC 20036

8. U.S. International Trade Commission, *The likely impact of a free trade agreement*, pp. xix, xx. Quotes U.S. Department of State telegram, Mexico City, October 4, 1990.

9. *Business Week* (November 12, 1990), p. 108. See also: Tim Ferguson, "Sun belt agriculture borders on nervousness", *Wall Street Journal* (February 5, 1991), p. A19.

10. "Canada to press for access to banks in talks on North American trade pact", *Wall Street Journal* (June 10, 1991), p. B6.

11. "U.S., Mexico, Canada seek to revive trade talks", *Wall Street Journal* (October 24, 1991), p. A13.

12. "Corn may be snag in trade talks by Mexico, U.S.," *Wall Street Journal* (December 27, 1991), p. A4

13. 100th Congress of the United States, *U.S.-Canada Free Trade Agreement*, House Document 100–216; pp. iii-iv; letter of transmittal from President Ronald Reagan to Speaker of the House Jim Wright, July 25, 1988.

14. U.S. Department of Commerce, *United States Trade Performance in 1988* (September 1989), Appendix A, Ann H. Hughes, "U.S.-Canada Free Trade Agreement", pp. 57–60.

15. Information given by Mahmood Zaidi, University of Minnesota, in a talk at First Unitarian Society in Minneapolis in January 1991.

16. *Federal Register*, Vol. 56, No. 136 (July 16, 1991), p. 32455.

17. U.S. International Trade Commission hearings, "Probable economic effect on U.S. industries and consumers of a free-trade agreement between the United States and Mexico", on April 10, 1991, at the Knickerbocker Hotel in Chicago. Testimony of Harry A. Foster, secretary-manager, Michigan Asparagus Growers; William Libman, secretary-treasurer, Libman Co., Arcola, Illinois; Donald Marquart, exec. vice president, Square D Co., Chicago.

18. "Mexico poll on trade plan", *Wall Street Journal* (October 31, 1991), p. A14. Poll was taken by Mexico's National Chamber of Commerce of Industries.

19. Lori Wallach and Tom Hilliard, Public Citizen's Congress Watch, *The consumer and environmental case against fast track* (Washington D.C.: May 1991), pp. 1, 18. See also: *GATT final draft text*, section on technical barriers to trade, pp. 44–72.

20. Ibid., p. 19. See also: *GATT final draft text*, "Sanitary and phytosanitary measures", Appendix D, p. 166.

21. Ibid., pp. 19–20. See also: Steven Shrybman, *Memorandum on GATT draft proposal*, Brussels, December 3, 1990; *GATT final draft text*, Article 2.9.1–4, Article 3.

22. Ibid., pp. 20–21. See also: *GATT final draft text*, Article 4.1.

23. Quoted in David Morris, *The Trade Papers, Trading our Future: Talking back to GATT* (Washington: Institute for Local Self-Reliance, 1991), p. 11.

24. Steven Shrybman, "Free trade and the environment", *Pro- Canada Dossier* (January-February, 1991), p. 7.

25. "Nestle ends 3rd world sales pitch", St. Paul *Pioneer Press* (January 27, 1984)

26. Morris, *The Trade Papers*, p. 14.

27. Shrybman, "Free trade and the environment", p. 6.

28. "All-American brawl", *U.S. News & World Report* (June 10, 1991), p. 30.

29. Morris, *The Trade Papers*, pp. 12–13.

30. Ibid., p. 12, 14–15. See also *Re: Disposable Beer Cans: E.C. Commission vs. Denmark*, the Court of European Justice, September 20, 1989.

31. Morris, *The Trade Papers*, p. 12.

32. U.S. International Trade Commission, *The likely impact of a free trade agreement*, p. 2–2.

33. U.S. Department of Commerce, *U.S. Foreign Trade Highlights 1990* (April 1991), pp. 11, 15.

34. U.S. International Trade Commission, *The likely impact of a free trade agreement*, p. 2–3.

35. U.S. Department of Commerce, *United States Trade Performance in 1988*, p. 57.

36. Robin Alexander, *Memorandum to the General Executive Board, United Electrical, Radio and Machine Workers of America* (November 28, 1990), pp. 6–7.

37. "Canadians seeking rescue from leader they 'despise' ", (Minneapolis) *Star Tribune* (November 14, 1991), p. 4A. Based on Gallup Poll.

38. John Dillon, "Trade talks are the key to the 'new world order' ", *Pro-Canada Dossier* (March-April, 1991), pp. 17- 18.

39. Ibid., pp. 16–17.

40. Keith Martin, Canadian Chamber of Commerce, "The North American Free Trade Negotiations and the Canada-United States Free Trade Agreement: Revisiting Unfinished Business", p. 2. A paper presented at a conference held in Minneapolis, Minn., on November 19–20, 1991, sponsored by Twin City Area Labor-Management Council and the University of Minnesota Industrial Relations Center, entitled "North American Free Trade: Labor, Industry and Government Policy Perspectives."

41. Laurell Ritchie, Common Frontiers (Toronto), testimony presented at seminar on "Social Issues", conference on "North American Free Trade: Labor, Industry and Government Policy Perspectives", Minneapolis, November 20, 1991.

42. Calman Cohen, Emergency Committee for American Trade, testimony presented at seminar on "The Impact of Free Trade on Industry", conference on "North American Free Trade", Minneapolis, November 20, 1991.

43. "Mexico: a new era", *Business Week* (November 12, 1990), p. 108.

44. U.S. International Trade Commission, *The likely impact of a free trade agreement*, p. 2–4. See also: Jeffrey Schott, "The Mexican free trade illusion", *The International Economy*(June-July, 1990), p. 32; submission to Commission by Instituto Technologico Autonomo de Mexico on November 29, 1990.

45. Calman Cohen, testimony presented at conference on "North American Free Trade", Minneapolis, November 20, 1991.

46. Kay R. Whitmore, "Snapshots of American Pioneers in Mexico", Manager's Journal, *Wall Street Journal* (May 13, 1991).

47. "Free Trade or Free Workers?", fact sheet prepared by American Labor Education Center, Washington, D.C., January 1991.

48. Christopher Whalen, letter to the editor, *Wall Street Journal*(April 30, 1991).

49. "The coming emergence of three giant trading blocs", International Monetary Fund, *IMF Survey* (April 1, 1991), p. 95.

50. Henry Ford, interview with Samuel Crowthers, *Monthly Labor Review* (December 1926), p. 1166.

51. Joe W. Pitts, "Pressing Mexico to protect intellectual property", *Wall Street Journal* (January 25, 1991), p. A11.

52. Susan W. Sanderson and Robert H. Hayes, "Mexico—opening ahead of eastern Europe", *Harvard Business Review* (September-October, 1990), p. 34, 40.

53. "Mexico braces for rush of U.S. lawyers", *Wall Street Journal* (October 10, 1991), p. B10.

54. "Is free trade with Mexico good or bad for the U.S.?", *Business Week* (November 12, 1990), p. 113.

55. Lloyd Bentsen, "Agreement with Mexico is an opportunity that United States can't afford to miss", Dallas *Morning News* (February 17, 1991).

56. Louis Uchitelle, "Outsiders' role in Mexico pact", Business Scene, *New York Times* (May 21, 1991), p. C2.

57. "Firms alter Mexican strategy", *New York Times* (September 22, 1991)

58. "GM plans to close 21 more factories, cut 74,000 jobs, slash capital spending", *Wall Street Journal* (December 19, 1991), p. A3; "Uncertainty of GM closing stirs tension", *Wall Street Journal* (December 20, 1991), p. A2.

59. *Free Trade or Free Workers?*, a memorandum prepared by American Labor Education Center, January 1991.

60. Quoted in Morris, *The Trade Papers*, p. 2.

61. "Who has special access to fast-tracked trade talks?", Public Citizens Congress Watch", appendix B to *The consumer and environmental case against fast track*, May 1991.

62. "Bush trade concessions pick up some support", New York *Times* (May 2, 1991)

63. "Congress extracted price for extension of president's trade-negotiating powers", *Wall Street Journal* (May 28, 1991), p. A2.

64. "Trade adjustment assistance — time for action, not false promises", AFL-CIO, Washington, D.C., *AFL-CIO Reviews the Issues*, Report No. 53, September 1991. See also: C. Michael Aho, Jonathan D. Aronson, *Trade Talks — America Better Listen!* (New York: Council on Foreign Relations, 1985), pp. 69–70.

65. Michael G. Matejka, alderman, Bloomington, Ill., testimony presented at U.S. International Trade Commission hearings in Chicago on April 10, 1991.

66. Mike Kostyal, Teamsters Local 912, Watsonville, Calif., personally told to the author during telephone conversation in November 1991.

67. *Labor Notes* (January 1992), News Watch, p. 4.

68. Public Citizen, Washington, D.C., *Why NEPA environmental impact statements are crucial: some potential health, safety and environmental impacts of Uruguay Round of GATT and North American Free Trade Agreement*, background paper presented with NEPA Lawsuit, August 1, 1991, p. 10.

69. Ibid., pp. 9–10. Quoted from Bush Administration's plan announced on May 1, 1991.

70. Seattle *Post-Intelligencer* (August 21, 1991), p. B5. Reports Carla Hills' press conference in Seattle on August 20, 1991.

71. Public Citizen, *NEPA Lawsuit*, August 1, 1991, background paper, p. 11.

72. Ibid., p. 2–3. See also: 16 U.S.C. 1531, 1821(e)(2)

73. Wallach and Hilliard, *Consumer and Environmental Case against Fast Track*, p. 15; "Two disputes cloud N. America trade talks", *Journal of Commerce* (September 5, 1991).

74. Public Citizen, press release, August 1, 1991, "Summary of Legal Arguments", pp. 1–2.

75. Public Citizen, *NEPA Lawsuit*, August 1, 1991, background paper, p. 12.

76. Paul A. Samuelson, *Economics*, Ninth Edition (New York: McGraw-Hill, 1973), p. 668.

77. "Atari to idle 1,700 at California site, move jobs to Asia", *Wall Street Journal* (February 23, 1983), p. 10.

78. Conversation during luncheon at conference, "North American Free Trade", Minneapolis, November 20, 1991.

79. Morris, *The Trade Papers*, p. 5.

80. Peter F. Drucker, "From world trade to world investment", *Wall Street Journal* (May 26, 1987), p. 32.

81. Ibid. See also: Peter F. Drucker, "Low wages no longer give competitive edge", *Wall Street Journal* (March 16, 1988), p. 30.

82. Peter F. Drucker, "Insulating the firm from currency exposure", *Wall Street Journal* (April 30, 1985), p. 30.

83. Quoted in Morris, *The Trade Papers*, p. 10.

84. Drucker, "Low wages", *Wall Street Journal*, (March 16, 1988), p. 30.

85. Perry D. Quick of Quick, Finan & Associates, letter to the editor, *Wall Street Journal* (April 26, 1988), p. 31.

86. B. Bruce-Briggs, Hudson Institute, "The coming overthrow of free trade", *Wall Street Journal* (February 24, 1983), p. 28.

87. Bernard Lewis, "The 'sick man' of today coughs closer to home", *Wall Street Journal* (December 26, 1991), p. 6.

88. "With communism dead, now it's capitalist vs. capitalist", *U.S. News & World Report* (December 30, 1991), p. 51.

89. Drucker, "Low wages", *Wall Street Journal* (March 16, 1988).

90. John Maynard Keynes, quoted in Morris, *The Trade Papers*, p. 8.

Part Two

1. "Canada's unions: progress in adversity", *International Labour Reports* (January-February, 1989), p. 7.

2. Robin Alexander, *Memo to executive board, United Electrical, Radio and Machine Workers*, November 28, 1990, p. 3.

3. Daniel LaBotz, *A Strangling Embrace: State Suppression of Labor Rights in Mexico* (Washington, D.C.: International Labor Rights Education

and Research Fund, 1992), chapter entitled "Historical Background of Mexican Labor", pp. 3–4.

4. Kim Moody, "Mexican-U.S. Economic Integration: Past, Present, Future", *Labor Notes* staff paper, fall 1990, pp. 4–5.

5. Ibid., p. 4. See also: Frente Autentico de Trabajo (FAT), Mexico City, "Dominant Trends of Mexico's Conjunction", September 1990, p. 2.

6. John Dillon, "Turning Mexico inside out", *Pro-Canada Dossier* (January-February, 1991), pp. 21–23. See also: Robin Alexander memo of November 28, 1990, quoting Kim Moody of *Labor Notes*.

7. Robin Alexander memo, November 28, 1990, p. 5.

8. Dillon, *Pro-Canada Dossier* (January-February, 1991), p. 21- 23.

9. Ibid.

10. Moody, *Labor Notes* staff paper, p. 7.

11. Alexander memo, p. 7.

12. Moody, *Labor Notes* staff paper, p. 10. Wage figures from *Handbook of Labor Statistics 1989*, p. 578. See also: FAT, "Dominant Trends", p. 9.

13. Alexander memo, p. 8; FAT, "Dominant Trends", p. 8.

14. "Latin crisis: with Mexico focusing on debt repayments, ports and roads suffer", *Wall Street Journal* (June 11, 1986), pp. 1, 26.

15. "Latin crisis: as debt turmoil ebbs and flows in Mexico, human misery persists", *Wall Street Journal* (June 12, 1986), p. 1.

16. U.S. International Trade Commission, *The likely impact of a free trade agreement*, p. 1–5, 1–8, 5–5, 5–6. See also: "Framework of principles and procedures for consultation regarding trade and investment relations", agreement between Mexico and the United States reached November 6, 1987.

17. La Botz, *A Strangling Embrace*, chapter 2, pp. 1, 4–5.

18. Ibid., chapter 2, pp. 1–2.

19. "Mexico's union boss, ally of Salinas, is a stumbling block in trade talks", *Wall Street Journal* (February 12, 1991), p. A8.

20. La Botz, *A Strangling Embrace*; chapters on labor struggle at the Cananea Mining Co., Modelo Brewery, PEMEX, and Tornel Rubber Company.

21. Ibid., chapter on Cuautitlan Ford workers.

22. *Labor Notes* (September 1991), News Watch, p. 4.

23. La Botz, *A Strangling Embrace*, chapter on maquiladoras. See also: *El Financiero* (January 7, 1991), footnote 6.

24. "Boom and despair: Mexican border towns are a magnet for foreign factories, workers and abysmal living conditions" by Sonia Nazario, *Wall Street Journal* (September 22, 1989), p. R26.

25. The Latin American Working Group (Toronto), *Open for Business: Canada – Mexico – U.S.*, L.A.W.G. Letter No. 45, January 1991, p. 10.

26. "Border boom's dirty residue imperils U.S. Mexico trade", *New York Times* (March 31, 1991), p. 16.

27. La Botz, *A Strangling Embrace*, chapter 2. See also: Diane Lund-

quist, the San Diego *Union* (May 28, 1991), p. 1; Jorge Carrillo, "Transformaciones en la industria maquiladora de exportacion".

28. Alan Brown, letter to the editor, *Star Tribune* (December 6, 1990).

29. Slide show by Jack Hedrick, UAW Local 249 (Kansas City, Mo.), at conference, "Competition vs. solidarity in an era of free trade", in St. Paul, Minn., January 26, 1991.

30. La Botz, *A Strangling Embrace*, chapter on maquiladoras, p. 11. See also: Jorge Carrillo and Alberto Hernandez, "Mujeres fronterizas en la industria maquiladora", p. 129–30.

31. "Boom and despair", *Wall Street Journal* (September 22, 1989), pp. R26–27.

32. La Botz, *A Strangling Embrace*, chapter on maquiladoras. From Carrillo, Transformaciones, p. 49.

33. "Weighing pros and cons of Asian processing zones", *ILO Information*, No. 3 (August 1983), p. 2. Report based on R. Maex, *Employment and multinationals in Asian export processing zones*, working paper No. 26 (Geneva: ILO, 1983).

34. La Botz, *A Strangling Embrace*, chapter on maquiladoras.

35. Deborah Bourque, "Women in the maquiladoras", *Pro-Canada Dossier* (January-February 1991), p. 33.

36. "Boom and despair", *Wall Street Journal* (September 22, 1989), p. R26.

37. New York *Times* (March 31, 1991), p. 16.

38. *Wall Street Journal* (September 22, 1989), p. R27.

39. Bruce Rubinstein, "Corporate Shangri-La", *City Pages* (December 26, 1990), p. 5

40. *Wall Street Journal* (September 22, 1989), p. R26.

41. New York *Times* (March 31, 1991), p. 16.

42. Ibid.

43. *Wall Street Journal* (September 22, 1989), p. R26-R27.

44. "Poisoning the border", *U.S. News & World Report* (May 6, 1991), p. 35.

45. David Morris, talk given at the Central America Resource Center in St. Paul, Minn. on March 23, 1991. See also: New York *Times* (March 31, 1991), p. 6.

46. Rubinstein, *City Pages* (December 26, 1990), p. 4.

47. Bill Cavitt, director, office of Canada, U.S. Department of Commerce, statement made at conference, "North American Free Trade", Minneapolis, November 19, 1991.

48. New York *Times* (March 31, 1991), p. 16.

49. LAWG Letter No. 45 (January 1991), p. 3. See also: John Ralston Saul, "Canada Today, Mexico Tomorrow" in Laurier Lapierre, ed., *If You Love this Country*, pp. 188–92.

50. "U.S., Canada and Mexico to negotiate a North American free-trade pact", *Wall Street Journal* (February 6, 1991), p. A8.

51. "Reagan, Mulroney sign U.S.-Canada trade pact", *Wall Street Journal* (January 4, 1988), p. 36.

52. "Bush, Mexican president discuss free trade", *Star Tribune* (April 8, 1991), p. 2A.

53. "Canada facing long, severe recession", *Star Tribune* (March 3, 1991), p. 1D.

54. *Pro-Canada Dossier* (January-February 1991), p. 9. Estimate by Bruce Campbell, Canadian Labour Congress.

55. Andrew Jackson, "The manufacturing crisis", *Action Canada Network Dossier* (September-October 1991), p. 5. Figures are from Statistics Canada Cat. 72–002 and Cat. 15–001. See also: "Southern exposure: Canada suffers exodus of jobs, investment and shoppers to U.S.", *Wall Street Journal* (June 20, 1991), p. 1.

56. Mary Williams Walsh, "The hard times are even harder north of the border", Los Angeles *Times* (February 24, 1991), p. D7.

57. Bruce Campbell, " goin' south — 2 years under free trade", *Canadian Dimension* (January-February 1991), p. 20–23.

58. Ibid., pp. 21–22.

59. "Canadian firms, fleeing the high costs at home, relocate south of the border," *Wall Street Journal* (February 7, 1991), p. A2.

60. *Canadian Dimension* (January-February 1991), p. 21–23.

61. *Pro-Canada Dossier* (January-February 1991), p. 8. Quotes letter to employees of Hartz Canada.

62. "Southern exposure", *Wall Street Journal* (June 20, 1991), p. 1.

63. *Canadian Dimension* (January-February 1991), pp. 18–19.

64. Scott Sinclair, *Free trade and regional development: two years on.* Article adapted for LAWG Letter, p. 20, from paper presented to the Coloquio Mexico-Canada sponsored by P.A.N., October 1990.

65. Ibid., p. 18. Quoted from *Canadian Forum* (June 1990), p. 10. See also: Andrew Anderson, "Piecemeal trade reform cited as dangerous", *Report on Free Trade*, May 21, 1990, p. 6; Sinclair, p. 21.

66. Steven Shrybman, *Selling the environment short: an environmental assessment of the first years of free trade between Canada and the United States*, pp. 1–4. Quotes federal minister for international trade, fall of 1987. Publication available from Action Canada Network.

67. Ibid., pp. 6–7.

68. Ibid., p. 5. From *Globe and Mail* (October 9, 1990), report on business.

69. Ibid., p. 8. See also: *Corrosion Proof Fittings, et al. vs. Environmental Protection Agency and William K. Reilly*: Brief of Canadian government, Fifth Circuit Court of Appeals, May 22, 1990.

70. Ibid., p. 9. See also: *GATT Fly*, "U.S. companies use FTA to attack regional and environmental aid", Toronto, September 1989.

71. Ibid., pp. 5–6. See also: *In the matter of Canada's landing requirement for Pacific coast salmon and herring*, October 16, 1989. 2TCT 7162.

72. Ibid., p. 9.

73. Ibid., Schedule 7, Chapter 7, *U.S.-Canada Free Trade Agreement* concerning pesticide regulation.

74. Ibid., pp. 9–10.

75. Maude Barlow, *Pro-Canada Dossier* (January-February 1991), pp. 4–5. Adapted from speech given at Canada-Mexico Encuentro, October 5, 1990.

76. Cuauhtemoc Cardenas, *Pro-Canada Dossier* (January-February 1991), p. 35. Speech given to the convention of the British Columbia Federation of Labor, Vancouver, November 30, 1990.

Part Three

1. Arnold Toynbee, *Civilization on Trial* (New York: Meridian Books, 1958), p. 153.

2. Mikhail Gorbachev, "Political report of the party central committee to the 27th Congress of the Community Party of the Soviet Union". *USA Today* (March 19, 1986), p. 5A. Paid advertisement of the Soviet embassy to the United States.

3. U.S. Department of Commerce, *Statistical Abstract of the United States 1988*, Table 508, p. 317; *Statistical Abstract 1979*, Table 587, p. 364.

4. Jude Wanniski, "The Laffer Curve and foreign policy", *Wall Street Journal* (March 2, 1981), p. 14.

5. Ibid.

6. St. Paul *Dispatch & Pioneer Press* (January 2, 1986), p. 11.

7. Victoria L. Hatter, "Who is buying developing countries' manufactures?", *United States Trade: Performance in 1985 and Outlook* (Washington: U.S. Department of Commerce, 1986), pp. 81–84.

8. Kenichi Ohmae, "Toward a regional globalism", *Wall Street Journal* (April 27, 1990), p. A12.

9. Adam Smith, *Wealth of Nations*, 1776. Quoted in Paul Samuelson, *Economics*, ninth edition, 1973, p. 41.

10. Adam Smith, *Wealth of Nations* (New Rochelle: Arlington House), pp. 293–325, p. 421

11. Lori Wallach and Tom Hilliard, *The consumer and environmental case against fast track*, Public Citizens Congress Watch, May 1991, p. 9. See Pat Choate, "Political advantage", p. 53.

12. Pat Choate, "Political advantage: Japan's campaign for America", *Harvard Business Review* (September-October 1990), pp. 87, 91, 93.

13. Michael McCauley and Anna Sochocky, "Task force seeks ways to wrest Congress from funders' grip", St. Paul *Pioneer Press* (March 10, 1991)

14. "Bush's domestic cul-de-sac", *U.S. News & World Report* (March 18, 1991), p. 17.

15. "Top dollar: Corporate chiefs' pay far outpaces inflation and the gains of staff", *Wall Street Journal* (March 28, 1988), p. 1.

16. *Wall Street Journal* (December 4, 1990), p. 1. Column by Selwyn Feinstein.

17. New York *Times* (May 3, 1991), p. A7. Excerpts from Pope John Paul II's encyclical, "Centesimus Annus", released May 2, 1991.

18. Ibid.

19. "Why are labor unions doing themselves in?", *Wall Street Journal* (February 2, 1986), p. 29. From column, "Speaking of Business", by Lindley H. Clark, Jr.

20. Jeremy Brecher and Tim Costello, *Global Village vs. Global Pillage: A One-World Strategy for Labor* (Washington, D.C.: International Labor Rights Education and Research Fund, 1991), pp. 13–14, 33; American Labor Education Center, *$4 a day, no way!*

21. "Amnesty International condemns Mexico abuses", Des Moines *Register* (September 18, 1991). Quotes John Healey, executive director of Amnesty International, U.S. branch. Amnesty International issued report entitled "Mexico: torture with impunity".

22. Martin O. Sabo, "Income disparities: Part II. What can Congress do?", *Congressman Martin Olav Sabo Reports*, September 1991.

23. Pat Choate, "Political Advantage", *Harvard Business Review* (September-October 1990), p. 103.

24. "The recession's end won't cure First World unemployment", *Wall Street Journal* (July 30, 1991), Labor Letter, p. 1.

25. "Women's gains on the job: not without a heavy toll", New York *Times* (August 21, 1989), p. 1. New York Times poll of 1,497 adults taken June 20–25, 1989.

26. "Family values strong but outlook troubling", St. Paul *Pioneer Press* (October 10, 1989). Massachusetts Mutual Life Insurance Co. national survey of 1,200 people conducted June 1989, reported in Chicago *Tribune*.

27. Adam Smith, *Wealth of Nations* (New York: The Modern Library, 1937), p. 315.

28. "USA has most behind bars", *USA Today* (January 7, 1991). See also: *Statistical Abstract 1988*, Table 305, "Federal & state prisoners: 1950 to 1986), p. 175.

29. "Private police: the role of the private sector in law enforcement grows", *Wall Street Journal* (October 15, 1991), Labor Letter column, p. 1.

30. *Wall Street Journal* (December 11, 1990), p. 1. Source: McCann-Erickson.

31. "Marketers' mantra: reap more with less", *Wall Street Journal* (March 22, 1991), p. 1B.

32. "That sales pitch interrupting dinner is by a real con man," *Wall Street Journal* (January 2, 1992), p. 1, 34.

33. Benjamin Franklin, letter to Benjamin Vaughan, July 26, 1784. Quoted from *A Benjamin Franklin Reader* (New York: Thomas Y. Crowell, 1945), pp. 791–92.

34. See George Will, "A land fit for heroes?", *Newsweek* (March 11, 1991), p. 78.

Part Four

1. "U.S.-Mexico trade pact is pitting vast armies of Capitol Hill lobbyists against each other", *Wall Street Journal* (April 25, 1991), p. 16A.

2. Ibid.

3. M. Delal Baer, "Put free-trade talks on the fast track", *Wall Street Journal* (January 4, 1991), p. A7.

4. *Star Tribune* (November 15, 1991), p. B7, and author's personal conversation.

5. Action Canada Network, MODTLE, and Mexican Action Network on Free Trade; Final Declaration, International Forum, "Public opinion and the free trade negotiations—citizens' alternatives", Zacatecas, Mexico, October 25–27, 1991.

6. "Development and trade strategies for North America"; Mobilization on Development, Trade, Labor, and the Environment (MODTLE.), Box 74, 100 Maryland Ave., N.E., Washington, DC 20002.

7. Memo from MODTLE to organizations interested in NAFTA, November 8, 1991.

8. "Social issues pact doesn't belong in trade agreement, Hills argues," Seattle *Post-Intelligencer* (August 21, 1991), p. B5.

9. U.S. Trade Representative, "Hills announces acceptance of 1991 GSP petitions", news release on August 21, 1991; Annex II, "U.S. Generalized System of Preferences listing of country practice petitions 1991 annual reviews", Document No. 001-CP-91. See also: U.S. Trade Representative, Trade Policy Staff Committee, "1991 GSP annual review, worker rights review summary, Case: 001-CP-91, Mexico", November 1991.

10. Response by Timothy Kehoe, professor of economics, University of Minnesota, to question asked at "North American Free Trade", conference in Minneapolis, Minn., November 20, 1991, seminar 3B; response to same question by Calman Cohen, Emergency Committee for American Trade.

11. Ibid., statement of Laurell Ritchie, Common Frontiers (Toronto), seminar 2C.

12. "Political will boosts hope of N. America trade pact", *Financial Times* (December 17, 1991), p. 5. See also: "Free-trade pact's priority low—U.S. politics and economy push Latin agreement to back burner", *Arizona Republic* (November 27, 1991), p. B6.

13. House Concurrent Resolution 246, introduced by Reps. Henry Waxman and Richard Gephardt, November 21, 1991.

14. "The coming emergence of three giant trading blocs", *IMF Survey* (April 1, 1991), p. 94. Quotes John Zysman, professor at University of California at Berkeley.

15. "Canada in the 'permanent war economy' ", interview with Tony Clarke, Pro-Canada Network chair, *Pro-Canada Dossier* (March-April 1991), p. 15.

16. "Guiding hand: in Asia, the Japanese hope to 'coordinate' what nations produce", *Wall Street Journal* (August 20, 1990), p. 1, 4.

17. "Baker urges Asians to be wary of new trade and security pacts", New York *Times* (July 25, 1991)

18. Leonard Silk, "Trade bloc war?", New York *Times* (April 26, 1991), Economic Scene column, p. 2C.

19. Letter to author from Motoyuki Miyano, Leisure Development Center, Tokyo, dated August 20, 1990.

20. "Paris club pact to forgive half of Polish debt", *Wall Street Journal* (March 15, 1991), p. A2, A14.

21. U.S. International Trade Commission, *The likely impact of a free trade agreement*, February 1991, p. D4. Cites a government-sponsored study by Prof. Raul Hinojosa Ojeda, then at University of California at Berkeley, using computer general equilibrium analysis.

22. "Forgive debt, finance nature", New York *Times* (July 16, 1991), editorial, p. A10; "Mexico, U.S. approve debt-for-nature pact", *Star Tribune* (February 20, 1991).

23. New York *Times* (July 16, 1991), p. A10.

24. S. 1435, a bill to amend the Foreign Assistance Act of 1961 and the Arms Export Control Act, etc., introduced by Sen. Christopher J. Dodd, July 2, 1991.

25. Henry Ford, interview with Samuel Crowthers, *Monthly Labor Review* (December 1926), p. 1166.

26. Bernard Wysocki, Jr., "Study may help Japan soothe trade tensions," *Wall Street Journal* (April 23, 1987).

27. "Lust for labor: Japanese officials mount frenzied effort to persuade the nation's workers to take it easy," *Wall Street Journal* (April 21, 1986), section 4, pp. 9D-10D.

28. Letter to the author from Reinhard Dombre, Deutscher Gewerkschaftsbund Bundesvorstand, September 9, 1991.

29. *Social Security* (Bonn: Federal Minister of Labour and Social Affairs, May 1989), especially pp. 28–29.

30. Letter to the author from Reinhard Dombre, September 9, 1991. See also: *Tarifbericht*, "Arbeitszeitkalender 1990", D.G.B., Dusseldorf, November 1990.

31. Commission of the European Communities, Community *Charter of the Fundamental Social Rights of Workers*, Luxembourg, 1990; introduction by Jacques Delors, p. 3; Title I, section 7, p. 14.

32. European Parliament, *Session Documents*, Strasbourg. Report of the Committee on Social Affairs, Employment and the Working Environment by Adrian Zeller, rapporteur; December 20, 1990; amendment 12, p. 7.

33. Melanie Kirkpatrick, "The Japanese — more and more like us", *Wall Street Journal* (December 6, 1991), p. A14.

34. Leisure Policy Study Group, Ministry of International Trade and In-

dustry (MITI), Tokyo, *A forecast of leisure-related demand in the year 2000 and current tasks*, a report issued May 1991, pp. 17, 19.

35. 1990s Policies Committee, Industrial Structure Council, MITI, *International trade and industrial policy in the 1990s — toward creating human values in the global age (summary)*, July 5, 1990, pp. 5, 11, 18.

36. Planning Subcommittee on Improving the Quality of Life, 1990s Policies Committee, Industrial Structure Council, MITI, *Interim Report*, May 9, 1990, p. 4, 14.

37. Ibid., pp. 15, 20.

38. *Documents considered at the Tripartite Symposium on Working Time in Industrialised Countries* (Geneva: International Labor Office, 1988), Table 10, "Annual hours of work", p. 24. See also: MITI, *A Forecast of Leisure-Related Demand*, p. 4.

39. "Task force backs microeconomic policy coordination", *IMF Survey* (February 4, 1991), p. 41.

40. *The GATT Negotiations and U.S. Trade Policy* (Washington, D.C.: Congressional Budget Office, June 1987), p. 15, 17.

41. Ibid., p. 17, 20.

42. Kenneth W. Dam, *The GATT: Law and International Economic Organization* (Chicago: University of Chicago Press, 1970), p. 238.

43. Ibid., pp. 236–42.

44. Ibid., pp. 244–47.

45. Keith Martin, "The North American Free Trade Negotiations", paper delivered to conference in Minneapolis, November 20, 1991, p. 4.

46. "A Free-trade agreement that preserves the nation's interests", statement by Manuel Garcia Urrutia, Frente Autentico Trabajo, Mexico City, to Asociacion Metropolitano de Licenciados in Relaciones Industriales, May 1991, item 3.4.

47. *Worker Rights under the U.S. Trade Laws* (New York: Lawyers Committee for Human Rights, 1989), p. 66. Statement by Ambassador Michael B. Smith at Workers' Rights and Trade Adjustment Assistance Program hearings on S. 490 and H.R. 3 before U.S. Senate Finance Committee, 1987.

48. "US urges examination of relationship of labor standards to international trade", *GATT Focus*, October 1990, p. 3.

49. See International Labor Office, *Documents at Tripartite Symposium on Working Hours*, 1988, p. 38. In western Europe, roughly one-tenth of productivity gains since 1960 have been translated into shorter work hours.

50. International Labor Office — Washington, D.C. Branch, "Private panel recommends stronger U.S. role in ILO", *ILO Washington Focus*, Vol. 4, No. 3, August 1991, pp. 1, 4.

51. MITI, *International Trade and Industrial Policy in the 1990*, pp. 6, 12–14.

52. Rudolph Oswald, AFL-CIO, statement on April 7, 1987; Hearings before U.S. Senate Committee on Finance on S.490, S.636, and H.R.3, 100th Congress, 1st session, pp. 54–59.

53. Lawyers Committee for Human Rights, *Worker Rights under the U.S. Trade Laws*, pp. 13–14. Refers to Trade Act of 1974, Section 502(a)(4), as amended.

54. Ibid., pp. 11–12, 39. See also: Executive Proclamation No. 5605 (1988).

55. Ibid., pp. 17–32 (GSP); pp. 33–34 (CBI).

56. Ibid., pp. 51–64 (Section 301); pp. 74–77 (IEEPA).

57. Ibid., pp. 64–66 (Section 301); pp. 74–77 (IEEPA).

58. Ibid., pp. 53–55 (mandatory action); pp. 55–57 (discretionary action); 62–63.

59. Jeffrey Schott, *Completing the Uruguay Round: A Results-Oriented Approach to the GATT Trade Negotiations* (Washington, D.C.: Institute for International Economics, September 1990), pp. 186–87.

60. Lawyers Committee for Human Rights, *Worker Rights under the U.S. Trade Laws*, p. 69.

61. 19 U.S.C., Chapter 17, Section 2901, paragraph 14.

Figures

1.1. *Pro-Canada Dossier* (March-April 1991), p. 18.

1.2. "Trade Adjustment Assistance: Time for Action, not False Promises", *AFL-CIO Reviews the Issues*, Report No. 53, September 1991.

2.1. U.S. International Trade Commission, *The Likely Impact of a Free-Trade Agreement*, p. 2–3 (GDP figures). *The World Almanac and Book of Facts 1992* (New York: World Almanac, 1991), pp. 40, 384, 745, 783 (population and territory).

2.2. LaBotz, *A Strangling Embrace*, chapter on maquiladoras. Source: figures supplied by the Mexican Secretary of Commerce as published in *El Financiero* (January 7, 1991).

2.3. *Wall Street Journal* (September 22, 1989), p. R27. Sources: Department of Labor, WEFA Group (1965 to 1988). LaBotz, *A Strangling Embrace* Source: Mexican National Institute of Statistics, Geography and Information (INEGI) for December 1990 as published in *La Jornada* (December 29, 1990), p. 11.

2.4. Adapted from chart accompanying "Comparing recessions shows FTA's role in job losses", *Action Canada Dossier* (September-October 1991), #33, p. 5. Compiled by Andrew Jackson from figures supplied by Statistics Canada Cat. 72-002, "Employment, Earnings and Hours" and Cat. 15–001, "G.D.P. by Industry".

2.5. From tables compiled by Bruce Campbell, "Selected closure (& partial closures) of US branch plants", *Canadian Dimension* (January-February 1991), pp. 20–21.

3.1. Cartoon by Jerry Fearing, St. Paul *Pioneer Press* (October 2, 1991), editorial page.

3.2. Calculated from data in *Handbook of Labor Statistics* (Washington: U.S. Department of Labor, December 1980), Table 72, p. 151; Table 1, p. 5; and *Employment and Earnings* (January 1988 and January 1991), Tables A-1 and B-1.

4.1. *Monthly Labor Review* (August 1991), p. 36. Table 1, "Indexes of hourly compensation costs for production workers in manufacturing, 30 countries or areas and selected economic groups, 1975, 1980, 1985, and 1988–90."

4.2. "Mean hours worked by all persons at work, 1943–1976 annual averages", unpublished table compiled by U.S. Bureau of Labor Statistics; *Employment and Earnings*, January issue 1977–1991, Table 30, persons at work by hours of work and type of industry."

4.3. *Tarif Bericht*, Arbeitszeitkalender 1990 (Dusseldorf: D.G.B., November 1990), Table "Tarifvertraglich vereinbarte Wochenarbeitszeit". Source: WSI-Tarifarchiv. Based on a survey of 1,000 employers in various industries.

4.4. Leisure Policy Study Group, Ministry of International Trade and Industry, *A Forecast of Leisure-Related Demand in the Year 2000 and Current Tasks* (Tokyo: MITI, May 1991), pp. 13- 16.

INDEX

Action Canada Network (formerly Pro-Canada Network), 20, 128, 137
advertising, 118
Advisory Committee on Trade Policy and Negotiations, 31
AFL-CIO, 32, 123
agriculture: Mexican avocados, 6; U.S. corn exports, 7–8; U.S. position on food embargo, 16; some exempted products, 32; breakdown of Mexican communal farming, 54; impact of Canada-U.S. free trade on, 76; production oversupply, 113; reduced U.S. employment in, 116–17; NAFTA alternative agenda, 129; MODTLE recommendation, 131
American Express Co., 123
Amnesty International, 111
arms race with Soviet Union, 88–89, 92, 119
asbestos regulation, 77
ASEAN nations, 138–39, 165
Asia: NAFTA designed to help U.S. compete against, 29; female workers in export production, 62; trading bloc, 137; locked into trade competition with, 142
association, right of, 131, 169, 172
Atari Democrats, 37
Australia, 163
automobiles, 7
avocados, 6

Baker, James, 28, 138–39
Bakker, Rev. Jim, 102
Baldridge, Malcolm, 73
Ball, George, 40

banks: Canadian access to U.S. market sought, 6; privatizing Mexican, 24; dictating national economic policy, 90–91; overextended with Third World loans, 91; cost of bailout, 96–97; lax government regulation, 103; debt-for-nature swaps, 144–45
Barlow, Maude, 80
Baucus-Danforth Amendment, 74
Bentsen, Lloyd, 28, 124
Bhagwati, Jagdish, 139
Black, Hugo, 115
Bloomington, Ill., 33
Blount County, Tenn., 34
Bolivia, 145
border-crossing procedures, 10–11
Bourque, Deborah, 62
bracero program, 50, 59
Brady, Nicholas, 53
branch-plant economy, 69
Bretton Woods conference, 162
British North American Act of 1867, 46
Brock, William, 124
broom industry, U.S., 13
Brown, Alan, 61
Buchanan, Pat, 134
Bush, George, 5, 19, 28, 31–32, 68, 101, 124, 126, 134, 151
business: as third power center, 84–86; political pendulum favoring, 93; political motives in, 95; totalitarian tendencies, 100–04; epochal rivalry with government, 100; usurping government's domain, 101; high salaries of corporate executives, 102; appropriate functions, 111–13; lobbying for fast-

track extension, 123–24, 126; against cutting work hours, 150
business consultants, 66
Business Roundtable, 124
business services: in Canada-U.S. FTA, 10; U.S. objective to liberalize trade in, 21; whether U.S. can develop comparative advantage in, 38

Cable News Network, 93
Calles, Elias Plutarcho, 50
Campbell, Bruce, 70
Canada: joins U.S.-Mexico trade talks, 6; negotiating objectives in NAFTA, 6–7, 21–22; some national characteristics, 45; historical overview, 47–48; unions, 48–49; some consequences of free trade with the United States, 68–78; lessons of 1988, 135–36
Canada-United States Free-Trade Agreement: stillborn as source of Canadian idealism, 4; Reagan transmittal to U.S. Congress, 8–9; preempts authority of Canadian provincial governments, 16; political opposition to, 49; Reagan heralds, 68; effect on Canadian employment, 68–70; used to threaten striking workers, 73; not strictly a "commercial accord", 75; repudiation supported in NAFTA alternative agenda, 130
Canada-United States Trade Commission, 11
Canadian Chamber of Commerce, 21
Canadian Chemical Producers Association, 78
Canadian Pacific Railway, 48
Cananea copper mines, 57
capital flight: from Mexico, 26; from Canada, 69
capital investment: intense competition for funds, 23–24; drives Mexican economic boom, 26; production capacity added in Mexico, 30; no loyalty to nations, 31; more important to world economy than trade, 38
Cardenas, Cuauhtemoc, 19, 47, 80, 142
Cardenas, Lazaro, 47, 50, 56
Caribbean Basin Economic Recovery Act of 1983, 169
Caribbean Basin Initiative, 163, 169–70
Carlson, Arne, 126
Carrillo, Jorge, 61
Carter, Jimmy, 19, 111
Cavitt, Bill, 66
Centesimus Annus, 106–07
cheap labor: in Mexico, 4, 24; tapped by Asian firms, 29–30; no longer dominates international investment decisions, 38; less important to a nation's development, 43; in maquiladoras, 60; AFL-CIO concerns, 123; NAFTA alternative agenda, 129 ; in regional trading blocs, 137; a form of dumping, 164–65; alternative to free labor, 176.
child labor, 123, 131, 169, 172
Child Labor Coalition, 123
Choate, Pat, 98–99
Christianity: conflict with the Roman state, 84; center of resistance to totalitarian power, 106
Chrysler Corp., 30
Citicorp, 145
Citizen Trade Watch, 126
civilization, development of, 83
Clarke, Tony, 137
Coalition for Justice in the Maquiladoras, 127
Codex Alimentarius Commission, 15
Cohen, Calman, 23, 25, 133
Columbus, Christopher, 167
Commodity Credit Corporation, 145
Common Frontiers, 22, 133
comparative advantage: U.S. aspirations regarding intellectual properties, 27–28; doctrine stated, 36; in harassing attorneys, 37
competitiveness: allegedly enhanced with free trade, 1, 23; Canadian

problems, 69; motive for NAFTA, 142; Japanese efforts to mitigate, 147–48; and denial of worker rights, 174
Confederation of Mexican Workers (CTM): formation of, 50; bureaucratic violence, 56–59
Congress, U.S.: will decide NAFTA, 5; battles over fast-track extension, 123–27; Riegle and Waxman-Gephardt resolutions, 125, 134; authority to regulate foreign and interstate commerce, 168–69, 174
Congress of Labor, Mexican, 57
Congress Watch, 17
Congressional Budget Office, 162
Conservation International, 145
conservative economic policies: political support for, 19; advanced through debt crisis, 90–91; on the offensive in the 1980s, 92–93
Consumer and Corporate Affairs, Canadian Department of, 78
convict labor, 169, 171–72
Conyers, John, 114
cooperation between trading nations: alternative to free trade, 136; a framework of principles supporting, 140–41; to enforce labor and environmental standards, 141; to promote economic growth in developing countries, 147–49; focus on Germany and Japan, 150–56; international organizations, 161–67; to stabilize commodity prices, 163–64; labor standards and trade policy, 164–67; coordinating ILO and GATT, 166, 175; undermined by unilateral U.S. action , 172
Cooperative Commonwealth Federation, 48
co-production, 137
corn: U.S.-Mexico trade to disrupt small-scale farming, 8; declining Mexican production, 54
countervailing duties: national laws continued under Canada-U.S. FTA,

11; U.S. tendency to impose, 75, 158
creative destruction of obsolete industries, 36–37
Cuautitlan Ford assembly plant, 58–59
cultural industries: under Canada-U.S. FTA, 6, 9, 21; U.S. ambitions, 27–28; commercial television, 101–02; recommendation to exclude from NAFTA, 128–29
currency-exchange rates: fluctuations drive international investment, 39; Canadian and U.S., 73

Dam, Kenneth W., 164
Davis, Martin S., 31
Deaver, Michael, 98
debt: Mexico's foreign, 23–24, 51–52; meeting creditors' demands, 53; its impoverishing result, 54–55; crisis of Third World, 89–92; World Bank and IMF, 90; in alternative agenda, 128; a driving force behind NAFTA, 142; forgiveness in exchange for environmental protection, 143–45
debtors' cartel, 91
de-industrialization of America, 108
Delors, Jacques, 153
democratic processes, threatened by free trade, 22, 25, 176
Denman, Catalina, 66
deregulation: conservative agenda of, 15–16; essence of free trade, 23; through U.S.-Canada FTA, 74; NAFTA self-contradictions, 134; U.S. philosophy coming to Europe, 150
developing countries: in different economic situation, 139; needed transfer of wealth, 140–41; shorter work hours and imports from, 146–47, 149; a brake on exports from, 156–60; concessions in GATT, 162–63; trade-preference programs, 163; against including labor standards in GATT, 165–66; General

ized System of Preferences and Caribbean Basin Initiative, 163, 169–70

development, economic: NAFTA may hurt Mexico's, 13; protectionist achievements, 41; Japanese approach to, 42; 19th and 20th century patterns, 42–43; India and Italy as models, 43; at the core of trade negotiations, 80–81; origin of Third World debt, 89–90; focus of NAFTA alternative agenda, 128; framework of global principles, 140–41; GATT exceptions for developing countries, 162–64

dialectical movement, 104–05

Diaz, Porfirio, 46, 49

Diaz de Leon, Jesus, 57

dispute-resolution procedures: NAFTA negotiating objectives, 5; complicated by differing legal systems, 7; in Canada-U.S. FTA, 11; in GATT draft, 15; ruling against dolphins, 35; rulings under Canada-U.S. FTA, 78–80; GATT principles, 162

divided power: characteristic of western society, 86–87; Gorbachev's gamble, 88; healthy model of society, 89; overcome by business, 101–02; papal recommendations, 107; children's hand game, 110

Dodd, Christopher J., 145

dolphins, 35

Dombre, Reinhard, 150

Dorgan, Byron, 125

Douglas, C.H., 48

Drucker, Peter F., 38–43

Duke, David, 134

Economic Dislocation and Worker Adjustment Act, 33

Economic Policy Council of United Nations Association, 27–28

education: alleged U.S. comparative advantage, 27–28; corporate support for Mexican, 28; privatization of, 101; appendage to the career system, 102

Egypt, 144

"El Charro" (the cowboy), 57

election fraud in Mexico, 19

Emergency Committee for American Trade, 23, 133

employment: in the maquiladoras, 59–60; rosy predictions of gains with free trade, 68; job loss with Canadian recession, 68–69; shift to less useful production, 116–17; U.S. business efforts to cut cost of, 150

energy: export provisions in Canada-U.S. FTA, 11; ownership of Mexican oil, 20–21; environmental impact of Canada-U.S. FTA, 75–78; consumed in packaging and transporting food, 76

Enterprise for the Americas Initiative, 145

Environmental Protection Agency, U.S., 34

environmental regulation: justified, 2; hurt by free-trade agenda, 16; lax enforcement in border region, 63–65; deleterious effect of Canada-U.S. FTA 76–78; supplements free-market activity, 113; MODTLE's position on, 129; financed by debt forgiveness, 144–45; enforced by tariffs, 159

Escobar, Raul, 2

European Community: Canada-U.S. FTA compared with, 3–4; decision by Court of Justice, 17–18; protection of agriculture, 37; its union unlike NAFTA, 132; Maastricht meeting, 135; regional trading bloc, 136; policy toward shorter hours, 152–53

European Parliament, 153

Export-Import Bank, 145

export-oriented production: investment motive in Mexico, 25–26; multinationals gearing up for, 30; in maquiladoras, 50; Canadian energy supplies, 75–76; to accumulate funds for debt service, 142

Fair Labor Standards Act of 1938,
114–15, 158, 168, 173
Fair Trade Campaign, 127
Fair Trade Caucus, 125
family life, insufficient time for, 115
fast-track authority to negotiate trade
agreements, 31, 123–27, 134
Federal Board of Conciliation and Arbitration, Mexican, 58–59, 61
Federal Reserve Bank, U.S., 52, 97
Federation for Industrial Retention
and Renewal, 127
financial regulation: John Maynard
Keynes, 96–97; reaching its limits,
96–97; and economic reality,
119–20; international control
mechanisms, 161
fishing industry: Mexican suit against
dolphin ban, 35; elimination of
Canadian domestic-processing rules,
72, 74; landing requirements for
herring and salmon, 77; RMALC
position, 130.
food-safety standards, 15; seen as
trade barrier, 78
Ford, Henry, 26–27, 147
Ford Motor Company, 30, 59
foreign ownership of business, in
Canada, 69
Forest Resources Conservation and
Shortage Relief Act of 1990, 34
Fortress North America, 137
Foster, Harry A., 13
Franklin, Benjamin, 119
free enterprise: global prerogatives of,
16; ideological leaning of trade
negotiators, 31; 89; Adam Smith's
theories, 94; postwar mixed economy, 96; overcome by public largesse, 101; papal critique of, 107;
functions of business and government, 111–12; attempt to harness
authoritarian government, 111–12
Freeman, Harry, 123
free trade: applauded, 1; and

prospects for democracy, 22; Salinas policy reversal, 24; means
lower social and environmental
standards, 79; props up an
authoritarian regime, 80; trinational
opponents, 127–28
Friends of the Earth, 35
furniture industry: fled Los Angeles to
escape air-pollution standards, 65;
higher costs in Canada than the
U.S., 71–72

General Agreement on Tariffs and
Trade (GATT): falling tariff rates,
11; some types of nontariff trade
barriers, 14–15; preempts local-
government authority, 17; excludes
agriculture and textiles, 136; its
background and purpose, 161–62;
aid to the developing countries,
163–64; commodity price support,
163–64; introduction of labor standards, 165–66; collaboration with
international bodies, 166–67; fair
labor standards, 169; Section 301
authority as violation of, 171;
Presidential mandate to negotiate
improved worker rights, 174–75
Generalized System of Preferences, 18,
133, 149, 163, 169–70, 173–75
General Motors Corp., 30
Gephardt, Richard, 125, 134
Germany: a leader of European trading bloc, 137; social benefits for
workers, 152; manufacturing work-
week, 152, 156
global economy: deregulation of, 16;
investment competition in, 23–24;
comparative advantages in, 36–37;
importance of investment in, 38;
efficient use of resources, 40; international labor solidarity, 109–10.
Gorbachev, Mikhail, 88
government: comparative advantage
created by, 39–40; one of three
power centers in society, 83; economic policies dictated by international bankers, 90–91; its purpose

questioned, 93; Adam Smith's definition of functions, 95; repeated financial emergencies, 97; revolving door with private-sector careers, 99; its basis of power, 99–100; corrupted by money, 100–01; too close to business, 103; economic functions of, 112–13; public-sector professions, 112; less useful employment, 116–17; need for self-reform, 120–22; able to regulate labor supply, 146; flexible and coercive regulatory techniques, 158

government procurement: provisions in Canada-U.S. FTA, 10; access to Mexican oil, 20; other U.S. objectives, 21

Gray, Harry J., 16

Green Giant, 33

Greenpeace, 123

Group of Seven, 136, 144, 161

Hamilton, Alexander, 41

Harmonized System, 160

Hartford Convention, 42

Hartz Canada, 73

Health and Welfare Canada, 78

health insurance: Canadian program called unfair trade subsidy, 17; can be avoided in Mexico, 66; public or private, 111

Hebert, Raymond, 3

Hedrick, Jack, 61

Hernandez, Alberto, 61

Hernandez, Edwviges Ramos, 62

Hills, Carla, 8, 34, 98, 132–33

Hoover, Herbert, 98, 115

hours of labor, shorter: to control production oversupply, 114, 146; federal legislation, 114–15; tradeoff with employment, 116; Benjamin Franklin's theory, 119; impact on wages, 119–20; to help developing countries, 141, 146–49; new Japanese policy, 148, 154–56; ILO conventions, 150; in United States, 151; in Germany, 152–53; international statistics, 156; in tariff index,

159; like an accelerator to imports, 160; consistent with GATT supply-management rules, 164; role of ILO in improving standards, 166; relevance to trade law, 168; possible inclusion in GATT, 173–75

human-oriented international trade and industrial policies, 167

human rights agenda, 111, 128, 131, 133

immigration, Mexican: Salinas' warning, 2; effect of U.S. corn exports upon, 7–8; NAFTA alternative agenda, 129–30

individualism, Canadian disdain for U.S. value of, 4; Japanese policy favoring, 156

Institutional Revolutionary Party (PRI), 46, 56

intellectual-property protection: U.S. negotiating objectives, 5; Mexico's tightened, 27; easily evaded, 37; retaliation under U.S. trade law, 171–72

interest rates, Canadian, 69, 73

International Business Machines, 30

International Emergency Economic Powers Act of 1977, 171

International Labor Organization, 115, 150, 160, 165–66, 175

International Monetary Fund, 90, 136, 162

International Trade Commission, U.S.: report to Congress, 5; hearings in Chicago, 13; NAFTA's limited potential to stimulate trade, 18; effort to liberalize Mexico's investment policies, 25

International Trade Organization, 162, 169

interstate-commerce clause, 168

Investment Canada, 10

investment regulation: goal to relax Mexico's, 6; elimination of performance requirements in Canada-U.S. FTA, 10; U.S. wants national treat-

ment in Canada, 21; Mexican liberalization of, 25
invisible hand, 94, 113

Jackson, Andrew, 42
Jackson, Henry, 124
James Bay hydroelectric development, 75–76
Japan: investing in Mexico, 30; a different development model, 42; U.S. lobbying efforts, 98–99; culture of affluence, 139–40; attitude toward shorter work hours, 153–56; leader of Asian trading bloc, 137; mercantilist policies abandoned, 148; new MITI approach, 154–56; strengthening international cooperation, 166–67
Jefferson, Thomas, 41
Job Training Partnership Act, 33
John Paul II, 106–07

Kaptur, Marcy, 125
Keefe, Robert, 124
Kehoe, Timothy, 133
Keynes, John Maynard, 43, 96–97
Khomeini, Ayatollah Ruhollah, 106
Kimberly-Clark Corp., 30
King, Mackenzie, 47

labor standards: linked to NAFTA, 125; in trinational declaration, 129; in MODTLE statement, 131; NAFTA proponents' attitudes toward, 133; in EC social charter, 153; reflected in tariff rates, 158–59; discussion topic at GATT, 165–66; proposed right to shorter work hours, 166; injected into trade laws, 168–76; ILO's role in creating GATT code, 175
labor theory of value, 95
labor unions: to be appeased by trade-adjustment assistance, 31; link to Mexican government, 50, 56–57; repression in Mexico, 57–59; in maquiladoras, 60–61; union-busting in Canada, 73; resisting

totalitarian state, 108; democratic and bureaucratic tendencies, 108–09; global competition with business, 109–10; need to become more ideological, 109; lobbying against NAFTA, 123, 126; affirmation of labor's right to organize, 129, 131, 169, 172; suppressed in developing countries, 165
Labor, U.S. Department of, 1
Laney, Tom, 2
Law to Promote Mexican Investment and Regulate Foreign Investment, 25
lawyers: set to invade Mexico, 28; U.S. comparative advantage in, 37; excessive fees, 103; proposed public-sector alternative, 112
League of Nations, 166
leisure: needed for family life, 115; stimulates increased consumption, 147; Japanese preparations for, 154
Leisure Development Center, 148, 154
Levi Strauss, 34, 130
Lewis, Bernard, 42
Libman, William, 13
Lincoln, Abraham, 176
Linneman, Peter, 108
List, Friedrich, 41
locking in conservative gains: motive for NAFTA, 19, 25
looting: by corporate executives and professionals, 98–99, 102–03, 112
luxury good, economists' attitude toward human rights, 133

Mackenzie Delta natural-gas production, 75
Madrid, Miguel de la, 19, 53
Majors, John, 135
malnutrition of Mexican children, 55
maquiladoras: customs regulations, 18; health hazards, 34; inspired by Asian export-processing zones, 43; their beginning, 50; harbinger of NAFTA, 55–56, 66; their explosive growth, 59–60; wages and benefits,

60–61; working conditions, 61–62; sexual harassment, 62; squalid communities, 63; water and air pollution, 63–65; a paradigm of business totalitarianism, 105

Marine Mammal Protection Act, 35

market economy: uncoupling production and consumption, 26–27; its development in western society, 85–86; has outlasted socialism, 87; Adam Smith's observations, 94; political decisionmaking in, 95, 102–03; papal critique, 107; proposed restrictions upon, 112–13; enjoys global consensus of support, 140

Marquart, Donald, 13

Marshall, Ray, 166

Martin, Keith, 21

Marx, Karl, 95

Mayekawa committee, 148

McCloskey, Michael, 34

McKinley Tariff Act of 1890, 169

mercantilism: historical perspectives on, 41–42; new Japanese trade policies, 148

Metcalf, Richard, 63

Mexican Border Industrialization Program, 50

Mexican Investment Board, 30

"Mexican miracle", 51

Mexican Revolution of 1917, 49

Mexico: negotiating objectives for NAFTA, 6; making policy changes irreversible, 25; economic expansion based on investment, 26; engineering graduates, 28; lacks resources to enforce environmental regulations, 34; some national characteristics, 45; its postwar industrialization, 50–51; squandered oil revenues, 51–52; corporative state, 56; labor unrest and violence, 58–59; maquiladora program, 59–66; its totalitarian state, 105, 108; charged with human-rights violations, 111; lobbying for NAFTA, 124; NAFTA war chest,

126; would resent human-rights criticisms, 133; trade policies driven by debt, 142; debt-for-nature swap, 143–45; beneficiary of Generalized System of Preferences, 170

MEXUSCAN Solidarity network, 109

Michigan Asparagus Growers, 13

Ministry of International Trade and Industry (MITI), 154, 156, 166

Minnesota Fair Trade Coalition, 127

Mitterrand, Francois, 151

Miyano, Motoyuki, 148

Mobilization on Development, Trade, Labor, and the Environment (MODTLE), 126–28, 130–32

Modelo Brewery, 57–58

money: origin of Third World debt, 90; has corrupted political process, 98, 100–01, 120; basis of business power, 100; unifying influence in society, 100, 102; and big government, 103; self-discipline required by public servants, 120–21

Morris, David, 17

Mosbacher, Robert, 2, 28

Most-Favored-Nation treatment at GATT, 162–63, 165, 169

Mulroney, Brian, 19, 21, 49, 68, 74, 133

multinational corporations: friends in government, 20; able to escape government regulation, 29; expanding production facilities in Mexico, 30; need to establish global presence, 38; appropriate corporate structure, 39; reassurances to locate in Mexico, 66; a corporate bill of rights, 80; and international labor solidarity, 110; proposed code of conduct for, 132

Nader, Ralph, 123, 126

Nakasone, Yasuhiro, 148

National Action Party (PAN), 47

National Autonomous University Workers Union of Mexico (STUNAM), 130

National Environment Policy Act, 35

nationalism: Canadian and Mexican,
3; lack of corporate, 30–31, 159
national treatment, in services, 10, 21
National Wildlife Federation, 123
Nestle, 16
New Democratic Party (NDP), 46
nontariff trade barriers: in negotiating
agenda, 5; their variety, 14–15;
conservative deregulatory agenda,
15–16; U.S. interpretations, 17, 74;
some remaining Mexican, 23;
Canadian environmental rules,
76–77; GATT commitment to reduce, 161–62
North American Free-Trade Agreement (NAFTA): editorial comment,
1; unequal bargaining positions, 4;
patterned after Canada-U.S. FTA,
8; negotiating agenda, 5–11; elimination of tariffs, 12–13; locking in
investment opportunities, 25; U.S.
negotiating objectives, 20–21, 23;
Canadian objectives, 21–23; Mexican objectives, 23–24; win-lose
proposition, 28–29; proposed
safeguards for labor and the environment, 31–36; precedent of maquiladoras, 55–56; and Canada-
U.S. FTA, 76–78; negotiations announced, 68; opinions of Maude
Barlow and Cuauhtemoc Cardenas,
80–81; and business totalitarianism,
105; a spur to international labor
solidarity, 110; boost to the political left, 121–22; battle over fast
track, 123–25; negotiations,
125–26; groups for and against,
126–27; alternative agendas,
127–32; whether social criteria
should be included, 132–33;
whether linked to worker rights,
135; a product of trade-bloc competition, 137; about the future of
democracy, 176
Nutrition Labeling and Education
Act, 14

Obregon, Alvaro, 49

Ochoa, Zenaida, 62
Ohmae, Kenichi, 93
oil: U.S. covets Mexican, 6, 20–21;
foreign ownership prohibited under
Mexican Constitution, 49; brought
income and debt to Mexico, 51–52;
union leader arrested, 58
Ojeda, Dr. Raul Hinojosa, 7, 144
Omnibus Trade and Competitiveness
Act of 1988, 124, 169–71, 174
O'Neill, Joseph, 124
Ontario Chamber of Commerce, 78
Organization for Economic Cooperation and Development (OECD),
113, 136, 167
Ostry, Sylvia, 26
Ottoman Turks, 42
outsourcing of production: more expensive than it seems, 40; organized
by regional trading blocs, 137;
denial of worker rights and competitive advantage, 137

Packwood-Magnuson Amendment to
Fisherman's Protection Act, 35
parental leave bill, 151
Party of the Democratic Revolution
(PRD), 47
PEMEX, 20, 24, 58
Persian Gulf war, 121, 173
pesticide standards: in trade agreements, 15–16, 78; California's criti-
cized, 17
Peter the Great, 88
Petroleum Workers Union (Mexican),
58
Poland, 144–45
politics: favoring NAFTA, 19–20; in
three North American countries,
46–47; in economic decision-
making, 95; corrupted by campaign
financing, 100–01; criteria for corporate promotions, 102–03; in the
fast-track decision, 123–25
Portillo, Lopez, 19, 52
poverty: Mexico's debt-induced, 54;
in maquiladora communities, 63
printing industry: Canadian subsidies

for, 72; U.S. recycling laws, 76–77
prisons: privatization of, 101; rising
rates of incarceration, 118; telemar-
keting by inmates, 119
privatization: undertaken in Mexico,
19, 24, 53; of education and prison
management, 101; to thwart public-
sector unions, 109, 112
Procter & Gamble Co., 123
production oversupply: insoluble by
free market alone, 113; and reduced
work time, 114; a possible solution,
146–47
productivity: creates need for shorter
hours, 114; and wasteful employment, 116; produces labor displacement, 119; effect on labor supply,
147; right of workers to receive fair
share of gains, 166
PRONASOL, 54
protection, trade: for steel and textiles, 7; necessary for certain industries, 13; historical perspectives on,
41–42; Canada's past sins of, 69;
U.S. reliance on harassing lawsuits,
74–75; in pre-Salinas Mexican
economy, 51; various forms in
Canada, 72; permitted developing
nations in GATT, 163; labor standards seen as form of, 165
Proxmire, William, 101
Public Citizen, 35–36, 123, 126
"publicization", 112

Quick, Perry D., 40

racism, allegations against NAFTA
opponents, 1–2
rationalized production, 23
Reagan, Ronald, 8, 19, 68, 88, 97,
98, 112, 170–71
Red Mexicana de Accion Frente al
Libre Commercial (RMALC), 128,
130, 164–65
reference pricing system, 53
reforestation program in British
Columbia, 17

Regional Confederation of Mexican
Workers (CROM), 57
regional trading blocs: emergence of
three, 136–39; social policies in Europe and Japan, 151–56
regulation: how to evaluate, 2; tariffs
a tool for social, 13; notification requirements in GATT, 15; trade
agreements undermine local
authority, 17; multinational corporations escape, 29; self-regulated
professions, 103; Hills rejects social
and environmental, 132; to relieve
development pressures, 142; targeted to individual employers, 132,
159, 173; flexible or coercive, 158;
both a brake and accelerator, 160;
labor standards and trade policy,
164–76
religion: conflict with the Roman
state, 84; struggle between Pope
and Emperor, 84; resistance to
totalitarian state, 106, 110
Renewal Act of 1984, 169
returnable bottle law (Denmark), 18
Revolutionary Confederation of Workers and Peasants (CROC), 57–58
Revolutionary Workers Confederation
(COR), 57, 59
Ricardo, David, 36
Richardson, Bill, 134
Riegle amendment, 125, 127, 134,
176
Riegle, Donald, 125
risk-benefit model for pesticide regulation, 16, 78
Ritchie, Cedric, 69
Ritchie, Laurell, 22–23, 133
Roosevelt, Franklin D., 47, 115
Rostenkowski, Dan, 123
rules of origin: U.S. wants tough,
6–7; in Canada-U.S. FTA, 10; Sa-
linas ignoring U.S. wishes, 29–30

Sabo, Martin, 112
Salinas de Gortari, Carlos, 2, 5, 19,
23–24, 29–30, 53, 57–58, 68, 92,
126, 133–34

Samuelson, Paul, 36
Saul, John Ralston, 67
Scheele, Nicholas, 57
Schott, Jeffrey, 172
Section 301 of Trade Act of 1974, 171–73
Section 502 of Trade Act of 1974, 170
Section 503 of Renewal Act of 1984, 169
security firms, private, 118
Serra Puche, Jaime, 2
Shah of Iran, 16
Shrybman, Stephen, 16, 78
Sierra Club, 35
"silent integration" of U.S. and Mexican economies, 51
Sinclair, Scott, 74–75
Smith, Adam, 41, 94–96, 99, 117–18, 121
Smith, Michael B., 173
Social Charter, 3, 132–34, 152–53
Social Credit, 48
social dumping, 130, 164–65, 174
socialism: U.S. mixed economy, 96; and business totalitarianism, 104; Pope's assessment, 107; and regeneration of political left, 121–22
solidarity, international: a result of free-trade controversy, 81; to cope with business in global economy, 109–10; NAFTA opponents seek, 127
Solidarity (Polish trade union), 106, 151
Solidarity Pact, 54
South Africa, 171
Soviet Union: its Byzantine totalitarian structure, 87–88; possible alternative to western economies, 92; similar to Mexican system, 105
Spratt, Susan, 135
Steptoe & Johnson, 124
Strauss, Robert B., 98, 124
structural adjustment program (SAP), 53
supply-management programs: for

Canadian dairy industry, 72; undermined by U.S.-Canada FTA, 76; cure for production oversupply, 113; applied to labor, 164
Supreme Court, U.S., 115
tariff rates: U.S. and Canadian, 10; international comparisons, 11; U.S. and Mexican, 18; drop in Mexican, 53; and aid to developing countries, 149
tariffs: elimination proposed in negotiating agenda, 5, 12; in Canada-U.S. FTA, 8, 10; source of tax revenues, 13; effect of eliminating, 18–19; Canadian yogurt and ice cream, 76; labor and environmental standards in developing countries, 157–60; formulation of an index, 159–60; GATT negotiations, 161–62; preferential treatment for developing countries, 163, 170–71
taxes: maquiladora employers reluctant to pay, 63; higher in Toronto than in New York City, 72; Reagan's avoidance of, 97
technical regulations, in GATT, 14–15
Tecumseh, 47
Texas: would benefit disproportionately from NAFTA, 28; toxic waste from maquiladoras, 64
Theophilus, 87
Third Rome, 87
"tigers", four Asian, 42, 170
timber industry: British Columbia reforestation programs, 17, 77; special tax on Canadian exports, 72
Tornel Rubber Company, 58
totalitarianism: prone to absolute corruption, 86–87; Byzantine origin, 87–88; business-government partnership, 98; money-centered culture, 101–02; business, 103; hardcore and soft-core types, 104; fight against, 104–06; Mexican state and foreign corporations, 105; resisted

by organized labor and religion,
106 10; new opportunity for the
political left, 121–22
Trade Act of 1974, 163, 169
trade-adjustment assistance: Bush
promises regarding, 31; experience
from past programs, 32–33
Trade and Development Committee at
GATT, 163
Trade Expansion Act of 1962, 32
Trade Policy Staff Committee, 170
training, job: for displaced workers,
31–33; U.S. subsidies to business,
71–72; in Germany, 152
travel, Japanese overseas , 154
Trudeau, Pierre Elliott, 19
Truman, Harry S., 162

Uchitelle, Louis, 29
unemployment: in Canada, 68–69;
OECD predictions, 113; safeguards
in Germany, 152
United Nations, 136, 166
United Nations Association of U.S.A.,
166
United States: values repugnant to
neighbors, 3–4; negotiating objectives in NAFTA, 6–7, 20–21; relations with two continental neighbors, 45–46; took most Latin
exports, 92; springboard for business totalitarianism, 105; expenditures for advertising and crime,
118; no hours reduction, 150–51;
manufacturing workweek, 156; influence on international trade
policy, 173
Universal Declaration of Human
Rights, 128
University of Minnesota, 126
UN Conference on Trade and Development, 1964, 163
Uruguay Round of GATT negotiations, 134, 136, 165

vacations, paid, 150, 152, 166
Velazquez, Fidel, 57–58
Villa, Pancho, 49

Volcker, Paul, 52

Wachter, Michael, 108
wages: differential between Mexican
and U.S., 4; falling Mexican, 19,
53; effect of job-training programs,
33–34; precipitous drop in Mexican
purchasing power, 57; in the maquiladora plants, 60; in Canada and
U.S., 72; of U.S. corporate executives, 102; self-defeating gains for
labor, 108; and reduced working
hours, 119–20; North American
equalization, 129; a minimum level,
131, 148; in tariff index, 159
Walesa, Lech, 151
Walker, Charls, 124
Walsh-Healey Act of 1936, 115
Wanniski, Jude, 90
waste, economic, 116–19
waste disposal: in maquiladoras,
63–64; NAFTA alternative agenda,
129
Watzman, Nancy, 17
Waxman, Henry, 134
Waxman-Gephardt resolution, 134
wealth redistribution: need for, 103,
120; between developed and developing countries, 140–41; has
both accelerator and brake, 160
Webb, Richard, 55
Whitmore, Kay R., 25
"win-win" situation, claimed for
NAFTA, 28
Wofford, Harris, 134
worker rights, internationally recognized: NAFTA opponents' support
for, 129–31; NAFTA proponents
oppose linkage to trade, 132–33;
developed nations as guardians of,
142; ILO conventions, 150; European social charter, 152–53; enforced by selective tariffs, 158–60;
discussions at GATT, 165–66; in
U.S. trade law, 168–76
World Bank, 26, 90, 136, 162
World Health Organization, 16
women: employed in maquiladora

plants, 62; shortchanged by inadequate free time, 115; NAFTA alternative agenda, 129
Wriston, Walter, 52

Yeutter, Clayton, 17
yutori, 140

Zapata, Emiliano, 49